The Search for the Grail

Also by Graham Phillips
with Martin Keatman

The Green Stone
Eye of Fire
King Arthur – The True Story
The Shakespeare Conspiracy

The Search for the Grail

Graham Phillips

ARROW

First published by Arrow in 1996

1 3 5 7 9 10 8 6 4 2

Arrow Books Limited
Random House, 20 Vauxhall Bridge Road, London SW1V 2SA

Random House Australia (Pty) Limited
16 Dalmore Drive, Scoresby
Victoria 3179, Australia

Random House New Zealand Limited
18 Poland Road, Glenfield
Auckland 10, New Zealand

Random House South Africa (Pty) Limited
Box 2263, Rosebank 2121, South Africa

Random House UK Limited Reg. No. 954009

A CIP catalogue record for this book
is available from the British Library

Papers used by Random House UK Limited are natural, recyclable
products made from wood grown in sustainable forests.
The manufacturing processes conform to the environmental
regulations of the country of origin.

ISBN 0 09 953941 1

Typeset by Deltatype Ltd, Ellesmere Port, Cheshire
Printed and bound in Great Britain by
Cox & Wyman Ltd, Reading, Berks

Contents

Illustrations

Acknowledgements

Graham Phillips would like to thank Mark Booth, Anthony Whittome, Lyndsay Symons, Elizabeth Rowlinson, Karina Attar, Tracey Jennings, Dan and Susanna Shadrake, Malcolm Ordover, Steven Griffin, Melissa Marshall, Victoria Palmer, Jean Astle, Kerry Harper, Caroline Wise, Steven Wilson, the management and staff of Hawkstone Park, Francesca Price, Michael Hurll Television Ltd, Brian Blessed, Martin Keatman, the Edwards family, Mrs Sheila Lea, Geophysical Surveys of Bradford, Mike Stokes and Roger White, for all their invaluable help.

Introduction
The Holy Grail

> And as they were eating, Jesus took the bread, and blessed it, and
> broke it, and gave it to the disciples, and said, Take, eat; this is my
> body. And he took the cup, and gave thanks, and gave it to them,
> saying, drink ye all of it. For this is my blood of the new testament,
> which is shed for many for the remission of sins.

> Matthew 26: 26–8

The Grail has occupied a unique place in the Western imagination since
the dawn of the Middle Ages. Even today it remains a central recurring
theme in modern literature. It has inspired writers, artists and musicians
for centuries, and now it exerts its enchanting influence from the cinema
screen and on television. A sacred chalice said to hold the power to cure
all ills and bring peace and prosperity to the world, the Grail embodies a
promise of immortality and the fulfilment of dreams and aspirations.

Over the years the search for the Grail has become as important a
motif as the sacred artefact itself. In the literature of the Middle Ages
medieval heroes sought the Grail in scores of epic poems and romantic
adventures, each gaining worldly insight and spiritual enlightenment
from the tasks given them during the quest. It became almost
unimportant that the Grail itself was not discovered; the real search was
for knowledge, and the understanding of the inner self was the true
prize. In many medieval stories the Grail was merely a beacon to lure the
hero into the ultimate game of life, to discover his true place and
purpose in the world. This is the Grail as it was eventually portrayed in
the Gothic revival of the nineteenth century, in the paintings of the Pre-
Raphaelites and in the verses of the romantic Victorian poets. It is the
image that has become the theme of today's novelists and Hollywood
scriptwriters. But what exactly is the Holy Grail? Did – or does – it really
exist?

To most people today the Grail occupies the realm of legend.
However, during the Middle Ages it was not portrayed simply as

another magical artefact, but as the most sacred Christian relic. As such, belief in the Grail's existence was not a matter of profane superstition, but of profound religious faith.

In most medieval Grail romances, from the thirteenth century onwards, the Grail was portrayed as the cup used by Christ himself at the Last Supper, in which the wine became his blood. It was said to have been kept by the disciples during the Roman persecutions, before being brought to Britain, where it was later sought by King Arthur and his knights. Millions of Christians throughout the world firmly believed that Jesus was the Son of God and that the miracle of the Last Supper really occurred. From the Christian perspective there was no doubt that the cup of the Last Supper actually existed, and during the Middle Ages many believed that it still survived.

Usually, holy relics were the earthly remains of saints: their bones or, in some cases, a mummified appendage. Relics were believed to hold divine power: they could heal sickness, protect against evil and secure spiritual well-being. In the Middle Ages relics were highly sought-after, their acquisition becoming an international obsession. For many monks it was a sacred duty to seek them out and return them to their abbots. In abbeys throughout Europe relics were displayed in public shrines, to be visited by thousands of pilgrims in the hope that they might be helped, cured or enlightened by their close proximity to the remains. Pilgrims were prepared to pay to view or touch the relics, and vast wealth was donated to the churches, abbeys and cathedrals which contained the bones of the most famous saints. Often a religious centre would grow rich and powerful solely from the proceeds of its relics.

An excellent example is Glastonbury Abbey in Somerset. The impressive ruins of the abbey date from the late twelfth century, replacing much older buildings destroyed by fire in 1184. Following the fire, the abbey was desperately in need of funds for rebuilding, and the only sure way to raise the money was to attract large numbers of pilgrims. In 1190, during renovations to the abbey ruins, the monks claimed to have discovered in the foundations the bones of at least three famous saints: Patrick, Gildas and Dunstan, all thought to be early patrons of the abbey. The relics were put on display and attracted generous donations from multitudes of worshippers. So wealthy did the abbey become that it was reconstructed as one of the most splendid in England.

During the Middle Ages any relics were big business, but the most prestigious were those thought to have been associated with Christ himself. As the Bible relates that Jesus ascended bodily into heaven, his bones could not exist on earth. It was therefore items associated with Jesus that became his relics. Many splinters from the cross were claimed as genuine, as was the famous Turin Shroud in which Christ's crucified body was said to have been wrapped. If it had survived, however, the holiest of all relics would be the vessel which had once contained the very blood of Christ – the cup of the Last Supper.

The oldest surviving reference to the Grail as the name for the cup of Christ was by the Burgundian poet Robert de Boron, in his *Joseph d'Arimathie*, composed around the year 1200. The Bible relates how Joseph, a rich merchant of Arimathea, laid the body of Christ in the tomb after the Crucifixion. According to Robert, Joseph of Arimathea obtained the cup of the Last Supper from Pilate and used it to collect drops of blood from Jesus' crucified body. In the poem, Joseph eventually embarks on a series of adventures, leading ultimately to the Grail being brought to Britain, to the 'Vales of Avalon'.

In the following decades, other writers composed scores of similar romances, in which the Grail was portrayed as a fabulous jewelled chalice made of gold and silver. If a cup used at an impromptu meal in first-century Palestine really had survived intact, it seems highly improbable that it would be such a spectacular artefact. More likely, it would have been a simple drinking vessel made of wood, stone or pottery. Moreover, it is difficult to equate such an opulent receptacle with Jesus, the humble carpenter who renounced material wealth.

Yet regardless of the Grail's supposed appearance, did it really survive intact to be hidden somewhere in the British Isles?

The name that is inextricably linked with the Grail is that of King Arthur. In nearly all the medieval stories of the Grail quest Arthur and his warriors are the central characters.

It is the Knights of the Round Table who search for and discover this holiest of relics. Consequently, before we can begin to evaluate the authenticity of any of the Grail stories, we must first investigate King Arthur himself. Was he simply an invention of the medieval imagination? Or did he really exist?

PART ONE
THE SEARCH FOR KING ARTHUR

1

The Arthurian Romances

The story of King Arthur which we know today was the work of the English knight Sir Thomas Malory, printed in 1485 under the title *Le Morte d'Arthur* (*The Death of Arthur*). Malory did not invent the story, however, he simply collected together a wide variety of existing tales and retold them. The stories were already popular at the time and, as one of the first books to be set in print, Malory's version established itself as the standard presentation. Yet during the Middle Ages, the era of jousting, chivalry and knights in armour, the period in which the tales are set, there are no records of such a king, either in England or elsewhere in Christendom. Even if we go back to the Norman Conquest of 1066 we find no King Arthur. If we go back still further to the ninth century, when Athelstan became the first Saxon king of all England, again no such monarch exists. So who was Arthur? How did such an elusive and obscure character become so famous?

In addressing this question we must trace the development of the narrative itself, examining how the story evolved in the romantic literature of the Middle Ages. The earliest detailed account of Arthur's life was written around 1135 by the Welsh cleric Geoffrey of Monmouth, who later became Bishop of St Asaph. Geoffrey's work, the *Historia Regum Britanniae* (*History of the Kings of Britain*), became the foundation upon which all the later stories of King Arthur were constructed. As its title suggests it was not intended to be read as fiction. On the contrary, it was presented as an accurate historical record of the British monarchy. But at a time when accurate historical records were almost non-existent, and history was not seen as it is today, as a discipline dependent solely on the interpretation of proven facts, writers often felt free to embellish history as they saw fit. It is thus difficult to distinguish between fact and invention in the works of Geoffrey of Monmouth.

Written in Latin, Geoffrey's *Historia* traces the development of the isle of Britain, culminating with the golden age of King Arthur.

According to Geoffrey, Arthur is born at Tintagel Castle in Cornwall, the son of the British king Uther Pendragon. Having become king while still in his teens, Arthur quickly asserts authority by defeating his barbarian enemies at the battle of Bath. Wielding a magical sword, Caliburn, said to have been forged on the mystical isle of Avalon, Arthur subsequently defeats the Scots in the North and unifies the nation. Having gone on to conquer Ireland and Iceland, Arthur reigns peacefully for twelve years, his queen Ganhumara at his side. He establishes an order of knights, accepting notorious warriors of all nations, before conceiving the ambitious notion of conquering Europe. When Norway, Denmark and Gaul (an area which once covered Northern Italy, France and Belgium, together with parts of Germany, the Netherlands and Switzerland) have fallen easily to his armies, Arthur returns home to a period of peace, holding court at the city of Caerleon in South-East Wales.

Eventually, Arthur is again drawn into war, setting off to fight in Burgundy. But all does not go well. He is soon forced to return to Britain to quell a revolt led by his nephew Modred, unwisely left to rule as regent in his absence. Although he succeeds in crushing the rebellion at the battle of Camlann, somewhere in Cornwall, Arthur is mortally wounded and taken to the isle of Avalon for his wounds to be tended. Geoffrey fails to tell us what then became of King Arthur.

Second only to Arthur in importance in Geoffrey's *Historia* is the magical Merlin, of whom he also wrote two poetic works. In the *Prophetiae Merlini* (*Prophecies of Merlin*) and the *Vita Merlini* (*Life of Merlin*) Geoffrey portrays Merlin as the guiding influence behind the throne.

Geoffrey's work quickly captured the popular imagination, and before long the adventures of King Arthur inspired writers from all over Europe. The first was the Jersey poet Wace, who in 1155 composed *Roman de Brut* (the *Romance of Brutus*). Written in French, this poetic rendering of Geoffrey's account was the first of the Arthurian romances and contains an important addition to the Arthurian story, namely the Round Table. Said to seat fifty of Arthur's knights, its purpose according to Wace was to promote a sense of equality amongst Arthur's noblemen.

Although Geoffrey of Monmouth popularised the Arthurian saga, and Wace poetically elaborated it, it was the French writer Chretien de Troyes who was chiefly responsible for establishing it as a fashionable subject of romantic literature. In his five Arthurian stories, written between 1160 and 1180, Chretien imaginatively develops the events by introducing all the medieval notions of chivalry and courtly romance. Not only is Chretien responsible for creating many of the knights (for example, Sir Lancelot), he uses the more lyrical-sounding Guinevere as the name for Arthur's queen and introduces Camelot as King Arthur's court. Most importantly, however, Chretien is the first known romancer to include the Grail in the Arthurian story. Unfortunately, he fails to explain what the Grail actually is, and it was left to his contemporary Robert de Boron in the late 1190s to reveal that it was the cup of the Last Supper. Said to possess miraculous healing properties, the lost Grail is sought by Arthur's knights, who gain both worldly experience and spiritual insight during their epic quest.

With the notion of the Grail quest, the stories of King Arthur gained a Christian acceptability, and many clergymen were inspired to write Arthurian works. Around 1200, the English priest Layamon was the first to relate the saga in native English. In his work *Brut*, an adaptation of Wace's *Roman de Brut*, Layamon elevates King Arthur into a messianic figure. In his version, Arthur survives as an immortal on the secret isle of Avalon, with the promise that he will one day return.

By the beginning of the thirteenth century, the remaining themes were added to what ultimately became the accepted Arthurian story. Between 1215 and 1235 a large number of garrulous Arthurian stories, known collectively as the Vulgate Cycle, were compiled. Anonymously composed, the Vulgate Cycle is chiefly responsible for many of the embellishments to the story, in particular the theme of Excalibur being thrown to the Lady of the Lake as Arthur lies dying.

With the Vulgate Cycle marking the change from verse to prose, and successive writers adding further themes, the story culminates in the fifteenth century with the best known version of the Arthurian legend, *Le Morte d'Arthur*, by Thomas Malory from Newbold Revel in Warwickshire. Completed in 1470, it was printed by William Caxton in 1485 and is in fact eight separate tales, which Malory originally entitled *The Whole Book of King Arthur and his Noble Knights of the Round Table*. Although *Le Morte d'Arthur* was originally only the name of the last story, this more convenient title for the entire work has survived to this day.

Le Morte d'Arthur opens with Arthur conceived as the illegitimate son of Uther Pendragon. After being brought up in secret, Arthur proves himself king by drawing the sword from the stone. He marries Guinevere, founds the Knights of the Round Table at Camelot (which

Malory identifies as Winchester) and begets Modred in unknowing incest. Following a period of prosperity, Arthur's knights commence a quest to discover the Grail, during which time Lancelot has consummated an adulterous affair with Queen Guinevere. Ultimately, the couple are discovered and Arthur pursues Lancelot into France, leaving Modred behind as regent. At the end of the story, Arthur discovers an attempt by Modred to seize the throne and returns to quash the rebellion. In a final battle, Modred dies and Arthur receives a mortal wound, after which he is transported on a barge to the Vale of Avalon. Following the battle, Arthur's sword Excalibur is reluctantly cast to the Lady of the Lake by Sir Bedivere, while both Lancelot and Guinevere enter holy orders and live out their lives in peace.

This, then, is the literary evolution of the Arthurian story. But is that all it is, straight fiction? Although they may have used artistic licence in their Arthurian epics, the medieval romancers appear to accept the historical reality of King Arthur. Conversely, however, they seem uncertain when it comes to dating the events. This is unfortunate, for if we are to unravel the truth it is critical to discover when Arthur is supposed to have lived. At face value the tales appear to be set during the Middle Ages; the knights wear elaborate armour, fight with broadswords and observe the rules of chivalry. It must be remembered, however, that when medieval writers transposed an ancient story, such as the legends of Greece or Rome, they invariably portrayed the characters in familiar terms, locating them in their own historical context.

If we are to identify the real Arthurian period we must return to Geoffrey of Monmouth's account. Unlike the later romances, Geoffrey's version of events was not intended to be read as fiction. His work, during the early twelfth century, was presented as an accurate historical rendering, stating in its preface that it is translated from 'a certain very ancient book written in the British language', given to him by Archdeacon Walter of Oxford. But is Geoffrey reliable? Since no trace of this 'very ancient book' exists today, we are left with the content of Geoffrey's work to make its own case.

Although Geoffrey tells us that Arthur died in A.D. 542, he presents a number of historical inconsistencies concerning this date. For example, we are told that Arthur fought a Gallic campaign during the reign of Leo I, emperor at Constantinople from 457 to 474. This suggests that Arthur was around a hundred years old at the time of the battle of Camlann. However, this may have arisen as a result of confusion between two alternative systems of dating used at the time. The Victorious calendar, prevalent in the fifth century, began the first year at Christ's Crucifixion, whereas the *Anno Domini* calendar, used by Geoffrey, begins year 1 at the birth of Christ, this latter system not becoming popular until the late sixth century. If Geoffrey has confused these two calendars, then Arthur may have died around 510, only thirty-six years after the Gallic war.

Other inconsistencies arise when we examine Arthur's contemporaries described by Geoffrey. Although history provides no record of Arthur's father, Uther Pendragon, Arthur's two uncles in Geoffrey's account seem to be based on historical characters. The problem is that they lived in different countries and at different times. Geoffrey tells us that Uther was the brother of Aurelius Ambrosius. Since this was most likely to have been Ambrosius Aurelianus, a known historical warlord who fought the Anglo-Saxons during the late fifth century, Geoffrey's placing of Arthur during this period would seem consistent. However, this does not tally with Uther's second brother, Constans. Since Geoffrey gives details of his life as a monk, Constans can be identified as the son of the Roman emperor Constantine III, a monk who, like Geoffrey's Constans, was persuaded to leave his monastery to become joint ruler with his father. Unfortunately, this historical Constans lived over half a century *before* Ambrosius.

Even during Geoffrey's lifetime there was considerable speculation as to when King Arthur supposedly lived. Wace, for example, locates Arthur's death a hundred years later than Geoffrey. We are therefore left to search a broad historical epoch spanning a quarter of a millennium: possibly as early as 400, perhaps as late as 650. Although by Malory's time Arthur was portrayed as a feudal king, if he had lived in the fifth or sixth centuries, he and his warriors would have been very different from the Knights of the Round Table. The warlords of the period wore Roman-style armour, and their fortifications were not huge Gothic castles, but wooden stockades.

The contemporary historical sources covering England and Wales at this time are limited principally to the work of the sixth-century monk Gildas, the writings of a few visiting foreigners and early monastic records which tell us little of military affairs. Yet with all the fame that Arthur was later to achieve, it is surprising to discover that none of these sources make any reference to him. So was Arthur, after all, a myth originating in the fertile imagination of Geoffrey of Monmouth?

Although there is no historical evidence to support much of

Geoffrey's Arthurian story, he certainly did not invent King Arthur. Some ten years before the *Historia*, in 1125, William of Malmesbury, a monk from the abbey of Malmesbury in Wiltshire, wrote the *Gesta Regum Anglorum* (*Acts of the Kings of the English*) in which he briefly mentions Arthur. William tells us that Arthur aided Ambrosius Aurelianus in holding back the advancing Angles, led the British at the battle of Badon, and had become mythologised in British folklore.

Additionally, in the British Library there are two manuscripts dating from the early 1100s which also include Arthur. In the *Welsh Annals* it is stated that around 518 A.D. Arthur won the battle of Badon, and about 539 A.D. he was slain with Medraut at the battle of Camlann. The second work, the *Historia Brittonum* (*History of the Britons*) includes a list of Arthur's battles, but at first glance tells us little more. However, together with William of Malmesbury, they help us narrow down the Arthurian period; evidently sometime between the late fifth and early sixth centuries. Unfortunately, since this was the historical Dark Ages, an era from which almost no written records survive, we are left with Geoffrey of Monmouth's account alone to provide us with any details of Arthur's life.

In the *Historia*, Geoffrey makes many historical claims known to be inaccurate from reliable contemporary sources. For instance, he begins by telling us that the British nation was founded by Brutus, who established a colony of several thousand Trojans freed from slavery in Greece. He goes on to deny that Britain was ever conquered by the Romans, concluding with a description of how the Saxons eventually invaded England with the help of an army of Africans. Not only does Geoffrey fail to mention many of the great British leaders who did exist, but some of those he does name were kings of other countries entirely. However, this is tame in comparison to Geoffrey's more fanciful notions. For example, he explains how Britain was once inhabited by a race of giants and that Merlin was the son of a demon.

Still, as we have seen, Geoffrey did not invent King Arthur. Perhaps the most intriguing question is why he made such an issue of King Arthur at all. Moreover, why did so many others follow suit? Why should an obscure warrior of the Dark Ages rise to become such a popular figure of romance six centuries after his death?

The principal reason seems to have been political: King Arthur became a crucial figure in a medieval propaganda exercise. The kings of England, of Norman blood following the battle of Hastings in 1066, needed to prove their divine right to govern. The continental Capetian dynasty was repeatedly laying claim to the English throne, further pressurising the Normans to legitimate their rule. And at a time of poor communications, it required more than merely armies to maintain order; the monarchy needed the support of the Church.

Many Saxon noblemen could rightfully claim descent from the true kings of England, such as Alfred the Great and King Athelstan; the Norman aristocrats thus required their own heroic and majestic ancestor. Having grounds to prove succession from the ousted pre-Saxon Celtic warriors – the Britons – many of whom had fled to France and settled in Normandy during the fifth and sixth centuries, the Normans looked to them. Unfortunately, there was no evidence that any of these could really be titled 'kings' in the medieval sense. The closest contender was the fabled warrior Arthur. With this aristocratic seal of approval on the Arthurian saga, Geoffrey's *Historia* was well received, particularly by the English king, Henry I.

Whatever documentation may have been available to Geoffrey and others in their reconstructions of Arthur's life, little has survived for us to examine today. From the medieval historians cited above we can assume an approximate dating for the supposed Arthurian period – the fifth or sixth century. But what of location? If he existed, where was Arthur born? where was his Camelot? and where was he laid to rest?

The Arthur of popular imagination was born at Tintagel Castle on the north coast of Cornwall. Anyone who visits the tiny village during the holiday season will find it teeming with sightseers of all nationalities. The ruins of the castle itself stand just outside Tintagel, on what is virtually an island surrounded by foaming sea, linked to the mainland by a narrow ridge of rock. The ridge crumbled long ago, so that any visitor to the ruins today must cross a footbridge and ascend a long flight of steps.

The earliest reference to Tintagel in association with King Arthur appears in Geoffrey of Monmouth's *Historia*, wherein Uther Pendragon has designs on Ygerna, the wife of Gorlois, Duke of Cornwall. Aided by a magic potion, prepared for him by Merlin the magician, Uther is transformed for a time into the form of Gorlois, and as such he visits the Duke's castle at Tintagel and makes love to the Duchess. Thus Arthur is conceived. On the death of Gorlois, Uther makes Ygerna his queen and Arthur is born at Tintagel Castle.

Tintagel's tourist industry and its thousands of patrons seem unaffected by the simple historical fact that this castle could not have been the birthplace of a warrior who had lived centuries before the

Battle of Hastings (1066). It was built only in the early twelfth century for Reginald, the Earl of Cornwall. The story was probably concocted by Geoffrey, who wished to please the Earl, the wealthy brother of his patron, Robert the Earl of Gloucester. Although in defence of Geoffrey it has been suggested that Arthur was born in a castle that previously occupied the site, modern excavations have shown that the promontory had then been the home of an early monastic community, an unlikely place for the birth of anyone.

With this shadow cast across his traditional place of birth, we turn to Arthur's magnificent castle of Camelot. Unlike Tintagel, there is no evidence that a place with the name Camelot ever existed. In fact, Geoffrey makes no mention of it at all, and neither does Wace. The earliest use of Camelot as the name of Arthur's court originates with the twelfth-century poet Chretien de Troyes. It appears in only one of Chretien's works, *Lancelot*, and is mentioned only once and in passing. The name Camelot may therefore simply have been Chretien's literary invention.

During the thirteenth century, later romancers began to make much more of Camelot, describing in graphic detail the splendid city and its impregnable castle. But although they differ considerably in their descriptions, they are united in their failure to specify its whereabouts. According to Malory, however, it was sited at Winchester in Hampshire, and in the Great Hall of Winchester Castle the most famous of all Arthurian relics, 'The Round Table', still exists.

Eighteen feet in diameter, made of solid oak and weighing approximately one and a quarter tons, it is now a table top without legs, hanging on a wall. 'The Round Table' resembles an enormous dartboard, painted in green and white segments, said to be the places where the king and his knights once sat. From the late fifteenth century many considered it to be genuine, and Winchester Castle was generally believed to be the site of Camelot's fortress. Unfortunately, once again, the castle is not old enough to be of the Arthurian period. Although a little older than Tintagel, it is still much too recent, having originally been built as late as the eleventh century by William the Conqueror.

But what of the table itself? The painted design was added well after Malory's time, during the reign of Henry VIII, although the structure is much older. In 1976 scientific tests were conducted in an attempt to establish its authenticity. Examination of tree ring patterns in the wood, analysis of its method of carpentry and radiocarbon dating were all employed. The results showed it to have been made during the reign of

Edward III, probably in 1340 when the king planned to revive the Round Table knighthood. Once again, there is no link with the real Arthur. However, the table does serve to demonstrate the considerable influence of the Arthurian legends during the Middle Ages.

Not only in England is there a town with pretensions to the title of Camelot. There are those who cite the small town of Caerleon, on the river Usk in South-East Wales. Geoffrey mentions Caerleon as the place where Arthur holds court for a time after his first campaign in Gaul. It is probably also the site of one of Arthur's battles, referenced in the *Historia Brittonum* as the City of the Legion, this being the direct translation of the name Caerleon. In Roman times it was called *Isca Silurum* and was a military outpost with a large civilian population, and as late as Geoffrey's time the impressive Roman ruins could still be seen. Modern excavations have uncovered a number of Roman remains, including an amphitheatre that was claimed by some to be the origin of the Round Table. However, although a case could be made for Caerleon having authentic Arthurian associations, in Geoffrey's account Arthur merely holds court there for a short time, while the *Historia Brittonum* simply includes it as a battle site.

Returning to England, in the country of Somerset an Iron Age hill-fort, Cadbury Castle, was for many years proposed as the site of Camelot. The oldest such reference dates back to Henry VIII's chief antiquary, John Leland, in 1542. Leland appears to have arrived at the conclusion based on a legend which existed at the time, together with the word Camel being found in the names of two nearby villages: Queen Camel and West Camel. Although the fort dates from well before the time when Arthur seems to have lived, there is no evidence to connect him with the place other than Leland's reference. The word Camelot, almost certainly being the poetic invention of Chretien de Troyes, does little to bolster the claim. Nonetheless, large-scale excavations were conducted at Cadbury in the late 1960s, under the directorship of the archaeologist Leslie Alcock. Although they showed that the camp, like many other similar sites, had been used during the period in question, no evidence was unearthed to associate it with the historical King Arthur.

If Camelot seems to be spurious, what can we make of modern associations with Avalon, Arthur's fabled resting place?

The first to mention Avalon was Geoffrey. In the *Historia*, he calls it *Insula Avallonis*, referring to it twice. He says that Arthur's sword Caliburn was forged on the island and that after his last battle he was carried there so that his wounds might be tended. In his poetic *Vita*

Merlini he also calls the island *Insula Pomorum*, the Isle of Apples. According to Geoffrey, it lies somewhere over the western sea and is the home of Morgan (a kindly enchantress and not the witch of later stories) who heads a sisterhood of nine maidens. After the battle, Arthur is carried there and placed on a bed of gold, where Morgan offers to heal him in return for his promise to remain with her on the island.

The site that springs immediately to mind whenever Avalon is mentioned is the West Country market town of Glastonbury. Beside the main roads entering the district, signboards welcome the tourist to 'The Ancient Avalon'. The town's claim to be the mystical isle of Avalon, Arthur's final resting place, has long been the subject of controversy. Nestling amidst a small cluster of hills, with much of the surrounding countryside once submerged, Glastonbury was almost an island in early Christian times. It is certainly an imposing location. Its highest hill, Glastonbury Tor, with its solitary stone tower at the summit, can be seen for miles around on the fertile Somerset plain.

Glastonbury's link with King Arthur arose as a result of a discovery said to have been made there in the late 1100s within the grounds of the abbey. As we have seen, the original abbey burned down in 1184, and after the fire the monks claimed to have unearthed the bones of Saints Gildas, Patrick and Dunstan. Additionally, however, they also claimed to have found the bones of a far more famous figure – King Arthur himself. In 1190, during reconstruction of the abbey, a grave was apparently discovered containing the bones of a tall man, together with some smaller bones and a scrap of yellow hair. A lead cross was said to have been found with the remains, which bears the Latin inscription:

HIC IACET SEPULTUS INCLYTUS REX ARTHURIUS IN INSULA
AVALLONIA CUM UXORE SUA SECUNDA WENNEVERIA

'Here lies the renowned King Arthur in the isle of Avalon with his second wife Guinevere'

Neither the bones nor the cross exist today, so unfortunately nothing can be proved. However the incident is at best suspicious. The discovery of the grave was, to say the least, fortuitous. The abbey was in desperate need of funds for rebuilding, and the only sure way to raise money was to attract large numbers of pilgrims. Stories of King Arthur were so widely popular at the time that nothing else could hope to bring in so many visitors. The inscription on the cross was also convenient, telling the world that not only was Arthur buried there, but that Glastonbury was also the secret island of Avalon.

The mention of Guinevere as Arthur's second wife was an additional 'stroke of luck', for at the time there were two separate and equally popular stories in circulation. One, that Arthur's queen was called Guinevere, the other that she was called Ganhumara. The reference to Guinevere being his second wife just so happened to satisfy everyone. A few years later, however, when it was generally accepted that Arthur had only had one wife, it was claimed that the cross had simply said:

HIC IACET SEPULTUS INCLITUS REX ARTHURIUS IN INSULA
AVALONIA

'Here lies the renowned King Arthur in the Isle of Avalon'

Conveniently, no mention of all of Guinevere!

In 1962, Dr Ralegh Radford excavated the site where the monks claimed to have dug, and found indications of an ancient grave; perhaps the brothers had discovered some bones, after all? Unfortunately, without the cross to examine, there is no way to verify that it was the body of Arthur that had been exhumed. However, we do have the purported inscription, which is itself controversial. It has been pointed out that the style of Latin betrays the cross as a twelfth-century fraud. According to the Oxford linguist, James Hudson, it varies from a sixth-century inscription by about as much as modern English varies from a Shakespearean text.

Today the affair of Arthur's bones is considered so suspect that few historians take it seriously. In all likelihood, the monks discovered an unmarked grave and subsequently someone had the idea to claim it as Arthur's. An inscribed cross was fashioned as 'proof' and the announcement made to an eager public. In other words, it was a medieval public relations exercise.

So how does Glastonbury tie up with this mystical isle? No evidence exists to suggest that anyone prior to 1190 associated Glastonbury with Avalon. On the contrary, early historians seem completely unaware of any such notion. William of Malmesbury, writing in the early twelfth century, compiled a history of Glastonbury. However, not once does he link it with King Arthur, nor does he refer to Glastonbury in connection with Avalon. Even more damning is Caradoc of Llancarfan who, writing around 1140, inscribed the earliest known text to associate the

Arthurian story with Glastonbury. He does not regard it as Avalon, however, saying only that the abbot of Glastonbury aided in the release of Guinevere from King Melwas of Somerset.

Much has been made of Glastonbury's link with the Holy Grail, but this only seems to have arisen following Robert de Boron's *Joseph d'Arimathie*. In the poem Joseph eventually embarks on a series of adventures, leading ultimately to the Grail being brought to Britain, to the Vales of Avalon.

Although Robert makes no reference to Glastonbury, the abbey monks soon suggested that this was where the Grail was hidden. In fact, in 1247 the monks produced a revised edition of the history of Glastonbury, compiled by William of Malmesbury a century before, in which it attempted to link the Grail historically with the abbey. Although in William's original treatise (*De Antiquitate Glastoniensis Ecclesiae*), written in 1130, he mentions nothing of Joseph of Arimathea, in the revised edition Glastobury church is said to have been founded by Joseph himself.

So the famous sites traditionally associated with Arthur do not withstand historical scrutiny. There is no contemporary document to prove Arthur's existence, and archaeologists have found nothing bearing his name. Considering that the medieval stories were romantic fiction, based to a large degree upon the less than reliable Geoffrey of Monmouth, what reason is there to look further? Is Arthur, after all, simply a medieval invention? To answer this question, we must first discover if there is any evidence for the existence of the Arthurian legend before the first romances were written in the twelfth century.

2
The Original Tales

From the *Welsh Annals*, the *Historia Brittonum* (both preserved in a manuscript dating from around 1120) and William of Malmesbury's *Gesta Regum Anglorum* (*circa* 1125), all written before Geoffrey of Monmouth, we know that the Arthurian legend was well established by the early twelfth century. Just how widespread was the legend?

It was certainly known in France by the early twelfth century. In 1113 a group of Church officials from the French city of Laon journeyed through England raising funds for the rebuilding of their cathedral. A few years later Hermann of Tournai wrote of the visit, describing the journey between Exeter and Bodmin. Somewhere along the route, he tells us, the local people informed the travellers that they were entering the land of Arthur. They drew attention to two landmarks, Arthur's Chair and Arthur's Ovens. Although we are not told what these were, they were more than likely rock fomations. Hermann also mentions a Cornish legend that Arthur was still believed to be alive.

Around the same period the legend had even taken hold as far away as Italy. In the north portal of Modena Cathedral in northern Italy, built between 1099 and 1140, an archway is carved with figures from an Arthurian scene. Known as the Modena Archivolt, the figures are identified from their accompanying inscriptions. The scene depicts a woman held prisoner in a castle, with three mounted knights attempting to rescue her. Beside one of the figures is the contemporary inscription *Artus de Bretania* – 'Arthur of Britain'.

For the legend of King Arthur to have been so widely disseminated by the early twelfth century, it must have been in existence for some considerable time. Accordingly there must have existed earlier Arthurian tales from which Geoffrey and the other medieval romancers wove their stories. Do any of them still remain to be examined today?

The first place to search is in early Welsh literature, as it was into Wales that the native Britons of the Dark Ages retreated after the invasion by the Anglo-Saxons. If Arthur really existed as a British warrior in the fifth or sixth century, then he may well have been celebrated in the stories of the Welsh. Arthur does appear in some of the oldest Welsh literature. However, none of the surviving copies of these works which include King Arthur date from the time before the Arthurian romances had become firmly established. Was this Celtic poetry and prose copied from much earlier material which predates Geoffrey and the Arthurian romancers?

The oldest surviving manuscript containing a Welsh poem that mentions Arthur is the *Black Book of Carmarthen*, compiled around the mid-thirteenth century. Now in the National Library of Wales, in Aberystwyth, it was probably the work of one scribe, and consists almost entirely of poetry supposedly copied from earlier documents or oral accounts. Like a number of medieval Welsh manuscripts, it takes its name from the colour of its binding. Although Arthur is included briefly in a few of the poems within the manuscript (for instance, the *Stanzas of the Graves*, which remarks how Arthur's burial place remains a mystery), he is only spoken of in detail in one, the *Pa wr yw'r Porthor*, commonly referred to as the *Dialogue of Arthur and Glewlwyd Gafaelfawr*. In this poem Glewlwyd Gafaelfawr is the guardian of a fortress to which Arthur attempts to gain entrance, being made to prove his worth before being allowed inside. Unfortunately, however, the tale supplies us with nothing concerning the historicity of Arthur, for the details concern only encounters with demons, monsters and mythical beasts. In fact, the only Arthurian inclusion within the *Black Book of Carmarthen* with any historical pretensions concerns Arthur's presence at the battle of Llongborth (in the *Stanzas of Geraint*) although, regrettably, the location can no longer be identified.

Slightly later than the *Black Book of Carmarthen* is the *Book of Taliesin* (also in the National Library of Wales), a manuscript dating from around 1300 containing poems attributed to, and about, a sixth-century poet of that name. Although it can be argued that Taliesin historically existed, the surviving manuscript is many times removed from the bard himself. Reference are made to Arthur in several poems within the *Book of Taliesin*, but once again only as passing allusions. However, one work, *Preiddiau Annwfn* – the *Spoils of Annwn* – is more detailed, concerning a raid by Arthur and his men into the magical land of Annwn to steal its treasures, a fabulous cauldron and a magical sword guarded by nine maidens.

The most important of all the Welsh manuscripts to include Arthur, the *Red Book of Hergest*, was compiled around 1400 and is now in the

Bodleian Library, Oxford. In this manuscript two tales are of particular interest, the *Dream of Rhonabwy* and the tale of *Culhwch and Olwen*. The former is the story of a warrior called Rhonabwy who is employed by the King of Powys in central Wales to seek out his renegade brother. During his search he experiences a dream or vision of Arthur's court on the eve of a great battle. In *Culhwch and Olwen* the hero Culhwch bids for the hand in marriage of Olwen, the daughter of the giant Ysbaddaden. However, the giant, intent on preventing their marriage, imposes a series of impossible tasks on Culhwch, which he must complete if he is to win his bride. On the advice of his father, the hero travels to the court of Arthur and acquires his assistance. For much of the story it is Arthur himself who leads the quest on Culhwch's behalf: he rescues the god-king Mabon, hunts down a giant boar and attacks Ireland, carrying off a magical cauldron.

An additional area of Welsh literature which must be considered in relation to King Arthur are the Triads. Taking their name from their groupings of themes or characters into threes, the Triads served as a mnemonic device summarising Welsh folklore. They were anonymously committed to writing during the Middle Ages by a group of Welsh writers, probably in the hope of preserving some of the Welsh oral tradition that was rapidly being lost. Not really poems in the true sense, they are basically outlines of what were obviously more detailed sagas. King Arthur is refered to in a series called the *Triads of Britain*, which also include a number of known historical characters from the Dark Ages. (Although dispersed through many Welsh manuscripts, the *Triads of Britain* were not brought together in one printed text until 1567. The surviving copy, *Y Diarebion Camberac*, is now in the British Library.)

The Triads are intriguing in that Arthur is not always depicted as the epitome of majestic virtue, in fact far from it. In the Triad the *Three Wicked Uncoverings* he is even blamed for the ultimate defeat of the Britons, being guilty of removing the head of the god Bran that had been buried on London's Tower Hill as a talisman against foreign invasion. Worse still, in the *Three Red Ravagers* Arthur is depicted as a curse upon the land itself; wherever he walks no grass will grow for seven years. Nor is he very successful in his exploits. In the *Three Powerful Swineherds* Arthur even fails dismally in an attempt to raid a herd of pigs belonging to a rival king. To add further confusion, his rank and position are often ambiguous; in the *Three Frivolous Bards*, for example, Arthur is included as one of the three bards (a bard being a court poet). However, the traditional King Arthur is also found in the Triads. The Battle of amlann, for example, is mentioned in the *Three Futile Battles*, as the outcome of a conflict between Arthur and his rival Modred.

An examination of Arthur in Welsh literature would be incomplete without consideration of the *Mabinogion*. The *Mabinogion* is often thought to be an ancient Celtic manuscript, instrumental in the search for an historical King Arthur. In reality, it was the title used by the Lincolnshire diarist Lady Charlotte Guest for her English translations of twelve medieval Welsh tales, published in three volumes between 1838 and 1843. They included eleven tales from the *Red Book of Hergest*, together with a story of the bard Taliesin (apparently from an eighteenth-century manuscript). As the tales include *Culhwch and Olwen* and the *Dream of Rhonabwy* they are indeed of Arthurian interest. However, they are simply translations of tales that can be examined at source. The word *Mabinogion* comes from the *Pedair Cainc y Mabinogi*, the *Four Branches of the Mabinogi*, the name previously given to just four of the tales in the *Red Book of Hergest* (*Pwyll, Branwen, Manawydan* and *Math*). The Welsh term *mabinogi* originally meant 'youth', but later came to mean 'a tale of youth' and finally 'a tale'. The first single volume of the *Mabinogion* appeared in 1877 and has since been republished many times. The *Mabinogion* is important in that it affords a wider readership to early Welsh literature, but from the Arthurian standpoint a study of the Mabinogion should be considered an investigation of tales within the *Red Book of Hergest*.

What conclusions can reasonably be drawn from this early Welsh literature? Was Arthur interpolated into Welsh folklore after he had already become a theme of popular romance? Or was it from such tales that Geoffrey and the romancers drew material to elaborate their own stories? Is there any evidence to date when they were originally composed?

Unfortunately, the *Triads of Britain* present us with problems. Unlike the other poems, there are no linguistic grounds on which to date the original stories which the writers were attempting to outline. Much of the lore may well have dated back to the early Dark Ages, yet all that can be said with certainty is that the Triads reflect the state of Welsh tradition by the thirteenth and fourteenth centuries, well after the Arthurian romances had become firmly established.

In the Triads, Arthur's role is strange indeed, as he is often portrayed as incompetent. This could hardly be seen as an attempt to cash in on the themes of the Arthurian romances and, as such, could constitute evidence of the survival of a separate Arthurian tradition. However, if the legends of Arthur had so negatively portrayed his character by the twelfth century, it seems unlikely that he would have become the central theme of medieval romance. It is more probable that the Triads represent the status of Welsh Arthurian folklore in the late Middle Ages. England had come to claim King Arthur as its own, and so the Welsh may have considered it expedient to debunk his supposed exploits.

Regarding the *Dream of Rhonabwy*, there is reason to doubt an Arthurian association earlier than Geoffrey and the romancers, for the surviving story can be dated with certainty. The King of Powys, who commissions the warrior Rhonabwy to seek out his brother, is named as Madog ap Maredudd, a known historical character who died around 1159. Based on this evidence, the *Dream of Rhonabwy* was almost certainly composed later than Geoffrey's *Historia*.

Culhwch and Olwen was certainly in existence about 75 years before the *Red Book of Hergest* was compiled, for it survives in fragmented form in the *White Book of Rhydderch* compiled around 1325 (now bound in two volumes in the National Library of Wales). Moreover, linguistic analysis has produced evidence for *Culhwch and Olwen* having originally been composed as early as the tenth century, over a hundred years before Geoffrey's *Historia* was written. The *Spoils of Annwn* may also be as old, as there are clear parallels between the two. The attack on Ireland to seize the cauldron in *Culhwch and Olwen* is reminiscent of the raid in the *Spoils of Annwn*, and Arthur's ship is called Prydwen in both tales.

Further indication that the *Culhwch and Olwen* and *The Spoils of Annwn* were composed much earlier than Geoffrey's time is that their themes seem to have been ancient Celtic concepts. The idea of nine saintly women living in seclusion in the *Spoils of Annwn* could certainly have been of Celtic origin. The first-century classical geographer Pomponius Mela, for instance, writes of nine priestesses living under a vow of chastity on an island off the coast of Brittany. These women were of a Celtic tribe similar to the Britons themselves, and were said to have the power to heal the sick and foretell the future. The same Celtic origins appear true of the magical cauldron which features in both tales. There are many examples of magical cauldrons in Celtic literature, such as the Cauldron of Dagda (Dagda being chief of the Tuatha de Dannan) in Irish folklore, indicating that the cauldron of the *Spoils of Annwn* could tally with ancient Welsh mythology. In fact, in the tale of *Culhwch and Olwen* it is to Ireland that Arthur went in pursuit of the cauldron. Moreover, the cauldron is said to belong to Di-wrnach, very possibly a Welsh rendering of the Irish Dagda.

In the *Spoils of Annwn* we read of Arthur's theft of the cauldron and sword from the land of Annwn. It could have been from this poem that Geoffrey created Avalon and the magical sword Caliburn. The similarities between them is difficult to ignore, particularly as Annwn is depicted as a land which lies across the water – a mystical land full of wonders and marvels that must surely bear some relationship to Geoffrey's isle of Avalon. In fact, the link between Annwn and Avalon is further substantiated when we see that within the poem the land is also called the 'fort of glass', a name associated with Glastonbury in the late twelfth century.

Five years after 'Arthur's remains' were unearthed by the monks at Glastonbury Abbey in 1190, a work entitled *De Principis Instructione* was written by the scholar Giraldus Cambrensis. In the text, Giraldus explains that the word Glastonbury meant 'fort of glass'. Although this assertion is unfounded (the name for the town more likely being derived from Glasteing, the personal name of the settlement's founder) it does suggest that the *Spoils of Annwn* existed around a century before the surviving *Book of Taliesin* was compiled, for it seems that Giraldus was attempting to bolster the town's claim to being the isle of Avalon. As such, Giraldus' assertion that Glastonbury was the 'fort of glass' demonstrates an acceptance by this time that Annwn and Avalon were one and the same.

Geoffrey's Avalon is so similar to the mystic land of Annwn that one is certainly based on the other. For instance, in Geoffrey's work the enchantress Morgan is the head of a sisterhood of nine women who act as guardians of the isle, whereas in the *Spoils of Annwn* Annwn is the home of nine maidens who are custodians of the magical cauldron. Additionally, in the *Spoils of Annwn* Arthur's ship is called Prydwen, while in Geoffrey's writing Prydwen is the name of Arthur's shield.

Even the name Avalon seems to be of Celtic origin. From Ireland there comes an ancient cycle of poems involving the sea god Manannan, who rules over a magical island described by the Gaelic word *ablach*, meaning 'rich in apples'. Geoffrey actually refers to Avalon as the 'Isle of Apples' (*Insula Pomorum*) in his *Vita Merlini*.

Geoffrey and the medieval romancers also seem to have interpolated other early Celtic material in their Arthurian stories – Excalibur for example. The word Excalibur was an adaption by Wace of Geoffrey's name for Arthur's sword, Caliburn, although nearly all the romancers that followed continued to use the now familiar and more lyrical Excalibur. Although it has been suggested that Geoffrey's term derived from the Latin word *chalybs*, meaning steel, Welsh legends indicate another origin of the name. In a number of Welsh tales (such as *Culhwch and Olwen*) Arthur's sword is called Caledfwlch, from the old Irish *caladbolg* meaning 'a flashing sword'. If Caliburn did come from Caledfwlch, then this would imply that the Excalibur theme may have been taken from an early Celtic legend.

The familiar story of Arthur's magical sword is not related by Geoffrey, however, who tells us only that it was forged on the isle of Avalon. It was not until a century after Geoffrey that the Vulgate Cycle introduced the Excalibur story we know today. In the Vulgate version, Arthur, who originally received Excalibur from a mysterious nymph, the Lady of the Lake, ultimately orders his knight Girflet to cast it into an enchanted pool as he lies dying on the field of battle. After twice disobeying the wishes of his king, the knight reluctantly consents. When the sword is thrown an arm rises from the lake, catches the weapon and takes it down into the watery depths. This, of course, is the tale elaborated by Thomas Malory, although in his version it is Bedivere and not Girflet who returns the sword to the Lady of the Lake. Although other romancers cast Galahad, Lancelot, or even Perceval in this role, the event itself had become firmly entrenched in the saga by the end of the Middle Ages.

There are clear Celtic undertones to the Lady of the Lake motif, suggesting that the writers of the Vulgate story may have been employing much earlier material. Archaeological excavations have unearthed many precious artefacts, including swords, that had long ago been thrown into sacred lakes and pools by the Celtic people of Northern Europe as votive offerings to water deities. One such dig, at Anglesey in 1942, recovered no less than 150 items that had been preserved for centuries in the mud of the dried up lake of Llyn Cerrig Bach. These artefacts were prized possessions, such as cauldrons, horse trappings and broaches, and as such had clearly not been discarded; rather they had been cast into the water as offerings over a period spanning some 250 years until the end of the first century A.D.

The theme of Excalibur being thrown to the Lady of the Lake may therefore have derived from the ancient Celtic practice of making a sacred offering to a water goddess, perhaps in the hope of restoring a warrior to health, or as part of a funerary rite. This hypothesis is further substantiated in the romances, where the Lady of the Lake is given the name Viviane. This name could well have been an adaption of a Celtic water goddess recorded by Roman writers under the name Covianna. A shrine to Covianna, under the Romanised name Coventina, can still be seen today on Hadrian's Wall in northern England. A well at the shrine has been excavated to reveal numerous votive offerings, particularly coins. From discoveries such as those at Coventina's Well, it can be deduced that the imperial soldiers stationed in Britain began to adopt British customs. Where the British warriors had offered their prize possessions, the Roman soldiers threw coins into the sacred pools, a practice that has survived to this day in the tradition of wishing wells.

The tale of Arthur drawing the sword from the stone may also be based on an ancient Celtic tradition. Despite the popular notion of the nineteenth century, now set firmly in the popular imagination by John Boorman's epic film *Excalibur*, it was not Excalibur that was drawn from the stone in the original romances, but a different sword entirely. Robert de Boron was responsible for introducing this theme around 1200, and may have taken it from the traditions of the Celtic warrior elite. In Roman times, if any dispute arose concerning the appointment of a new tribal leader, or the commanding chieftain of an alliance, the matter was resolved in combat. More often than not it would be decided by a duel, not necessarily to the death, between the rival candidates. As a sign that the loser or his supporters would abide by the outcome, a symbol of authority was presented to the victor. This was usually a sword consecrated by the pagan priesthood and laid upon a stone altar throughout the contest. The warriors believed that once the victor had attained the symbolic artefact, it would inflict a curse on any who broke the covenant. Such a tradition could have been the origin of the story of Arthur drawing the sword from the stone.

It seems, therefore, that Geoffrey and romancers employed Welsh tales, such as *Culhwch and Olwen* and the *Spoils of Annwn*, as the source material for some of their Arthurian themes. This original Arthur of Welsh legend, however, is quite different from the King Arthur portrayed in the medieval romances – he is a Celtic chieftain surrounded by demigods, demons and mythical beings.

Although it seems that the Arthurian story existed well before the time of the medieval romances, does this mean that King Arthur was originally no more than a fictional character from Celtic mythology? In order to discover if a real flesh-and-blood warrior does lie beyond the legend, we must now turn to the contemporary historical sources covering the Dark Ages and the period when Arthur is said to have lived.

3
Historical Manuscripts

One of the most important sources for Dark Age history is the *Ecclesiastical History of the English People*. Compiled around A.D. 731, this is the first English work that could genuinely be termed historical writing to cover the fifth to eighth centuries. Written by the monk Bede, at the monastery of Jarrow in Northumbria, it transformed the rough framework of existing material into an actual history book. Bede's work established the style for historians that followed and was the first to employ the A.D. system of dating for historical purposes. His sources were primarily ecclesiastical documents from the region of Kent, together with the work of Gildas and a wide variety of oral accounts.

The second important historical manuscript including the events of the fifth and sixth centuries is the *Anglo-Saxon Chronicle*, of which a number of versions survive. Although it appears to be based on early west Saxon monastic records, the surviving *Chronicle* was not compiled until the reign of Alfred the Great, between 871 and 899, seemingly under Alfred's personal supervision.

The fact that neither work contains reference to Arthur has long cast a shadow of doubt over his historicity. However, Bede may not mention Arthur for the simple reason that he is writing an ecclesiastical history of the Anglo-Saxons, and as such has no reason to include him. As for the *Chronicle*, since this was most likely Alfred's attempt to promote the successful exploits of his own Saxon ancestors, it is reasonable to assume that he would not have wished to draw attention to the accomplishments of the British opposition, of which Arthur was apparently one.

The surviving contemporary records of Britain during the supposed Arthurian period are few and far between, such as the writings of visiting foreigners and fragmentary monastic records. None mention Arthur, but as the former are chiefly travelogues of events in which the authors were personally involved, and the latter almost entirely concern themselves with eccelsiastical affairs, no conclusions can be drawn either way.

We come, therefore, to the most important work in the search for King Arthur, the *De Excidio Conquestu Britanniae* (*On the Ruin and Conquest of Britain*), written by Gildas in the mid-sixth century. Reputedly the son of a British aristocrat, Gildas appears to have attended a school in Wales founded by St Illtud. According to William of Malmesbury, Gildas eventually became a monk, spending some time at the monastery in Glastonbury. Since Gildas actually seems to have been alive during the Arthurian period, or if not immediately afterwards, the omission of Arthur in his work might at first seem damning. But, as with Bede and the *Chronicle*, there may well be another explanation for Arthur's exclusion.

Gildas' work was never intended as a straightforward textbook of history; indeed it is essentially a tirade. As the title suggests, it is primarily a criticism of his fellow countrymen, levelled at their petty squabbles which allowed superiority to the Saxons. In fact, he hardly mentions anyone by name prior to the time of his writing, except Ambrosius whom he seems to have admired. Gildas verifies the victory of the Britons at the Battle of Badon, referenced in the *Welsh Annals* and the *Historia Brittonum*, although he does not say that it was Arthur who triumphed there, omitting the name of the leader altogether. This omission means that the name of the British leader at the most important battle of the era is historically unknown.

Having briefly considered surviving sources contemporary with the era in which we place Arthur, at this point we need to return to writers of the twelfth century. How useful are the works of Geoffrey's contemporary William of Malmesbury in the search for Arthur? William is considered by modern scholars to be a far more reliable historian than Geoffrey. Although William says very little of Arthur, he does provide us with a reasonable idea of the status of the Arthurian myth at the time that Geoffrey was writing the *Historia*. To begin with, William's *Gesta Regum Anglorum* tells us that a variety of Arthurian stories were in circulation, but, unlike Geoffrey, William tends to regard them as fables. He does not, however, reject Arthur as an historical figure.

From William's work it is evident that very little was known about Arthur. But William does provide us with a starting point. For instance, he tells us that Arthur aided the warrior Ambrosius Aurelianus in fighting the Angles. Although Ambrosius is named in the *De Excidio* of

Gildas as the leader of Britons who launched a successful counter-offensive against the Saxon invaders sometime during the 460s or 470s, almost nothing is reliably known about Ambrosius, including how or when he died.

William of Malmesbury goes on to say that Arthur triumphed at the siege of Mount Badon. Since Gildas also mentions the Battle of Badon as the high point of the period of warfare initiated by Ambrosius, it would appear that William is implying Arthur to be the successor of Ambrosius. Whether or not the two ever fought alongside each other remains unclear. What is clear is that Arthur was believed to have been a Christian king, as is shown by William's description of Arthur bearing an image of the Virgin Mary during the Battle of Badon.

It is clear that William regarded much of what he heard about Arthur as suspect. For example, he derides the legend that at Badon Arthur single-handedly defeated nine hundred of the enemy. Not only is it apparent that Arthur had acquired a mythical status by the early twelfth century, but also that Arthurian relic-hunting seems to have become fashionable. For instance, William mentions that someone claimed to have located the tomb of Arthur's nephew a few years earlier, although he goes on to say that Arthur's own tomb still evaded discovery.

What can be deduced from William's common-sense approach? Only that in the early twelfth century Arthur was believed to have been a Christian king who lived some six hundred years before. Any further information appears to have been confined to legend. William's message is one of caution, for in his own words 'this is that Arthur of whom the Britons talk such nonsense even today'. All the same, he clearly believes that there is enough evidence of his existence, for he adds that in his opinion Arthur is worthy of inclusion in authentic history as one 'who long sustained his failing country'. But where did William obtain his information?

One of William's sources has survived in the form of the *Historia Brittonum*. Now preserved in the British Library in a manuscript catalogued as Harley 3859, the *Historia Brittonum* is an early-twelfth-century handwritten copy. However, the style of writing, together with older fragments of the work which still survive, indicate a much earlier date for its original compilation, sometime around 830 A.D. The *Historia Brittonum* is generally believed to have been the work of a ninth-century monk from Bangor in North Wales called Nennius.

In the *Historia Brittonum*, Nennius tells us:

I have heaped together all that I found, from the Annals of the Romans, the Chronicles of the Holy Fathers, the writings of the Irish and the Saxons and the traditions of our own wise men.

The result is disorderly, but certainly appears to be a genuine attempt by the writer to reconstruct a history. On the subject of Ambrosius, Nennius says virtually nothing, but of Arthur he tells us the following:

In that time the Saxons strengthened in multitude and grew in Britain . . . Then Arthur fought against them in those days with the kings of the Britons, but he himself was leader of battles.

The first battle was at the mouth of the river Glein. The second, third, fourth and fifth upon another river which is called Dubglas, in the district of Linnuis. The sixth battle upon the river which is called Bassas. The seventh battle was in the Caledonian wood that is Cat Coit Celidon. The eighth battle was in Fort Guinnion in which Arthur carried the image of St Mary, ever virgin, on his shoulders and that day the pagans were turned to flight and a great slaughter was upon them through the virtue of Our Lord Jesus Christ and through the virtue of St Mary the Virgin, his mother. The ninth battle was waged in the City of the Legion. The tenth battle he fought on the shore of the river which is called Tribruit. The eleventh battle took place on the mountain which is called Agned. The twelfth battle was on Mount Badon, in which nine hundred and sixty men fell in one day from one attack by Arthur, and no one overthrew them except himself alone. And in all the battles he was the victor.

It appears that William of Malmesbury took his information from Nennius, since his description of the battle of Badon corresponds with the *Historia Brittonum*, including an image of the Virgin (although ascribed to a different battle). William, however, does not take seriously the idea that Arthur alone killed over nine hundred men. This may only have been metaphorical, implying that no other British leader helped him in the fight; a possible indication that Arthur was let down, or that his army overcame considerable odds.

But how reliable is Nennius? There is much that is historically inaccurate elsewhere in the *Historia Brittonum*, which does nothing to bolster claims of historical authenticity. However, the content strongly suggests that not only William, but also Geoffrey of Monmouth, took

Nennius as his source. For example, Geoffrey's story of Brutus the Trojan, plus many of his other fanciful themes, appear in Nennius, often quoted almost verbatim. Geoffrey, however, is far more imaginative than Nennius, who does not appear to be deliberately trying to pull the wool over anyone's eyes. Nennius introduces his work:

> I ask every reader who reads this book to pardon me for daring to write so much here after so many, like a chattering bird or an imcompetent judge. I yield to whoever may be better acquainted with this skill than I am.

By his own admission he is claiming to be artless, an open confession which leaves one with the impression that the *Historia Brittonum* is an honest attempt by Nennius to present the information at his disposal.

So it seems that in Nennius we not only have William's source, but also the basic formula for Geoffrey of Monmouth. But where did Geoffrey find his account of other Arthurian episodes? It would seem that he took one of them from the *Welsh Annals*. Now in the same composite manuscript as the *Historia Brittonum* at the British Library, the *Welsh Annals* were also copied in their surviving form during the early twelfth century. The *Welsh Annals* appear to have originally been compiled on behalf of the kings of South Wales, for although they include a series of genealogies (family trees) of a number of British rulers, they conclude with a more detailed family tree of the South Welsh kings of the ninth century. Fundamentally of Welsh interest, they are also an attempt to catalogue the events throughout Britain.

Although the content of the *Welsh Annals* dates back to the mid-fifth century, from the style and spelling it appears that they were only kept as a contemporary record from around 800. In their present form, however, the fact that the last entry is dated in the 950s indicates that they were originally written at this time.

Regrettably the *Welsh Annals* are little more than an incomplete chronology of dates, coupled with brief notations on important incidents that occured. Written in Latin, the table spans a period of 533 years, although they do not use the A.D. system of dating. The *Welsh Annals* can be dated, however, because of an entry in year 9 saying 'Easter is changed on the Lord's day by Pope Leo, bishop of Rome'. This is known from other sources to have occured in A.D. 455, so if the ninth year is A.D. 455 then the first year must be 447. Whenever this calibration is tested against other dates, known from reliable sources, it appears to be accurate within a year or so either way. Consequently, the entries relating to Arthur, being inserted in the years 72 and 93, can be taken as A.D. 518 and A.D. 539. The first, in 518, concerns the Battle of Badon, referred to as:

> The Battle of Badon, in which Arthur carried the cross of our Lord Jesus Christ on his shoulders for three days and three nights, and the Britons were victorious.

Interestingly, there is no reference to Arthur fighting alone, although we do see yet another mention of a holy relic on his shoulders. On this occasion, however, it is a cross and not an image of the Virgin. It is now generally agreed that there has been an early confusion between the Welsh word for shoulders, *ysgwydd* (pronounced 'scuith') and *ysgwyd* (pronounced 'scuit'), meaning shield. The important point is that the *Welsh Annals* speak of a cross and not the image of the Virgin, suggesting that the compiler of the *Welsh Annals* was not reliant on the same source as Nennius.

The second and only other reference to Arthur in the *Welsh Annals* is the entry for the year 539:

> The strife of Camlann in which Arthur and Medraut perished, and there was plague in Britain and in Ireland.

Since Nennius does not mention Camlann (probably because he is only concerned with Arthur's victories), it could well have been from the *Welsh Annals* that Geoffrey took his information concerning this battle.

Before collating the information derived from the *Welsh Annals* and the *Historia Brittonum*, we must examine in greater detail Geoffrey's claim to possess an 'ancient book' from which he learned the truth about King Arthur. There is certainly evidence for Arthurian legends surviving into the Middle Ages, but aside from the *Welsh Annals* and Nennius, has Geoffrey drawn on any other historical sources?

Besides Geoffrey and William of Malmesbury, two of their contemporary historians endeavoured to place Arthur in an historical context. Less reliable than William, but more reliable than Geoffrey, they are Caradoc of Llancarfan and Henry of Huntingdon. Neither, however, can be taken as reliable sources of additional information on the historical Arthur. Henry bases his work concerning the Arthurian period primarily on Nennius and the *Anglo-Saxon Chronicle*. In his

Historia Anglorum, written around 1135, he includes Nennius' list of Arthur's twelve battles, inserting them between the *Chronicle's* entries for 527 and 530. He seems to have arrived at this dating because the *Anglo-Saxon Chronicle* indicates that the Saxon advance was halted for a time after 527. Caradoc, on the other hand, in his *Life of Gildas* (circa 1140) includes Arthur in the life of the monk. Once again, the inclusion of Arthur is unreliable, since an earlier and more accurate work on the life of Gildas fails to include him.

The relevance of Henry and Caradoc relates to Geoffrey's 'ancient book'. In a postscript to the *Historia* Geoffrey cautions them both, along with William, telling them to leave King Arthur alone, for only he (Geoffrey) has the 'ancient book in the British language'. Fine words maybe, but a lasting pity that he never seems to have produced the book as evidence. Without this book we are left with the *Historia Brittonum* of Nennius as the earliest document to provide us with any details concerning King Arthur.

Arthur does not appear to have been invented by Nennius. From the style of his writing, and his open confession of artlessness, he seems to have lacked the imagination or indeed the motive. He even includes a number of serious contradictions throughout his narrative, such as different versions of the same person's death. Nennius gives the reason for this himself, explaining that he is offering all the information he has collected, presumably to allow the reader to decide between conflicting accounts. Additionally there is the simple fact that Nennius provides no more detail of Arthur's life than is included in the above passage. If he had invented Arthur, surely he would have presented us with more particulars. For these reasons, we are left with the definite impression of an honest scholar simply transcribing what he has discovered.

The same can be said when examining the list of Arthur's battles; Nennius is unsure of their precise locations. If he had invented the hero, why does he provide so little detail? This lack of detail possibly points to Nennius' list being derived from an old British war poem. (Many such poems were composed during the Dark Ages, praising the battles of warriors who are known to have existed, such as the *Gododdin* and the *Canu Llywarch Hen*, examined later.)

What does the list of battles tell us in its own right? Surely it must provide some idea where and when the events took place? Unfortunately, aside from the battle of Badon, none of the others are historically verifiable, although some might be located with a little informed guesswork. The river Glein at the mouth of which the first battle was said to have been fought is probably the river Glen in South Lincolnshire. Linnuis, where the next four battles were fought, may well be Lindsey, also in Lincolnshire, and the Cith of the Legion is probably Caerleon (the direct translation of the Welsh name) although Chester is called Cair Legion in the *Welsh Annals*. Besides the Battle of Badon, which must have been in the South of England (as will be reasoned shortly), the only other probable location concerns the battle of the Caledonian Wood. Since Caledonia was the Roman name for Scotland, Cat Coit Celidon seems to have been fought somewhere in the far North.

What does Nennius tell us about Arthur? Firstly, he would seem to confirm William of Malmesbury's statement that Arthur aided Ambrosius in fighting the Angles. If Arthur was fighting in Lincolnshire, the probable area for the first five battles, he would indeed have been in an area occupied by the Angles by the late fifth century. Perhaps until Ambrosius' death Arthur was commissioned to fight in other parts of the country, while the main armies were busy in the South fighting the Saxons.

Nennius also tells us something about Arthur's rank. Arthur is introduced simply as the Britons' 'leader of battles', implying that Arthur was not a king himself. This implication is echoed in Nennius' assertion that Arthur fought 'with the British kings'. Elsewhere in the *Historia Brittonum* (see below), where Nennius mentions a legend concerning Arthur's dog, he describes Arthur simply as 'the warrior Arthur'. This ambiguity concerning Arthur's status prompts speculation that he may have been a foreign mercenary, which may account for his fighting in such widely spread locations, presumably for whoever was paying him at the time. Conversely, he may have been the commander-in-chief of Ambrosius' armies.

However, this is all speculation; all that can really be deduced at this stage concerns the legendary status of Arthur during the lifetime of Nennius. There are two legends of Arthur in an appendix of *Mirabilia* (Marvels) in the *Historia Brittonum*. One concerns a stone marked with the paw print of Arthur's dog, Cabal, said to lie on a pile of rocks in the region of Buelt (Builth) in Central Wales. According to Nennius, if anyone removes the stone it magically returns of its own accord. The other concerns a tomb which was said to change its size continually. It was in the district of Ergyng (Ercing), in what is now Herefordshire, and was thought to contain the body of Arthur's son Amr. These two inclusions suggest that Arthurian legends had become firmly established by the time of Nennius in the early ninth century.

What can reasonably be surmised from the *Historia Brittonum*, concerning the Arthurian legend that existed around 830 A.D.?

1. By the ninth century Arthur already featured in local folklore.

2. Arthur was believed to be a Christian warrior who fought the invading Saxons and perhaps the Saxon allies, the Angles in the East, or even the Picts of the North.

3. Arthur was believed to have consolidated a successful counter-offensive initiated by Ambrosius Aurelianus sometime during the late fifth and early sixth centuries.

4. The Battle of Badon, seemingly the result of a siege lasting three days, was considered Arthur's most important victory.

5. Arthur does not appear to have been thought of as a king at all; rather, as some form of war leader or commander-in-chief, perhaps the nearest equivalent in more recent history being the Japanese Shogun.

This, then, is all we know concerning the status of the Arthurian legend in the ninth century. Although considerably earlier than the Middle Ages of Geoffrey of Monmouth, it is still more than three centuries after the actual events appear to have taken place. But when exactly was the Arthurian era? At this stage, the only sure indicator of the period of Arthur is the Battle of Badon, an historical event attested to by Gildas himself, who wrote within living memory of the conflict. As the only historically verifiable event which has been associated with Arthur, it is therefore crucial to ascertain precisely when the Battle of Badon occurred.

4

The Arthurian Era

According to the *Welsh Annals*, the Battle of Badon occurred around 518. However the entries concerning Arthur must be treated with some caution, since they are two of a small number of British entries in the first century of the *Annals*, amongst a series of extracts from Irish annals. As we shall see, it seems that when the entry was inserted, a few centuries after the event, it was placed in the wrong year.

Since Gildas wrote at least 350 years before the *Welsh Annals* were compiled, almost certainly within living memory of the battle, he is surely the most reliable source. Unfortunately, Gildas does not supply dates. But, he does supply a vital clue as to when the Battle of Badon really occurred – although a certain amount of detective work is needed. Gildas writes that for a while in the late fifth century the Britons were successfully defeating the invading Anglo-Saxons:

> This continued until the year of the Siege of Badon Hill, virtually the last defeat of the rascals [the Anglo-Saxons], and certainly not the least. And this the forty-fourth year, inasmuch as I know, with one month by this time having passed and it was also the year of my birth.

What is Gildas actually saying in this rather confusing passage? Some scholars interpret Gildas as saying that the battle occurred forty-three years earlier; i.e. he was now forty-four and the battle had occurred sometime during the first year of his life. Gildas' *De Excidio* is thought to have been written in the 540s, as the work was composed before the death of Maglocunus, a king whom Gildas addresses personally and whose death is recorded during a plague that affected Britain in the late 540s. The *Welsh Annals* place the death of Maglocunus in 549, and as independent Irish records evidence plague in Britain at this time, it is probably accurate. From Gildas' references to Maglocunus, his criticism must have been compiled shortly before the death of the King.

So, according to this first interpretation, by dating the *De Excidio* to about 545, the Battle of Badon would have occurred some time around the year 500. However, there is a second, more convincing interpretation of Gildas.

Gildas actually says that the battle took place in the forty-fourth year of something or other, which seems a strange way of putting it if he really did mean forty-four years before the time he was writing. It seems more likely that Gildas is telling us that the battle took place in the forty-fourth year of some specific era, which also happened to be the year he was born. If so, what era could Gildas be referring to? The answer is provided by Bede in the early eighth century. Bede was certainly familiar with Gildas' *De Excidio*, for in one passage in his *Ecclesiastic History* he writes:

> Among other most wicked actions, not to be expressed, which their own historian, Gildas, mournfully takes notice of, they added this – that they never preached the faith to the Saxons.

Bede even quotes Gildas word for word on occasions. In similar fashion to Gildas, Bede talks of:

> . . . the siege of Badon Hill, when they (the Britons) made no small slaughter of those invaders about forty-four years after their arrival in England.

These invaders, explains Bede, were the Anglo-Saxons. Although it is clear that Bede is quoting Gildas in this passage, he must also have been employing an additional source, as he identifies the era as the Anglo-Saxon era, which Gildas neglected to do. To discover the date of Badon, we must therefore fix the date of the arrival of the Anglo-Saxons.

In 364 the Roman Empire had split into two; the Western Empire was governed from Rome, while the Eastern Empire was centred on Constantinople in what is now Turkey. The early years of the fifth century heralded the end of the Western Empire. Although it struggled on for a few more decades, the imperial establishment had all but collapsed. Its demise began with trouble amongst the Huns of central Asia in the early fifth century. Driven at first by a series of disastrous crop failures, these fierce and warlike barbarians surged towards the western Goths, who were in turn driven from their own lands. The vanquished Goths then crossed the Danube and the Rhine, compelling other nations to migrate still further westwards. With Rome on the defensive, the barbarian hordes across Europe began to break through the frontiers of the empire. One barbarian chief, Alaric, King of the Visigoths, reached Italy in 401, and by 408 was laying siege to Rome itself. To meet this challenge, the Romans were forced to withdraw troops from the colonial outpost of Britain.

With the Roman forces severely diminished, it was not long before problems arose on British soil. In the north, the Picts of Scotland began a series of increasingly daring raids across Hadrian's Wall, and in 410 the British administration appealed for reinforcements from Emperor Honorius in Rome. But the Emperor had troubles of his own, for in the same year Rome itself was sacked by Alaric's Visigoths. Not only did the British receive no reinforcements, but they also lost the legions they still possessed. With the empire in tatters, the Roman army withdrew completely from Britain.

Britain had been part of the Roman Empire for three and a half centuries, the fabric of government long reliant on its military support. This had provided stability for longer than anyone could remember. Now, suddenly, it was gone and anarchy threatened the country. Every freeborn Briton had long been a Roman citizen, and few would have been happy to see the legions leave.

The reason that so little is known of this period of British history is that the break from Rome removed Britain from the field of the Mediterranean writers, from whom we acquire much of our earlier information, and few contemporary native records have survived. It is therefore far from certain exactly what took place in Britain during the fifth century. The basic picture appears to be that the north was suffering repeated incursions from the Picts of Scotland, while the west was being invaded by the Irish. The greatest problem for the majority of Britons, however, was the struggle for regional supremacy between their own native chieftains. It was into this fragmented country that the Anglo-Saxons began their invasions.

As a result of the attack of the Huns on the Goths there were mass migrations right across the European continent, an unprecedented domino effect which continued until Attila, the King of the Huns, was ultimately defeated by a joint Roman/Visigoth army at Chalons (in Gaul) in 451. As a result, coastal dwellers from what is now part of Denmark and North Germany began to cross the Channel to settle in eastern Britain. These people were of mixed tribal groupings, Jutes,

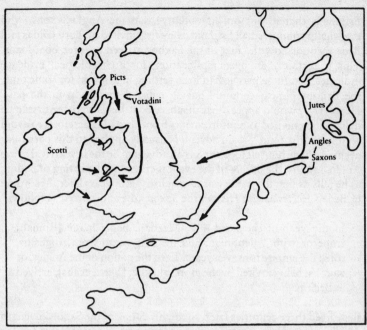

Invasions and Migrations in the Fifth Century

Angles and Saxons, later collectively called the Anglo-Saxons, or just Saxons.

It appears that rather than attempt to repel these migrants, one British chieftain enlisted their services as mercenaries, payment including land on which they could settle in South-East England. In return, a large part of Britain came under his control. Exactly who this man was, or his precise status, is something of a mystery. Gildas blames this leader for the eventual ruin of Britain but fails to name him, referring to him only as the 'proud tyrant'. Bede, on the other hand, calls him Vertigernus, while Nennius and the *Anglo-Saxon Chronicle* used the name Vortigern – which has since been used by most scholars. But this is unlikely to have been his true name; rather it was a title of some sort, which seems to have been derived from the Latin word *vertifernus*, meaning 'overlord'. It appears that for some time Vortigern was virtually the absolute ruler of Britain, suppressing his fellow chieftains and repelling the Picts and the Irish.

The reason that Gildas blames this 'proud tyrant' for the ruin of

Britain is that it was on his initiative that the Anglo-Saxons, who eventually conquered all England, were first invited in. Both Gildas and Bede recount how the first of the Saxons arrived in three boat-loads. This is certainly an oversimplification, for archaeological evidence indicates that these people had been settling in England for some time, the Britons almost certainly having enlisted their help in the past. However, it would appear that the three boat-loads were the first to be deliberately invited as reinforcements from abroad. Therefore, to avoid confusion, the term 'Saxon advent' is usually applied to this particular event. As Bede himself took the Saxon advent to be the first arrival of the Anglo-Saxons, the dating of the event is crucial to the dating of Badon, as he tells us that the battle was fought forty-four years later. According to Bede's *Ecclesiastical History* the Saxon advent occurred as follows:

> In the year of the Lord 449, Martian, being made [Roman] emperor with Valentinian, and the forty-sixth from Augustus, ruled the empire for seven years. Then the nation of the Angles, or Saxons, being invited by the aforesaid king [Vertigernus], arrived in Britain.

Bede lived three centuries later, so can his dating of the Saxon advent to 449 be trusted? The picture is confusing and different dates for the advent can be derived from the *Welsh Annals* and Nennius. The confusion seems to have arisen as a result of an original ambiguity concerning the date of a British plea for help referenced by Gildas, and later writers using it as a historical reference point. According to Gildas, some years after the Romans left Britain, events took such a turn for the worst that:

> The miserable remnants [the Britons] sent off a letter again, this time to the Roman commander Agitius in the following terms: 'To Agitius, thrice consul: the groans of the British.' Further on came the complaint: 'The barbarians push us back to the sea and the sea pushes us back to the barbarians; between these two kinds of death, we are either drowned or slaughtered.' But they got no help in return.

The reference to this letter is one of the only dateable events in Gildas' work. Although Gildas calls the Roman commander Agitius, he is actually referring to an officer named Aetius who was consul in Gaul. Not only are the names similar, but he is referred to as 'thrice consul', and Aetius was the only man (other than an emperor) to acquire a third consulship for over three hundred years. Considering that his third term began in 446, and the fourth in 453, the plea for help must have occurred at some point between these years.

So how long after this appeal was the Saxon advent? The events that follow the Aetius letter are described by Gildas:

> Meanwhile as the British feebly wandered, a dreadful and notorious famine gripped them, forcing many of them to give up without delay to their bloody plunders, merely to get a scrap of food to revive them. Not so others: they kept fighting back, basing themselves on the mountains, caves, heaths and thorny thickets. Their enemies had been plundering their land for many years; now for the first time they inflicted a massacre on them . . . [With the Britons now on the offensive] the impudent Irish pirates returned home, though they were shortly to return, and for the first time the Picts in the far end of the island kept quiet from now on, though they occasionally carried out devastating raids of plunder. So in this period of truce the desolate people found their cruel scars healing over.

This is probably the period of Vortigern, the transformation of events seemingly being organised by his ruthless efficiency. Following this there is a time of peace in which 'the island was so flooded with abundance of goods that no previous age had known the like of it'. Unfortunately, however, this age of abundance did not last. Gildas tells us that:

> a deadly plague swooped brutally on the stupid people, and in a short period laid low so many people, with no sword, that the living could not bury all the dead.

The problems that this natural catastrophe created weakened the country to such an extent that the Pictish and Irish raids recommenced. The Britons were thus forced to seek external assistance by convening 'a council to decide the best and soundest way to counter the brutal and repeated invasions and plunderings'. Together with their leader, the 'proud tyrant' (Vortigern), they decide to hire the Anglo-Saxons to fight for them as mercenaries.

It is quite clear from Gildas' narrative that the events separating the letter from the Saxon arrival must span at least a decade, perhaps two.

Time for the Britons to rally, probably under Vortigern, time for a period of wealth, and time for a plague to once again weaken the island. As Gildas has the Saxon advent occurring after all this, he is suggesting that it happened some time between 560 and 570. So why does Bede locate it in 449? The answer, it seems, is that Gildas inserted the passage on the Aetius letter in the wrong place in his text, and Bede realised that he had made a mistake.

The evidence for this comes from Gildas himself, for it is possible to date the plague he refers to in the above passage – an epidemic known from many foreign sources to have swept across the entire Roman world during the late 440s. As the Aetius plea occurred during the consul's third term, between 446 and 453, the letter could not have been sent a decade or two before the plague as Gildas' order of events requires. The letter to Aetius must, therefore, have been sent *after* the plague had weakened the country.

Gildas tells us that the Pictish and Irish invasions recommenced at this time, and that the British were forced to seek external assistance. In all probability, Gildas acquired a copy of the letter, which he could see referred to the invasions by the Picts and the Irish. Aware of the two periods during which the appeal may have been made – the first before Vortigern's period of prosperity around 420, and the second after the plague around 447 when the raids recommenced – he wrongly attributed it to the former. It would seem, therefore, that the appeal to Aetius was made immediately before deciding to invite in the Saxons, a decision that was forced upon the British after the consul refused them aid.

This seems to have been the conclusion reached by Bede: the Britons appealed for help from Aetius when the Pictish and Irish raids recommenced around 448, and the following year, after the appeal failed, their leader Vortigern decided to enlist the help of the Saxon mercenaries. Confirmatory evidence for this conclusion comes from Anglo-Saxon themselves, as the *Anglo-Saxon Chronicle* also records that they first arrived in 449. Consequently, by dating the Saxon advent to 449 it means that if the Battle of Badon occurred forty-four years later it must have been fought in 493.

With a date for the Battle of Badon, we now have a precise historical era in which Arthur is said to have lived: a time following the collapse of the Roman Empire in the West, after German warlord Odovacer had defeated the last emperor Romulus Augustulus in 476. By the 490s Britain had well and truly descended into the Dark Ages and the Anglo-

Saxons had invaded half the country. Does this fit with what Nennius – who provides the oldest surviving account of Arthur's campaigns – tells us about Arthur?

Many scholars have refused to consider the possibility of Arthur's historical existence because the medieval Arthurian romances are just too fanciful. However, Nennius' Arthur is not described in a context of magic and mystery, as he was in the later medieval tales, but in simple historical terms. Nennius is not portraying a romantic Arthur, he is merely writing of a British leader who once fought successfully against the Saxons. Moreover, when introducing the list of Arthur's battles, Nennius seems to be historically accurate, both chronologically and also concerning the contemporary warriors he names. According to Nennius:

> In that time the Saxons strengthened in multitude and grew in Britain. On the death of Hengist, Octha his son passed from the northern part of Britain to the kingdom of the Kentishmen and from him arise the kings of the Kentishmen. Then Arthur fought against them in those days . . .

The *Anglo-Saxon Chronicle* tells us that the Saxon advances into western Britain began around the year 455, starting in Kent, and were directed principally by Hengist himself until the 480s. This tallies precisely with Nennius' account, when he refers to Hengist being the Kentish leader shortly before Arthur began to fight the Saxons. Octha was also an historical figure. A ninth-century Saxon manuscript now in the British Library, known as the *Cotton Vespasian*, offers a list of the kings of the Dark Ages, including Octha, whom it records succeeding his father Hengist just as Nennius describes. Concerning dating, Nennius says that Arthur fought against the Saxons once Hengist had died. The *Anglo-Saxon Chronicle* gives the date of Hengist's death as 488, which accurately tallies with Arthur's campaigns if he fought the Battle of Badon five years later in 493.

As Nennius' dating is consistent with both the *Anglo-Saxon Chronicle* and the dating of Badon, and the two warriors he names along with Arthur appear to have been contemporary historical figures, there seems no compelling reason to doubt his reference to Arthur being the most important British leader of the period –around the last decade of the fifth century.

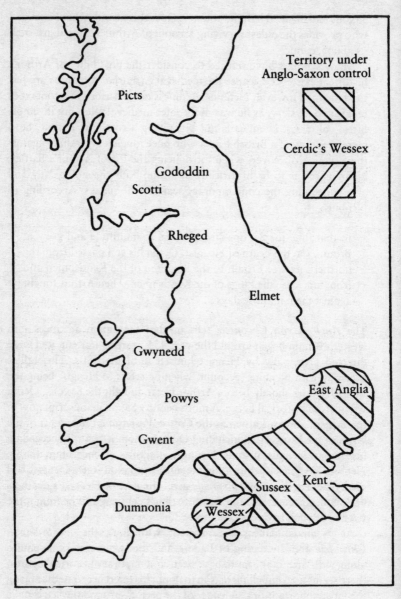

Britain at the Time of Badon

5

Prelude to Badon

Before we can begin to search for an historical Arthur around the end of the fifth century, we must reconstruct a picture of contemporary Britain, beginning with the arrival of Arthur's enemies the Anglo-Saxons.

It appears that in the latter half of the fifth century, in addition to the Saxon settlements in the South-East, the Angles began to arrive in large numbers in the area of the Wash in Lincolnshire and Norfolk. Although in the ensuing decades they were able to establish their own colonies as far south as Suffolk, they may well originally have been recruited as reinforcements for Vortigern's northern army.

The archaeological evidence, in the form of pottery from Yorkshire, Lincolnshire and East Anglia, tells us that the newcomers began arriving around 450. The Angles exhibit a slightly different culture from the southern colonists, indicating that they were originally from Schleswig in the northernmost part of Germany. Bede gives this area as their homeland, a territory which was then called Angeln.

Although the colonists in the South-East of England are usually described simply as Saxons, the very first of these settlers were the Jutes, from Jutland in Denmark. In fact, Bede tells us that it was the Jutes who initially established the kingdom of Kent, suggesting that the three boat-loads were not in fact Saxons at all. Alternatively, they may have been the first of the Saxons, invited to settle in the Jute colony. Either way, in the following decades the influx of true Saxons from the estuary of the river Elbe (adjacent to Angeln) overwhelmed the Jutish population, the minority being forced to integrate within a very short period.

In many ways the Jutes, Angles and Saxons were closely related to one another, the area from which they originally came being no larger than present-day Wales. For most purposes, therefore, the term Anglo-Saxon can safely be applied to the entire culture. Indeed the variations were tiny in comparison to the massive culture gap between themselves and the Romanised British, many of whom were practising Christians. The

Pagan newcomers had their own religious customs, which the majority of the Britons would probably have found abhorrent. In Roman terms the Britons were civilised and the Anglo-Saxons were barbarians. With such cultural differences, problems were bound to arise.

Trouble began around 455, when the Saxon colonies in the South East went into revolt. There were doubtless many reasons for the rebellion, although Gildas informs us that it arose over a question of payment for the mercenaries. Although he provides no details, he does explain the severity of the insurgency, saying that cities were destroyed and British inhabitants killed, enslaved or forced to flee. Bede gives the same account, although he adds the names of the revolutionary leaders – two brothers called Hengist and Horsa.

The Angles in the north also joined the rebellion, for Bede tells us that having 'entered into league with the Picts, whom they had by this time repelled by force of their arms, they began to turn their weapons against their confederates'. The degree of organisation in the Anglian revolt is difficult to ascertain. It is fairly certain, however, that the British were completely unprepared.

The rebellion appears to have begun with the overthrow of a British contingent in the north of Kent. The *Anglo-Saxon Chronicle* includes this initial Saxon victory in 455, saying that it took place at Aegaeles Threp, most probably Aylesford. But the *Chronicle* tells us that one of the Saxon leaders, Horsa, died in the battle. Nonetheless, this Saxon victory marks the establishment of the independent kingdom of Kent, since Hengist is proclaimed its king. The battle is also mentioned by Nennius (although he calls it Episford), who says that not only Horsa but also Vortigern's son Cateyrn perished.

As to the fate of Vortigern, Gildas gives us nothing to go on, except that in one passage he refers to him as the 'ill-fated tyrant'. Since Bede also offers no clues, we are left only with Nennius. Unfortunately, Nennius' 'heap' of all he could find includes almost as much from legend as it does from any written records he may have acquired. Even within these broad constraints he contradicts himself, in one place saying that after Essex, Sussex and Middlesex are conceded to the Saxons, Vortigern dies a broken man, whereas elsewhere he is consumed by fire.

Many scholars have deduced from Nennius, together with the various surviving legendary accounts, that Vortigern's failed policy with the Saxons, together with the general unrest in a post-plague nation, brought about his overthrow in civil war. One way or the other, he appears to have gone by 460. Nennius, for example, suggests that one Vitalinius was in command after Vortigern's death, probably a member of Vortigern's family since Vortigern's grandfather bore the same name. Whoever was actually leading the Britons at this stage, they certainly suffered a massive defeat.

When the literary and archaeological evidence is pieced together, it seems that by the time the rampage eventually ceased, the Saxon influence extended westwards from Kent, through Sussex and into Hampshire, and northwards through Middlesex to Essex. The Anglian influence, on the other hand, stretched northwards from the Wash, through Lincolnshire and Humberside, and southwards to Saxon Essex. Remarkably, it also extended as far west as Warwickshire. Defending an area half the size of England must have placed considerable strain on the Anglo-Saxon forces, for it appears that soon after having successfully routed the Britons, they retreated. This must have provided the British with a breathing space in which to organise their forces, as sometime around 465 they seem to have mustered a counter-offensive. Gildas says:

> After a time, when the cruel plunderers had gone home, God gave strength to the survivors . . . Their leader was Ambrosius Aurelianus, a gentleman who perhaps alone of the Romans had survived the shock of this notable storm . . . Under him the people regained their strength and challenged the victors to battle. The Lord assented and battle went their way.

Of the same period Bede says:

> When the victorious army, having destroyed and dispersed the natives, had returned home to their settlements, the Britons began by degrees to take heart, and gather strength . . . They had at that time for their leader, Ambrosius Aurelius, a modest man, who alone, by chance of the Roman nation had survived the storm . . . Under him the Britons revived, and offering battle to the victors, by the help of God came off victorious.

Once again, Bede is clearly using Gildas as his source, although it appears that he has drawn on additional material, considering that he gives Ambrosius' second name as Aurelius and not Aurelianus. Unfortunately, there is nothing more concerning Ambrosius. Aside from the fact that he is the only Briton of the period Gildas names, he remains as mysterious as Arthur himself. Whether or not he actually overthrew Vortigern (or his successor) or simply succeeded him is uncertain, all we know is that he began to turn the tide on the Anglo-Saxons.

It is reasonable to assume that this occurred somewhere around 465, for the *Chronicle* lists no battles between A.D. 465 and A.D. 473. This must have been a time of consolidation on both sides, when defences were prepared and personnel organised; a preparation for the decisive struggle that followed, an all-out confrontation in which a warrior called Arthur seems to have played a major role.

Unfortunately, everything we know from Gildas of this all-important period of conflict is contained in just two lines:

> From then on victory went now to our countrymen, now to their enemies. This lasted right up till the siege of Badon Hill.

Even Bede cannot help us, for he simply paraphrases Gildas:

> From that day, sometimes the natives, and sometimes their enemies, prevailed, till the year of the siege of Badon Hill.

We are left, therefore, with the *Chronicle*, which provides us only with the Anglo-Saxon side of the story, and the less than helpful Nennius.

It appears that once the war started, it was the Saxons who went on the offensive, consolidating their hold over Middlesex and moving westwards. According to the *Chronicle*, in 473 Hengist fought against the Britons and captured 'innumerable spoils', the enemy fleeing from them 'as they would from fire'. From the archaeological evidence, it seems that they consolidated their position in Surrey, pushing along the Thames Valley into Berkshire. However, the Britons seem to have held the advance at this stage and there appears to have been an uneasy stalemate in the South-East for the next decade. The war then shifts to a second front, in the east, against the Angles.

Here the fighting appears to have gone in favour of the Britons. In fact, the Angles in the Warwickshire area seem to have fallen quickly under British control. The archaeological evidence indicates a continutiy of British presence throughout this period, an undisturbed ceramic sequence (the same kind of pottery) together with uninterrupted burials. Also in Lindsey and Kesteven, respectively the north and south of Lincolnshire, archaeological discoveries indicate a survival of British power until the late sixth century. Many of the great dykes that dominated the south-western approaches to East Anglia were dug at this time to mark a fixed frontier. The linear Earthwork known as King Lud's Bank, for example, may represent a British attempt to control any further invasion, as it blocked the ancient routeway known as Sewestern Lane.

It was in the far North, however, that the fiercest fighting seems to have occurred, where Bede tells us that the Anglo-Saxons fought together with their allies the Picts. Here the archaeological evidence clearly shows that the initial colonies failed to establish themselves before the Britons totally reoccupied the area.

It is during this period that Arthur first appears in Nennius' account, on Hengist's death when 'Octha his son passed over from the northern part of Britain to the kingdom of the Kentishmen'. Nennius says that Octha was in command of the Saxon forces in the North, which suggests a working alliance between the Angles and the Saxons at this time. This being the case, perhaps Octha was forced to retreat after defeat in the north, regardless of the death of his father. Either way, there seems to have been fighting in the North around or just prior to 488.

The most likely locations of Arthur's battles from Nennius' list certainly seem to tally with what can be concluded from this assorted evidence. It seems that the first few battles on the list are fought in East Anglia, the period in which British control was regained and the construction of the great dykes undertaken. Following this, there is a battle in the far North (in the Caledonian Wood), presumably against the Picts and their Angle allies. Then the eighth battle, a particularly important victory judging from the fact that 'the pagans were put to flight on that day and there was a great slaughter upon them'. This, the Battle of Castellum (Fort) Guinnion, could be almost anywhere, although it may well have been the final battle in the North, possibly forcing Octha and his Saxon expeditionary force to return home.

This Eastern and Northern stage of the war may well have been the period of which William of Malmesbury wrote, when Arthur fought against the Angles. However, it is the ensuing period of the conflict which is most confusing, the period in which Ambrosius appears to have been succeeded by Arthur himself as the leader of the British forces.

As with Vortigern, we have no way of knowing what really happened to Ambrosius. However, Nennius provides evidence of a civil conflict at this juncture. Arthur may even have taken up arms against Ambrosius himself.

The Battle of Badon itself was fought some time around the end of the fifth century, a battle that was certainly against the Anglo-Saxons, as evidenced by Gildas. The battle marked a decisive defeat of the Saxons, resulting in a truce that was to last for more than half a century; in fact, right up until the time that Gildas was writing, as he tells us that after Badon war with the Anglo-Saxons had ceased.

In the half century that followed Badon, until the time of Gildas' writing, Britain enjoyed a period free from external attack. Indeed, there is archaeological evidence of a reverse Anglo-Saxon migration; considerable numbers returning to the continent, due no doubt to their precarious foothold in Britain. For instance, several types of characteristic English Anglo-Saxon pottery have been discovered in parts of Germany, dating from the early to mid-sixth century, indicating that these regions received newcomers direct from Britain. However, Gildas tells us that there was considerable civil strife amongst the Britons during this period, which he saw as heralding the ultimate ruin of Britain. Bede, in a less vehement manner, says:

> In the meantime, in Britain, there was some respite from foreign, but not civil war. There still remained the ruins of cities destroyed by the enemy, and abandoned; and the natives, who had escaped the enemy, now fought against each other.

Unfortunately for the Britons, Gildas was correct in his assessment of the situation; their precarious superiority over the Anglo-Saxons was not to last. Soon after 550 the Saxons were again pushing westwards, opening with a victory at a battle near Salisbury. It was not long before Buckinghamshire was overwhelmed, and in 577 the Britons in the South-West were cut off from the rest of Britain following a Saxon triumph at the Battle of Dyrham, when Bath, Cirencester and Gloucester were lost. For a time, the Britons appear to have struggled on in the Somerset marshlands, but in 614 the Saxons moved into Devon and by 682 were in effective control of the entire South-West peninsular, apart from Cornwall (which remained independent until 926).

The native British were gradually driven from England and reduced to three remnants of Celtic civilization: Wales, Cornwall and the North-West, while others fled across the Channel and settled in Brittany. Ultimately, even Cornwall and the North-West were conceded to the

Anglo-Saxons, leaving only the area we now call Wales as the surviving homeland of the native Britons. The Anglo-Saxons gained so much control over what is now England that they began to refer to the native Britons as Welsh, deriving from the Saxon word *weala* meaning foreigners. The Britons, on the other hand, began to call themselves *cymru*, meaning 'fellow countrymen'. From the tenth century onwards it was no longer a matter of Anglo-Saxon and native Britain, but two separate countries, England and Wales.

It was this division that enabled the stories of King Arthur to survive primarily in Wales until the time of the medieval romancers. It may also explain why the *Welsh Annals* include Arthur, while the English *Anglo-Saxon Chronicle* does not, and why the Welsh monk Nennius makes reference to him, whereas he is omitted from the work of the English monk Bede.

Returning to the end of the fifth century, however, we must now attempt to establish where the Battle of Badon – the most important battle of the era – was fought.

From the archaeological standpoint, the kingdom of Kent must have suffered a massive defeat some time around 493 as no evidence is found of Saxon burials in Essex, Hertfordshire and much of Buckinghamshire for some decades after. This indicates that they withdrew into Middlesex, Surrey and Kent by the turn of the century.

However, just prior to the 590s there was a considerable increase in Saxon influence in the South of England, a significant increase in manpower that began originally in 477. According to the *Anglo-Saxon Chronicle*, that year saw the arrival of a new wave of Saxon warriors who landed in strength at a place called Cymenesora, probably the Selsey Peninsular just to the east of Portsmouth. Led by the warrior Aelle, they quickly overpowered the Britons in the district, forcing them to flee. In 485, the *Chronicle* again records Aelle's victory over the Britons, this time at the River Mearcredesburna (possibly the Alun). Thereafter, Aelle seems to have gone from strength to strength until 491, when he besieged the fort at Anderida (modern day Pevensey). During this battle, the *Chronicle* tells us, his men slaughtered all those who had taken shelter within its walls, a massacre that marked the ultimate defeat of the British in the area, and saw the establishment of the Saxon kingdom of Sussex (South Saxons). Aelle had now reached the easternmost limits of his campaign, for he was now sharing borders with Octha's kingdom of Kent.

What happened next is unknown, although Bede tells us that Aelle became the first high king of Saxon-occupied Britain, a position the *Chronicle* refers to as *bretwalda*, meaning 'wide ruler'. The term may well infer that he was the senior partner in an alliance with the kingdom of Kent.

Unfortunately for Aelle, his kingdom did not survive for long. Both the literary and archaeological evidence clearly show the virtual annihiliation of Saxon Sussex. The *Chronicle* makes no further reference to Sussex or its kings for another one and a half centuries, while archaeology has discovered no Saxon burials in the area between the late fifth and late sixth centuries.

This, together with the withdrawal of Octha's Thames Valley Saxons, can only be explained by a successful British offensive sometime during the 490s; which tallies completely with what Gildas tells us of the Battle of Badon; the Saxons on the offensive until 491, Aelle establishing himself as chief Saxon warlord, and an eclipse of at least half the Saxon South-East within a few years. A major decisive battle fought sometime in the mid-490s fits perfectly.

All points considered, the Battle of Badon appears to have been fought against a Sussex/Kent alliance, indicating a possible strategic position in the Swindon area, about as far as the Saxon forces had pushed. If so, then a site for the Battle of Badon could be Liddington Castle, a prominent Iron Age hill-fort not far from Swindon, overlooking the village of Badbury. It is one of many such hill-forts reoccupied during this time, and lies in a central position between the main Anglo-Saxon settlements, as they existed in the 490s, and the British areas controlled by the cities of Gloucester, Cirencester and Bath. Moreover, it stands on a major trading route junction of the period, at the intersection of the Roman road, Ermine St, running to the south, and the ancient Ridgeway, cutting right across Central England.

Unfortunately, there is a major stumbling block in the case for Liddington Castle. The argument relies mainly on the name similarity between the village of Badbury and the word Badon. There are, in fact, over half a dozen places still called Badbury in Britain today, their names deriving from the Old English *Baddanbyrig* or *Baddanburg*, meaning the 'fort of Badda'. Since Badda is a Saxon name, probably a god or hero, it follows that these sites were so named by the Saxons. It is difficult to imagine Gildas, a native Briton writing within living memory of Badon, referring to the battle site by the name the foreigners used. In fact, the name may not have been pronounced Badon at all, but Bathon.

Many words in the British language, which later evolved into modern

Welsh, employed the syllable th. The Roman alphabet, in which English is still written today, had no single letter for this sound. Although we now use the combined letters T and H, this is a comparatively recent development. In fact, as late as the Middle Ages English writers employed a variant of the letter Y for the th sound, resulting in today's common misconception that our ancestors spoke 'Ye Olde English'. The truth is that THE was always pronounced with a TH and not with a Y. Returning to the Dark Ages, however, there was much confusion. Some Latin writers used the letters T and H, while others used the Greek letter Theta.

The problem, however, is further compounded. With certain place names and some personal names, the pronunciation of the th syllable had a different inclination. To distinguish between these sounds scribes would often emply a double D. This practice has survived to this day in modern Welsh. For example, the county of Gwynedd is pronounced as Gwyneth, and the village of Beddgelert as Bethgelert. To make things worse, the double D was sometimes dropped in favour of a single D. This could well have been the case with Badon, which may have been pronounced Bathon. Continuing to seek modern name similarities in the search for the battle site, we are drawn towards the city of Bath.

The city, called by the Romans *Aquae Sulis* (meaning 'The Waters of Sul'), was named Badanceaster by the Saxons who captured it in the late sixth century. Badan means 'bath' and so Badanceaster means 'city of baths', referring to the Roman baths still to be seen there. Indeed, the modern name Bath is derived from this Saxon name. However, it would appear that the Saxon name may have come from the original British word for a bath – *baddon* – which is still preserved in modern Welsh, where it is pronounced 'bathon'. In other words, to the early Welsh speaking Britons, the battle of Badon may simply have meant the battle of Bath. Interestingly, Bath is precisely where the Welsh-speaking Geoffrey of Monmouth tells us that Arthur fought his most celebrated battle.

It is in the *Historia Brittonum* that we find perhaps the most persuasive piece of literary evidence that the Battle of Badon was fought at Bath. Nennius again mentions Badon at the end of his work, but this time gives us two vital clues as to its location. In his list of 'Marvels' he tells us of a wonder of Britain which is a 'hot lake, where the baths of Badon are, in the country of the Hwicce'. These baths of Badon must surely be the Roman baths in the city of Bath. Although there may have been other Roman bath sites still visible during the time of Nennius, they are unlikely to have had a hot geothermal lake in the vicinity. The Roman baths of Bath were unique in Britain, as they were heated by natural springs of hot subterranean water. Moreover, there is evidence for the location from Nennius' reference to 'the country of the Hwicce'. The Hwicce were an Anglo-Saxon tribe recorded in the *Tribal Hidage*, a Mercian taxation document compiled by King Offa in the 760s, listing peoples subject to the Mercian king. This tells us that the Kingdom of the Hwicce covered the Worcester and Gloucestershire areas, along with what is now part of the county of Avon, including the city of Bath.

From this assorted evidence we can conclude that the battle of Badon was fought in the vicinity of Bath. But where? Although the *Welsh Annals* refer only to the 'Battle of Badon', both Nennius and Gildas are more specific. Nennius tells us of the 'battle on Mount Badon', while Gildas talks of the 'siege of Mount Badon'. These references to a mount, together with the reference by Gildas to a siege, imply that the battle was fought for the possession of a hill-top site, undoubtedly one of the hill-forts that were reoccupied at this time. If Badon was a hill-fort in the Bath area, vital for control of the city, then the most probable location is the huge triangular hill-fort on Little Solsbury Hill, overlooking the city just to the north-east. Indeed, excavations have shown that this fort was refortified by the British during the late fifth century.

If the Battle of Badon was fought here, it would mean that the Britons would previously have been in serious trouble. The Saxons would have been less than fifteen miles from the Bristol Channel, threatening to cut the entire British nation in two. This may explain why the Battle of Badon was so crucial – the whole future of the country was at stake.

It seems, therefore, that at Bath the advancing Saxons failed to take the hill-fort and during the resultant siege a counterattack by the British succeeded in routing the enemy. With the Saxon superiority broken, the way was open for a massive counter thrust into the South-East. Aelle may have been the Saxon commander at Badon, since Bede asserts that he became 'high king' of Saxon Britain. Conversely, although the *Cotton Vespasian* names Octha as Hengist's son, the *Chronicle* makes no reference to him. Perhaps the Saxons who later compiled the *Chronicle* chose to omit the name of the man who had led their army into the most damaging defeat of the entire era.

6

Arthur of Britons

We have investigated the Anglo-Saxon kingdoms of the late fifth and early sixth centuries, but what of the Britons? If we are to uncover Arthur's origins, we must discover more about the British and their leaders in the period leading up to Badon.

During Roman times Hadrian's Wall divided the unconquered Picts of Scotland from the occupied Celtic tribes in England and Wales; around sixteen in all, each led by a chief or king. Following the usual Roman policy, these occupied tribal zones became Roman administrative districts called the *civitates*, or provinces. But once the Romans left, at the beginning of the fifth century, central government came under strain and regional control gradually reverted to the tribal chieftains. One of these chiefs, who seems to have been the most successful, was Vortigern.

Aside from Gildas, Bede and the *Welsh Annals* (see below), the *Anglo-Saxon Chronicle* also records Vortigern as the leader of the British forces who fought Hengist and Horsa in 455. The only other inclusion of Vortigern in a Dark Age manuscript appears in the *Historia Brittonum* of Nennius. Here he is portrayed as reigning when the Saxon brothers Hengist and Horsa land with three ships. Vortigern allows them to live on the isle of Thanet, and invites other Saxons to join them if they will aid his struggle against the Picts and the Irish who are harassing Britain. Ultimately, Vortigern is tricked by Hengist into arranging a conference, at which many of his nobles are massacred and the war between the Britons and the Saxons begins.

Nennius provides a vital clue to the original province of Vortigern, suggesting that he is descended from 'Gloiu, who built a great city upon the banks of the River Severn that in British is called Caer Gloiu, in Saxon Gleucester' – the modern Gloucester. This implies a connection with the Cornovii tribe, who occupied an extensive area in the West Midlands (including Gloucester) and East Wales. Since the Cornovii province became the kingdom of Powys soon after Roman rule,

Vortigern seems originally to have been the King of Powys, an excellent strategic position from which to gain control of Britain.

The most important Dark Age reference to Vortigern, which supports the Powys conjecture, is an inscription on the Pillar of Eliseg, in Clwyd, North Wales. The Pillar of Eliseg is all that remains of an ancient stone cross standing in the Vale of Llangollen near the medieval abbey of Valle Crucis. Although the inscription is no longer visible, in 1696 the Welsh antiquarian, Edward Lhwyd, translated what could then be discerned. In this inscription Concenn, the king of Powys who is known to have died in 854, commemorates the emancipating exploits of his great-grandfather, proudly celebrating his line of descent from Vortigern himself. This shows quite clearly that the rulers of Powys of the late Dark Ages considered themselves descendants of Vortigern, the founder of their kingdom. Together with the evidence from Nennius, the inscription on the Pillar of Eliseg means that the kingdom of Powys is the most likely seat of Vortigern.

Sometime around 460, a new and altogether different type of leader appeared on the scene; a man who appears to have reorganised the country and turned the tide on the invading Saxons. He is someone who Gildas not only seems to have admired but even names. Although he only mentions him once, Gildas says:

> Their leader was Ambrosius Aurelianus, a genleman who, perhaps alone of the Romans, had survived the shock of this notable storm: certainly his parents who had worn purple, were slain in it.

Bede also refers to Ambrosius (see above, p43), as does Nennius but no other surviving Dark Age manuscript includes him.

Although only a brief reference, Gildas' passage gives further information about Ambrosius: for instance, that his parents wore purple. Since purple was the royal colour of the Roman emperors, this statement implies that he was a member of a high-ranking Roman family, as Bede points out. In addition, we see that his parents died during the storm, which can be taken to mean the Saxon onslaught to which Gildas previously referred. Also, since Gildas seems to have admired this 'gentleman', who was 'alone among the Romans', we can assume that he stood for some alternative viewpoint to Vortigern, the 'tyrant'. Nennius names Ambrosius as Vortigern's rival and relates a legend concerning their first meeting.

In the story, Vortigern is attempting to construct an impregnable fortress high in the Welsh mountains in the kingdom of Gwynedd, following his defeat by the Saxons. However, the work is constantly disrupted by a strange series of disasters. The king summons his magicians, who advise him that in order to complete the work he must first locate a boy with no earthly father. Having done so, he must kill the youth and sprinkle his blood on the site. Eventually, such a child is found, but in order to save himself the boy challenges Vortigern to tell him what lies beneath the foundations. When he cannot do so, the boy reveals a pool containing two dragons, one red and one white, which proceed to fight one another. Interpreting this mysterious omen, the boy tells Vortigern that the two creatures represent the Britons and the Saxons, and the victory of the red beast means that the Britons will eventually triumph. The king's admiration is assured when it is revealed that the boy's name is Ambrosius, the son of a Roman consul. At the end of the passage, Vortigern is persuaded to give Ambrosius authority over the western part of Britain.

What does this legend tell us? First, it can be seen as clarifying Gildas and Bede as to the nature of Ambrosius' royal family ties, since we are told that he is the son of a Roman consul. Second, that Ambrosius was brought up in secret, for some reason being kept from Vortigern. And third, Ambrosius assumed authority over the western part of Britain, initially from the kingdom of Gwynedd in North Wales. This concept of a Roman leader holding sway in this area in the late fifth century is supported by archaeology. Gwynedd is precisely where the most Romanised form of life is known to have continued. Tombstones, for example, imply a continuity of Roman thought, bearing inscriptions such as *magistratus* (magistrate) and *civis* (citizen). Such Roman terms would be meaningless unless a Roman style of organisation still survived.

From the standpoint that Amrbosius' power base was in northern Wales we return to Nennius, who also calls Ambrosius Gwledig Emrys – Gwledig meaning 'prince', and Emrys the Welsh rendering of Ambrosius. This version of his name is found at Dinas Emrys, an Iron Age hill-fort in Snowdonia in North Wales, where *The Tale of Ludd and Llefelys* in the *White Book of Rhydderch* locates Ambrosius. Although the surviving copy is fourteenth century, *circa* 1325, linguistic analysis has shown that the story is very much older. The fort was certainly reoccupied around the right period for Ambrosius and was perhaps the most important in the area. In 1954-56, Dr H.N. Savory of the National

Museum of Wales undertook an excavation of the hilltop fortifications, showing that a rich and powerful British chief was in possession towards the close of the fifth century. Whether or not Ambrosius was this warlord, this part of Britain, the kingdom of Gwynedd, is the most feasible location from which Ambrosius came.

What ultimately happened to Ambrosius is unknown. However, the successful counter-offensives he initiated against the Angles in the north were continued in the south by some unnamed successor. This is demonstrated, as we have seen, from both the archaeological and historical evidence, which clearly indicates a series of major British victories in southern Britain, starting with the triumph at Badon around 493.

Whoever was commanding the Britons by the last decade of the fifth century was without doubt a formidable leader. The fact that the Britons were stronger and more united than ever before during this period is evidenced not only in Gildas, Bede and the *Anglo-Saxon Chronicle*, but also in archaeology. For example, there are the huge dyke fortifications that were constructed at this time, such as those previously mentioned, in Lincolnshire and East Anglia. The positioning of the ditch to the eastern side is clear evidence that the dykes were intended to defend against attacks from the east. Excavations show that the builders used Roman-style pottery and wore boots with Roman-type hobnails. In orther words, it was the Britons who built them to counter any further advances by the Angles. On the Saxon front there are the linear earthworks around the Thames Valley, built by the Saxons to mark a fixed frontier. The British, whom they were digging in to resist, were a formidable threat.

Not only do the massive British fortifications evidence large reserves of manpower, and the Saxon earthworks attest to the Britons having a powerful army, but both these factors suggest a united nation and, more importantly, a strong and determined leader. However, contemporary records do not record the name of this leader – Ambrosius' successor. Was it really the historical King Arthur?

To attempt to solve this enigma, we must first try to ascertain from where this leader may have originated. In the century following the departure of the Romans, most of the old British tribes had re-established themselves as kingdoms, so his base must have been the most powerful of these. Which kingdom was it?

Many kingdoms can be discounted as a seat for Ambrosius' successor: The Cantii tribe in Kent were completely conquered by the

Saxons, as were the Trinovantes of Essex. Further north, in Suffolk and East Anglia, the Iceni, once the tribe of the warrior queen Boudicca, had been overwhelmed by the Angles, as had the Coritani and the Parisii to the north and east of them. Since these tribal areas had been effectively neutralised we must, therefore, turn to those which remained independent from the Anglo-Saxons in the mid-480s.

In the far north: the Novantae trible to the west of the country had established themselves as the kingdom of Rheged, and the Brigantes, to the south of them, had founded Elmet. These areas were not only suffering repeated incursions by the Picts, but were being continually subjected to raids by the Irish. None of these areas could have mustered the political and military muscle to unite and lead the rest of Britain.

In the far south: the Atrebates of Wiltshire and Berkshire had established a number of smaller kingdoms, as had the Durotriges of Dorset, the Belgae of Somerset and the Regenenses of Hampshire. Since these kingdoms were too small and fragmented to have supplied any form of strong leadership, the only kingdoms of real significance were the larger, more stable ones of the Midlands, the South-West and Wales.

Aside from a few tiny mountain kingdoms of South-Central Wales, such as Buellt and Brycheiniog, only five other kingdoms appear to have remained. In the west of Wales: Gwynedd in the north, the old tribal area of the Deceangli, and Dyfed in the south, the old tribal area of the Demetae. In the east of Wales: the Silures trible in the southern kingdom of Gwent, and in the northern and central part of the province the massive Cornovii kingdom of Powys, which also included a large section of the western Midlands. The remaining kingdom was Dumnonia, of the Dumnonii trible, in Devon and Cornwall.

Since little is known of these kingdoms in the fifth century, we will begin by considering the one which was the most powerful by the time of Gildas, a generation later. In the *De Excidio* Gildas addresses the five most influential kings. These were almost certainly from these five kingdoms. Of one of them he says:

> What of you, dragon of the island, you who have removed many of these tyrants from their country and even their life? You are last on my list, but first in evil, mightier than many both in power and malice, more profuse in giving, more extravagant in sin, strong in arms but stronger still in what destroys a soul.

This king, the most powerful of all, he names as Maglocunus, the chief who died of the plague in the 540s. As usual, almost nothing is known of him aside from his mention in the Welsh genealogies and selected comments from Nennius. In both he is called Maelgwn, the Welsh rendering of his name. In the *Historia Brittonum* Nennius says that 'Maelgwn ruled as a great king among the Britons, that is in the region of Gwynedd'. Some important indications concerning the status of the kingdom of Gwynedd can be gained from the clues supplied by Gildas in the above passage.

The term used by Gildas to describe Maglocunus is the 'dragon of the island'. Even without the genealogies, or the evidence of Nennius, this would place him very much in the kingdom of Gwynedd, for it was here, during the mid-sixth century, that the rulers of the kingdom adopted the symbol of the red dragon as their tribal emblem. This emblem, which was eventually adopted for the whole of Wales, was originally the standard of the later Roman emperors. Its use by the kingdom of Gwynedd is very much in keeping with what we have seen regarding the continuation of Roman influence in North Wales. In fact, the kings of Gwynedd are often found in early Welsh poetry being referred to as the 'dragons of Britain' or the 'head dragons'.

Geoffrey of Monmouth calls Arthur's father Pendragon, coming from the Welsh meaning 'head (or chief) dragon'. Of course this may not necessarily mean that Geoffrey had access to some record, or knew of some legend associating Arthur's family with Gwynedd; it could simply be implying a king of Wales generally. However, when this allusion is coupled with the apparent strength of Gwynedd in the post-Arthurian era, together with Ambrosius' association with the kingdom and Roman continuation, it certainly indicates the importance of this area in our search for Arthur's background.

Staying with Arthur's legendary father, when we consider that his forename, Uther, almost certainly derives from the Welsh word *uthr*, meaning 'terrible' (as in 'frightening'), his name must mean the 'terrible head dragon'. Once again, it would appear that like Vortigern, the 'overlord', Uther Pendragon is yet another by-name or designation. Perhaps Geoffrey of Monmouth knew only the title of Arthur's father, whom he claims became king upon the death of Ambrosius, and from it constructed his name. However, as we have seen, Geoffrey is forever mixing his historical characters and ascribing relationships out of time and place, as with Constans being the brother of Ambrosius. Nevertheless, we have also found half-truths in Geoffrey's work, such as Constans being the son of Constantine.

Regarding the relationship between Uther and Ambrosius, although they may not have been brothers (as Geoffrey portrays them) Uther could have assumed the regency of Gwynedd when Ambrosius became the overall British leader. The most important issue, however, concerns the ruler of Gwynedd's relationship to Arthur, be he Uther or anyone else. In other words, did Arthur succeed as king of Gwynedd? Nennius' oblique statement seems at first to rule this out. Since he tells us that Arthur fought 'with the British kings', it could be concluded that Arthur was not a king himself. However, there may be another explanation for this remark. Is Nennius telling us that although Arthur was a king, he was not a *native* Briton? If he was not a king why does Nennius not simply say that Arthur 'led the British kings', instead of saying 'he fought with the British kings', which implies he was their equal. Could Nennius be saying that Arthur was a foreign king?

This hypothesis draws us once again to the kingdom of Gwynedd. The kings who ruled this area do not appear to have been Britons in the strictest sense of the word, but came from Manau Guotodin, to the north of Hadrian's Wall in what is now Scotland. They were British inasmuch as they inhabited the isle of Britain, but they were not Britons, the name for the inhabitants of what is now England and Wales. Returning to Nennius' passage concerning Maelgwn (Maglocunus), he goes on to say:

> His ancestor, that is Cunedag, with his sons, eight in number, came previously from the northern part, that is from the region that is called Manau Guotodin one hundred and forty six years before Maelgwn ruled and expelled the Scots with a very great slaughter from these regions.

The Welsh genealogies at the end of the *Welsh Annals* also refer to this ancestor of Maglocunus and his occupation of North-West Wales. However, here he is called Cunedda. The *Welsh Annals* say that the newly adopted Welsh kingdom stretched 'from the river that is called Dubr Duiu (the Dee) up to the river Tebi (the Teifi, which joins the sea at Cardigan)'. In the *Annals*, however, we find a contradiction of Nennius' specific dating. Here we are told that Cunedda was Maglocunus' great-grandfather, meaning that only two generations separate the two men; surely not a period of 146 years as Nennius would have us believe.

Let us first consider the time in which Nennius places the arrival of Cunedda and his men, 146 years before Maglocunus ruled. Although the precise date of the beginning of Maglocunus' reign is unknown, the general consensus places it sometime around 520. 146 years before takes us back to the mid-370s, when the Roman legions were still in Britain. Concerning this period, archaeological excavations of the fortress of Segontium (Caernarvon), the principal garrison of North-West Wales, have revealed that its final buildings were erected about 370, intensive occupation ceasing around 385, when many soldiers were withdrawn to fight in a Roman civil war.

This could have been the time of the arrival of Cunedda's army. Perhaps they were invited to settle in the area to help guard it until the regular army could be strengthened. This was the general policy of the empire in its latter days: invite in one friendly barbarian army to hold an area against another, more hostile, tribe. However, there is a persuasive argument against this having occurred in North-West Wales at this time. The evidence concerning the district of Gwynedd would make it incompatible with what Nennius says. He tells us that Cunedda and his sons 'expelled the Scots with a very great slaughter from these regions'.

The Scots referred to in this passage are the Scotti, a Roman term for the Irish meaning 'raider' or 'bandit'. In the latter days of the empire the Scotti were settling in considerable numbers in South-West Scotland, and by the ninth century they had conquered the entire country. Indeed, it is from the Scotti that Scotland derives its name. Any notion that the Irish had managed to settle in North-West Wales, while Segontium was still being garrisoned, is unlikely considering the Roman military presence. In fact, the archaeological evidence shows that it continued to be garrisoned, although with a smaller force, until the final departure of the legions in 410.

Turning to the *Welsh Annals'* timescale of Cunedda's arrival: Maglocunus was the great-grandson of Cunedda. As Cunedda's son (Maglocunus' grandfather) was old enough to fight with Cunedda, we can assume that his son (Maglocunus' father) was born within thirty years of landing in Gwynedd. Add to this, say, another thirty years before the birth of Maglocunus, plus another thirty before the time of his reign, and we arrive at a generous ninety years, a hundred at the very most. This takes us back only as far as the 430s. By this time, Gwynedd was certainly suffering repeated Irish raids. Perhaps, therefore, it was Vortigern who invited in Cunedda.

However, this date was arrived at by deducing the longest period of time that could have elapsed between Cunedda's arrival and the start of Maglocunus' reign. It is far more likely that Maglocunus' father was born within ten years of Cunedda's arrival in Gwynedd, and Maglocunus himself within twenty-five years of this. Adding another twenty-five years before the start of his rule gives a more reasonable calculation of somewhere around sixty years in all. If this was the case, then it would take us back to sometime around 460, the time of Ambrosius, a far more likely period. From the evidence of Gildas and Bede, it can be deduced that the western part of Britain had been troubled by the Irish on and off throughout the first half of the fifth century after the Roman legions left. If the kingdom of Gwynedd was to have supplied the power base for Ambrosius, which it certainly appears to have done, some aid against the Irish must have been forthcoming.

What does all this tell us of Arthur? According to the *Welsh Annals*, well before Maglocunus' reign his grandfather, Enniaun Girt, became king of Gwynedd. The Cunedda family therefore ruled the kingdom for at least two generations before Maglocunus. Hence, if Arthur's roots were in Gwynedd, seemingly the most powerful British kingdom of the era, he is almost certain to have been a member of the Cunedda family.

Manau Guotodin, where Cunedda originated, was an area around the Firth of Forth in the district of Edinburgh, about the size of modern day Lothian, forming the northern part of the Celtic kingdom of Gododdin. Although its people were predominantly Pictish, they were of a tribe called the Votadini who, during the days of the empire, were the northern tribe most favourably disposed towards the Romans. This was because their kingdom fell within an area that, for the period of the Roman occupation of Britain, was never truly British or Pictish.

The word Pict does not denote a particular tribe; rather it is a Roman term meaning 'painted men', and was used to refer to anyone of the British tribes that fell outside the limits of the empire. Since the ancient British warriors who fought against the Roman invasion painted themselves in woad (a blue dye) before entering battle, the Pictish tribes of the North were so named because they continued this custom.

In 43 A.D., when Britain was conquered by Emperor Claudius and became an island province of the Roman Empire, it was found impossible to control the Scottish Highlands. The fierce northern tribes of this mountainous area were free continually to raid the Roman towns in the North of England and the Scottish Lowlands. At the beginning of the second century, when the Picts even sacked the city of York, defeating a legion of around 5,000 men, the Emperor Hadrian visited Britain and in 122 A.D. ordered that a great defensive wall be built across the North of England. When completed, between Newcastle and the Solway Firth, it was over seventy-three miles long, fifteen feet high and some eight feet thick, with sixteen forts along its length, each garrisoned by about a thousand men.

But Hadrian's Wall was not built at the limits of the empire. In fact, the Roman area of occupation stretched more than fifty miles further north. Roman forts already existed across this part of Scotland and, from the time of Claudius, they had been considered to be the frontier outposts of the empire. It was along this frontier that Hadrian's successor, Antoninus Pius, constructed another wall, spanning the thirty-six miles between the Clyde and Firth estuaries. Unlike Hadrian's Wall, which was built of brick, the Antonine Wall consisted of a huge linear earthwork surmounted by a wooden stockade and protected by a deep ditch. Around 200 A.D., however, this second Wall was abandoned and Hadrian's Wall became the final frontier of the Roman Empire.

Falling as it did between the Antonine and Hadrian's Wall, the kingdom of the Votadini had been part of the empire for well over a century. For this reason, throughout the next two and a half centuries relations between the Votadini and the empire were good. The Romans offered support against the hostile Picts, while in return the Votadini helped police this buffer zone. The same applied to the two other southern Scottish tribes, the Selgovae and the Damnonii. However, by the early fifth century, both of these tribes had been effectively neutralised. Even before the Romans left Britain, the Scotti had settled the South West of Scotland, overwhelming the Damnonii and threatening the Selgovae.

Shortly after the legions pulled out, the pro-British Votadini were experiencing trouble on three fronts. The Angles were raiding their coastline, the Picts were marauding from the North, and the Scotti were pushing ever closer from the West. The Votadini must certainly have been a formidable people, for they were able to hold out against these combined forces until the early seventh century.

It would not have been difficult for Ambrosius to persuade the Votadini to settle in the North West of Wales. In return for their military muscle against the Irish, the Votadini warriors and their families would have a new land in which to settle. Indeed, they would have had much in common with the imperialist faction of Gwynedd; no-one had greater reason for wishing to see the return of the legions than the people of Gododdin, who were facing annihilation on three fronts.

That Cunedda and the Votadini warriors colonized North-West

Wales by the late fifth century can be verified. Characteristic Votadini pottery has been discovered in Gwynedd dating from the second half of the fifth century, which not only supports a migration from Gododdin but also places the time of their arrival during the period of Ambrosius. Additionally, the identifying name-affix 'Cun', or in Welsh 'Cyn', of the Cunedda family is found on tombstones and in the genealogies of Gwynedd. For example, in the name of Maglocunus and his cousin Cuneglasus, whom Gildas also names. Furthermore, the genealogies show that Cunedda's ancestors bear a mixture of Pictish and Roman names.

The Cunedda migration, referred to by Nennius and in the *Welsh Annals*, is almost certainly an historical event. The important question, however, concerns the lineage of Arthur. Was Arthur's father one of the Votadini, perhaps Cunedda or one of his sons? The weight of evidence certainly seems to point in this direction. To recap:

1. Gwynedd was undoubtedly the most powerful kingdom by the time of Gildas. It is not unreasonable to assume that this was a legacy of the apparent Arthurian period.

2. The kingdom from which Ambrosius sprang was almost certainly Gwynedd and, as Arthur appears to have been Ambrosius' successor rather than deposer, it follows that Arthur was of the same kingdom.

3. The name of Arthur's father in Geoffrey of Monmouth's *Historia* is Uther Pendragon, meaning 'terrible head dragon', a title that would fit the king of Gwynedd in the late fifth century.

4. The Votadini appear to have arrived in Gwynedd at the time of Ambrosius, accounting for his military back up in ousting the Vortigern family. If Arthur's father was the king of Gwynedd he would, therefore, almost certainly have been a Votadini.

5. Nennius infers that Arthur was not a British king, perhaps not even a British national. However, he is an equal of the British kings. Such a description would sit with a king of the Votadini who, although not Britons, were a trusted people with a common enemy.

6. After the disastrous policy of the Vortigerns, and the final collapse of the Western Empire, a compromise leader would surely have been

essential to assure a unified following. A Votadini was ideally suited, considering the British leaders' distrust of one another.

7. If Arthur was a Votadini, he would certainly have made an ideal commander-in-chief of the British forces. He came from a hardy warrior race, whose people had much first-hand experience in fighting not only the Anglo-Saxons but also the Scots and the Picts.

The final evidence comes from Gildas himself, but before we examine this we should consider what is possibly the oldest of all Arthurian references, an ancient Celtic poem called the *Gododdin*. As its title suggests, it comes from the kingdom of the Votadini.

Accredited to a Votadini bard named Aneirin, this epic poem concerns the fate of a group of warriors from the kingdom of Gododdin, who set out to fight the Anglo-Saxons in Yorkshire. In one passage the poet praises the courage of a particular hero, Gwawrddur, saying that although he fought bravely 'he was no Arthur'. Why should this isolated Pictish tribe of Scotland choose to hold up the British warrior, Arthur, as a paragon of military valour? It is difficult to imagine a Votadini poet, who is praising the prowess of his tribe, admitting that one of their great heroes was not comparable with one of the Britons. Unless, that is, Arthur had been a Votadini himself.

Although it is not surprising to discover many Welsh poems containing references to King Arthur, it is strange indeed to find Arthur mentioned, almost casually, by a Pictish tribe on the eve of their demise. Moreover, the *Gododdin* appears to be considerably older than the Arthurian poems of Wales.

The *Gododdin* is set in a period around the end of the sixth century, when the Votadini fought gallantly, but unsuccessfully, against the Anglo-Saxon advance towards their kingdom. The mention of Arthur in the poem has thus led many scholars to conclude that he was in fact from this far northern kingdom. However, it could just as well be taken as evidence that Arthur was from Gwynedd in the North-West of Wales, also a kingdom of the Votadini.

The poem has survived in two mid-thirteenth century copies now in the Public Library in Cardiff. However, from the style of writing and spelling, it appears to have been copied from a ninth-century manuscript. Unfortunately, this means that the poem would probably have been recited from memory alone until someone decided to write it down in the 800s. However, the *Gododdin* is generally accepted to have been composed shortly after the end of the sixth century (for reasons such as the type and mode of warfare it describes) and the mention of Arthur is considered to have been in the original form. This is primarily because of the rhyme scheme; his name rhymes with the end of the previous line. In the British language the lines concerning Arthur read:

> *gochone brein du ar uur*
> *caer ceni bei ef Arthur*

The English translation is:

> He glutted black ravens on the wall
> of the fort although he was no Arthur.

In other words, he fed the ravens with the bodies of the dead enemy.

Given that the writer is lamenting the demise of the Votadini in the face of the Anglo-Saxons, the mention of Arthur in this context is perhaps recalling the heyday of the tribe, a time when there were successes against the Anglo-Saxons, led by a victorious warrior named Arthur.

The *Gododdin* not only suggests that Arthur was of the Votadini, it also attests to the links between Gododdin and Gwynedd. In fact, the poem relates that one of the chief warriors, Gorthyn, had come to Gododdin from Gwynedd along with a large company of soldiers. Why should he choose to do so, in a country that was so fragmented at this time, unless powerful ties existed between the two dynasties?

With the most likely origins for Arthur being in the kingdom of Gwynedd, we return to Gildas. Around 545 he names the king of Gwynedd, Maglocunus, as the most powerful British ruler. According to Gildas, Maglocunus had come to power by overthrowing his uncle in battle. In his *De Excidio* Gildas scolds Maglocunus, saying:

> In the first years of your youth, you crushed the king your uncle
> and his brave troops with fire, spear and sword.

As Maglocunus was well into middle age by the time Gildas was writing, and is described as a youth when he overthrew his uncle, the event must have taken place some time in the early sixth century, around 520. This means that his uncle was almost certainly of the same generation as the Britons who fought at Badon. Indeed, as Maglocunus became the most powerful king after defeating him, the uncle may actually have been the Britons' leader at the battle. Was Maglocunus' uncle therefore the historical Arthur? Unfortunately, Gildas fails to name him. All we can tell is that he appears to have been a valiant leader whom Gildas admired.

Interestingly, this uncle does have something in common with the legendary Arthur. A similar story of internecine strife occurs in the medieval romances, in which Arthur dies when his nephew attempts to seize the throne. Although in the romances the name of Arthur's nephew is Modred, was the original legend based on the historical Maglocunus?

Another powerful leader referred to by Gildas was Cuneglasus, who ruled a separate but unnamed kingdom at the same time that Maglocunus ruled Gwynedd. Cuneglasus is recorded in a genealogy in the *Welsh Annals*, where he is named as Maglocunus' cousin – in other words, Maglocunus' uncle was Cuneglasus' father. The fact that Cuneglasus was a powerful ruler in his own right appears to confirm that it was his father whom Maglocunus usurped. It therefore seems as though Maglocunus' uncle ruled a kingdom which divided into two separate kingdoms after his death – his son Cuneglasus directly succeeded him in one, while his nephew Maglocunus seized power in the other.

According to Gildas – the most complete contemporary historical evidence that still exists – this mysterious uncle is the most likely candidate for Britain's most powerful ruler during the apparent Arthurian era.

But who was he? In the *Welsh Annals* Maglocunus' uncle and Cuneglasus' father is named as Owain Ddantgwyn. There can be little doubt that this was indeed his name, as four separate Dark Age genealogies also record him. Does this mean that the most powerful leader at the time of Badon was not called Arthur after all?

7

Tracking the Bear King

What do we know about Owain Ddantgwyn – seemingly the most powerful British king at the time of Badon? Unfortunately, nothing more than is preserved in Gildas' *De Excidio*. However, Gildas does tell us something about him. In addressing Owain's son Cuneglasus, he writes:

> Why have you been rolling in the filth of your past wickedness ever since your youth, you bear, rider of many and driver of the chariot of the bear's stronghold, despiser of God and oppressor of his lot, Cuneglasus?

Twice he mentions the word bear. First he is calling Cuneglasus 'you bear', then that he is the charioteer of 'the bear's stronghold'. He seems to be saying that Cuneglasus is now in command of what had once been 'the bear's stronghold', and has assumed the title, 'the bear', for himself. As we know that Cuneglasus' predecessor was his father, Owain Ddantgwyn, it seems may also have been known as the 'bear'. Furthermore, Gildas tells us that Cuneglasus had inherited some particular military advantage, for Gildas goes on to ask him why he wages war against his fellow countrymen 'with arms special to yourself.'

We can deduce from Gildas that Owain Ddantgwyn seems to have possessed an effective military advantage; he held an important strategic fortress; and he was known by the title, the Bear. The first two deductions would tally with the Briton's commander at Badon; the third, however, implies much more. Namely that Owain Ddantgwyn *was* the historical Arthur. In the British language of the time, and still preserved in the modern Welsh, the first syllable from the name Arthur – *Arth* – actually means 'Bear'. Like Vortigern and Uther, could the name Arthur have originally been a title?

It seems to have been a common Celtic practice of the period for warriors to assume the battle name of an animal, in some way typifying the qualities of the individual. Not only are there many examples from Ireland and Gaul, as well as Britain, of various warlords assuming such epithets, but Gildas himself names a number of British kings and likens them to animals. Apart from Maglocunus, whom he calls the Dragon, there is Aurelius Caninus, the Dog, whose father seems to have been called the Lion (as Gildas also calls him the lion-whelp) and Vortipor, the Leopard. Moreover, the poem *Gododdin* describes warriors by battle names such as the Hound, the Wolf, and one is even called the Bear, clearly demonstrating that the name Bear was being used as a battle name by the Britons during the Dark Ages.

Various scholars have theorised that the name Arthur was a British derivative of the Roman name Artorius, in the same way as Ambrosius became Emrys, Vortigern became Gwrtheyrn, or as Maglocunus became Maelgwn in the later Welsh language. In fact, the notion has become popular since the twelve-part poem *Artorius*, by John Heath-Stubbs, was published in 1973, followed shortly afterwards by John Gloag's story *Artorius Rex*, published in 1977. Although it has been pointed out that a Roman soldier called Lucius Artorius Castus served as an officer in Britain during the late second century, and another called Artorius Justus was here in the third century, this does not constitute proof that Artorius was the original version of the name Arthur. The fact remains that no record including the name of Artorius, or anything like it, survives which could conceivably be linked with a warrior of the Arthurian period.

The name Arthur does not appear anywhere on record until the end of the sixth century. Around this time, no less than six of the various British genealogies include the name of Arthur, which seems to suggest that the royal families of the time were beginning to call their sons after a famous warrior of that name. By the same token, the fact that the name does not appear earlier than these genealogies suggests that the name had only been contrived shortly before. King Arthur, therefore, may have been the first person to hold that name, implying that it was originally a title. Indeed this seems to have happened with Vortigern, since a number of princes were christened with this name in the centuries after the original had lived.

The original name Arth could quite easily have been rendered as Arthur. Britain of the post-Roman era had two main languages: Latin, the Roman language, and native Brythonic, which later developed into Welsh. (Of the other languages of the British Isles, English was a later development of the language spoken by the Anglo-Saxons, while Gaelic, spoken by the Scotti who gradually spread throughout Scotland, was the language of the Irish.) The evidence of tombstones and other inscriptions from the fifth century provides evidence that many kingdoms were reverting wholly to Brythonic, while Gwynedd continued to use Latin. If his tribal title was the Bear, he may not only have used the Brythonic word Arth, but also the Latin word for bear, *ursus*. His original title may therefore have been Arthursus; later being shortened to Arthur, as Antonius is shortened to Anthony or Marcus to Marc. Indeed, Gildas refers to Cuneglasus, a Latinized name, which later became Cunglas or Cynglas in the Welsh (the syllable *cun* is spelt *cyn* in Welsh).

If the name Arthur was a battle name it would not be the first time that a leader had gone down in history under his title. The emperor Caius Caesar, for example, better known as Caligula, meaning 'little boot', a nickname he acquired as a child because he enjoyed dressing up as a soldier. Or the Mongol warlord Temujin, more easily recognised under his title Genghis Khan, meaning 'universal ruler'.

It seems therefore that with Owain Ddantgwyn we have the best candidate for the historical Arthur: a warrior who seems to have been the most powerful king at the time of Badon, and used the battle name the Bear – in the native British tongue, *Arth* – from which the name Arthur was derived.

Is there further evidence that Owain Ddantgwyn was the historical Arthur? Gildas tells us that Cuneglasus ruled from the 'bear's stronghold', seemingly the seat of his father Owain. If we can discover where this was we should be in a position to search for archaeological evidence concerning Arthur. If the 'bear's stronghold' was Owain's stronghold, and Cuneglasus was in command of it by the time of Gildas, then we must first discover over which kingdom Cuneglasus ruled.

We have already seen how the five most powerful British kingdoms of the sixth century were Gwynedd, Dumnonia, Dyfed, Gwent and Powys, and Gildas names the five most powerful kings who must have ruled these kingdoms. As Cuneglasus was one of these kings, which of them was his kingdom? Unfortunately, Gildas neglects to tell us. We must therefore examine the other four kings named by Gildas and consider which of these five powerful kingdoms can be eliminated.

Besides Maglocunus, who we know is from Gwynedd in North Wales, there are three others. First, Constantine, who Gildas tells us is from Damnoniae. Although arguably this could be referring to the

Tribes of Roman Britain

region of the Damnonii tribe in South-West Scotland, by Gildas' time this had been conquered by the Irish. It is more likely that he means Dumnonia, the kingdom of the Dumnonii in Devon and Cornwall. Next is Vortipori, whom he calls the tyrant of the Demetarum. This is certainly referring to the Demetae tribe's kingdom of Dyfed in South-West Wales, where a contemporary memorial stone inscribed with Vortipori's name has been discovered. The final king Gildas names as Aurelius Caninus. Unfortunately, as with Cuneglasus, Gildas offers us no clue to his home kingdom. All we can say is that, judging by his name, this man may have been a descendant of Ambrosius Aurelianus.

So Gwynedd, Dumnonia and Dyfed can be eliminated as Cuneglasus' kingdom, leaving us with either Gwent or Powys.

As we have seen, after Owain's death his kingdom seems to split into two separate kingdoms – Maglocunus ruling in Gwynedd and Cuneglasus ruling in the other. The second half of this kingdom could not have been Gwent, as Gwent and Gwynedd were divided by a series of smaller mountain kingdoms in Central Wales, such as Buellt and Brycheiniog mentioned in the previous chapter. We are therefore left with the kingdom of Powys, which actually adjoined Maglocunus' kingdom of Gwynedd on its eastern boarder. (From the archaeological perspective, the recent work of K.R. Dark, the editor of the *Journal of Theoretical Archaeology*, also associates Cuneglasus with Powys in his *Civitas to Kingdom*, published in 1994.)

So the 'bear's stronghold' – Owain's capital – would seem to been in Powys, a kingdom that covered the West Midlands and Central Wales. This would make historical sense. As we have seen, Powys was originally the seat of Vortigern, and a centrally strategic kingdom. We have reasoned that Ambrosius, from his powerbase in Gwynedd, and with the help of Cunedda's Votadini warriors, replaced the Vortigern administration in Powys. This must have meant that Powys had come under his direct authority, and after his death the Cunedda family must have continued to rule there as they did in Gwynedd. Indeed, there is archaeological evidence that the Cunedda family had annexed the kingdom of Powys by the end of the fifth century (see next chapter). If Cunedda's grandson, Owain Ddantgwyn, really was the British commander at the time of Badon, he would almost certainly have established his stronghold in the kindom of Powys, right in the heart of Britain, rather than in the more remote kingdom of Gwynedd.

Although it is difficult to determine exactly when the kingdom of Powys came into existence, it must have been soon after the Roman withdrawal. Once the Roman administration had gone, many of the old tribal areas seem to have made fairly rapid attempts to establish themselves as independent principalities. However, it was not long before a three-fronted threat forced the British chieftains into begrudging unity; the council of leaders referred to by Gildas.

The incursions of Germanic invaders in the east, the Picts in the north, and the Irish in the west considerably weakened the border and coastal tribes. The central position of the Cornovii tribe must therefore have afforded them a unique position of strength, providing time and resources to establish an autonomous kingdom long before their neighbours; a kingdom strategically situated to take control of a substantial area of the country. In all probability they discovered that surrounding tribes were all too willing to become satellites of the Cornovii, rather than submit to foreign invasion. In return for the protection of the central kingdom, the British tribal chiefs may have sworn allegiance to a Cornovii king as their 'overlord', Vortigern.

It is impossible to say at what point the kingdom first came to be called Powys, although the Welsh names for the sub-Roman kingdoms would not seem to have been in general usage until the late sixth century. Gildas, for example, refers to them only in tribal terms. However, the name Powys probably came from the Latin word *pagus*, meaning 'country district'. Regardless of its original name, during the Vortigern period the capital of Powys seems to have been the old Roman city of Viroconium, the *civitate* capital of the Cornovii.

During the Roman occupation of Britain, the country had been divided into provincial districts known as *civitates*, each founded on existing tribal areas and controlled from an administrative city or capital. Accordingly, the Cornovii of Central England and West Wales were subject to the administration of Viroconium Cornoviorum. Now in the county of Shropshire, Viroconium became the fourth largest city in Roman Britain, and was without doubt the most important trading centre in the Midlands.

Built on the fertile plain overlooking the River Severn, Viroconium was originally established as a military base to co-ordinate the Roman conquest of Wales. Sometime around 78 A.D., however, the western command of the island was transferred to the city of Chester and Viroconium became a thriving civilian town. Although it was to have all the provisions of other provincial capitals, such as cobbled streets, water supply and drainage system, the Cornovii city was far more elaborate and wealthy than most. Viroconium, with its law courts, market-place and other public facilities, became the principal city of Central Britain. Unlike the other main Roman cities – London, Lincoln and York – all that now remains of Viroconium are its ruined walls, standing in quiet farm land outside the tiny village of Wroxeter, a few miles to the east of Shrewsbury.

Standing as it does in the open countryside, the ruins of Viroconium have provided an excellent opportunity for excavation, and in the past century much archaeological work has been conducted. Today the dig is open to the public and a small museum stands at the site, where some of the excavated material is on display, although the majority is housed in Rowley's House Museum in Shrewsbury.

Located at an intersection between the old Roman Watling Street and the modern B4380, the visible ruins of Viroconium are the remains of a large bath-house complex erected around 150 A.D., one of the best surviving examples of its kind in Britain. The ancient brickwork that dominates the site, known locally as the 'Old Work', was once the south wall of a large aisled basilica that acted as an exercise hall for the baths themselves. It is remarkable that so much of the ruins have survived, as for generations local people used the stones from the old city to build their houses and, in particular, the parish church of St Andrews.

The public baths became the social centres of Roman towns, and in a damp climate like Britain the basilica served as an all year round recreation hall. Its main entrance overlooked Watling Street (which cut through the heart of the town), while the bath-house itself adjoined the exercise area by way of a large doorway which once stood in the gap that passes through the 'Old Work'. In addition to having surviving walls of the moist and dry saunas, and the cold plunge baths, the baths-complex at Viroconium provides one of the only two visible examples of a Roman swimming-pool in Britain, the other being in the city of Bath. Throughout the site of the bath-house the reconstructed tile columns, the *pilae*, can still be seen, which once formed part of the hypercaust or underfloor heating system.

Although the visible ruins exhibit only a tiny section of the once great city, which still remains to be excavated beneath the surrounding farm land, they do reveal what was once the city centre. Not only do we find the leisure complex, but also the administrative centre. On the opposite side of Watling Street from the bath site are a long line of column stumps, which once formed part of the eastern colonnade of the city forum, where debates were held and municipal decisions made.

All this, however, represents the Viroconium of the Roman era. But what of the early fifth century? Is there any archaeological evidence that Vironconium became the principal city of Vortigern's Britain?

Viroconium assumed a new strategic importance during the early fifth century, a time when the cities of the coastal provinces were suffering constant threat of invasion and pillage. London, for instance, the Roman capital of Britain, was easy prey for the Germanic raiders by route of the Thames. In fact, it was probably for this reason that Vortigern later installed Hengist and Horsa on the Isle of Thanet, to help protect the Thames estuary. York, on the other hand, was continually sacked by the Picts, whereas Lincoln was constantly under threat from the Angles and their repeated inland incursions from the Wash. Although other major cities such as Cirencester, Exeter or Bath could be considered safe from outside attack, they would not have been afforded the central expediency of Viroconium.

Vortigern's administration needed to co-ordinate forces on three fronts, and the location of Viroconium would have been ideally suited. Here Watling Street, arguably the most important Roman road in Britain, makes contact with the River Severn, one of the most significant waterways of the island. Upstream the Severn penetrates deep into the heartland of Wales, while downstream it arcs across the West Midlands, flowing to the sea through the Bristol Channel. Additionally, the Roman road network linked Viroconium with other important fortifications in the area such as Lavrobrinta (Forden Gaer) to the west, Bravonium (Leintwardine) to the south and Deva (Chester) to the north.

Not only did Viroconium occupy a site of vital strategic importance, but it was also situated in the centre of one of the country's most fertile agricultural areas. Archaeological excavations around the town and along the Severn Valley have revealed it to have been a remarkably rich Romano-British farming district, perhaps the most important reason for the apparent size and wealth of the city in Roman times. Whatever location was chosen by Vortigern for his power base, it would certainly need to feed itself in the event of any breakdown in relations with the allied tribes.

If Viroconium had become the capital of Vortigern's Britain we should expect to discover archaeological confirmation of the administration, such as intensive occupation of the city during this period. In fact, in recent years archaeology has unearthed remarkable evidence that not only supports this idea, but also reveals a highly urbanized city unique in Dark Age Britain.

Throughout the later Roman period, Viroconium declined in importance and, although it remained occupied, many of its buildings became
run down and dilapidated. The recreation basilica, for instance, once
the pride of the city, fell into such a state of disrepair that it finally
collapsed sometime around the mid-fourth century. Within a couple of
decades, even before the Romans left, the town was virtually abandoned.

Until recently this fragmentary picture was all that was known of
Viroconium. However, in the late 1960s, an extensive archaeological
excavation was initiated at the site. It was to last for well over a decade,
bringing to light a series of new and incredible discoveries. The dig, led
by archaeologist Philip Barker, was far more proficient than any that
preceded it, and produced a mass of evidence for the period following
the collapse of the baths-complex. The results showed that during the
final few years of Roman occupation the whole area was cleared and
completely rebuilt; a new city had been constructed on the ruins of
Viroconium.

From the excavation of post holes, and other tell-tale signs in the
foundations and substructure of the city, the new buildings were found
to have been made of timber, not bricks and mortar like the earlier
Roman town. However, when the evidence emerging from the dig was
gradually collated, these new buildings were discovered to have been
highly sophisticated. They were large and elaborate constructions of
classical design, with colonnades and orderly facades, many being at
least two storeys high. It appears, therefore, that in the closing days of
the Roman occupation Viroconium became Britain's most important
city, and could well have been Vortigern's capital soon after the
Romans left.

However, was the city still the capital of Powys at the time of the
Owain Ddantgwyn and the Cunedda family in the late fifth century?
The answer is almost certainly yes. At the excavation in 1967 a
tombstone dating from around 480 was discovered just outside the city
ramparts, bearing the inscription *Cunorix macus Maquicoline*, 'King
Cuno son of Maquicoline'. The *Cun* affix in his name clearly identifies
him as a member of the Cunedda family, as many of his descendants had
this same distinctive syllable, such as *Cun*eglasus and Maglo*cun*us. As
Cuno is actually identified as a king, it suggests that the Cunedda
dynasty was using Viroconium as its capital just prior to Owain's time.

So the archaeological evidence seems to confirm that Viroconium was
Owain's capital – the 'bear's stronghold' mentioned by Gildas. But is

there archaeological evidence at Viroconium to confirm that Owain Ddantgwyn was the historical Arthur? The archaeological evidence certainly indicates a period of much prosperity following the period of Badon, as the city was completely rebuilt in a manner unlike any in the country at the time.

The latest archaeological excavations in the vicinity of the Roman baths complex have shown that the area had been entirely reconstructed in the early sixth century, shortly after the time of Badon. Not only were new buildings erected and streets replanned, but the entire infrastructure of the city was also repaired. For example, a new drainage system and fresh water supply was installed through an elaborate arrangement of aqueducts. Long stretches of the Roman cobbled roads were also dug up and completely re-layered. Viroconium was restructured and a new kind of town came into existence, a dynamic trading centre and hive of industry. The nerve centre of this new Viroconium appears to have been a massive winged building constructed on the site of the old basilica. Accompanied by a complex of adjoining buildings and out-houses, this classical mansion appears to have been the palace of an extremely important chieftain.

The precise date of the rebuilding is at present impossible to determine with accuracy, but an approximate period is possible. The dating of archaeological sites is achieved in a number of ways, one widely used procedure being radiocarbon dating. Organic matter, in whatever form, either animal or vegetable, contains Carbon 14, and once the living organism has died the Carbon 14 gradually decays until some 60,000 years later it disappears altogether. From a chemical analysis the amount of Carbon 14 can be measured, enabling dating. Luckily there was an abundance of organic matter within the deposit strata of the final building phase at Viroconium; for instance, bones discovered amongst the rubble which was used to form the foundations of the last buildings. Unfortunately, radiocarbon dating is only accurate to within some fifty years, so a number of sample readings were necessary to gain a more precise date. In this way an average central date around 500–550 was obtained by cross-referencing a series of radiocarbon tests on various finds from the Viroconium dig.

This remarkable revitalisation of the city required considerable wealth and powerful leadership. Who had wielded the influence to organise and motivate such an endeavour, sometime between 500 and 550 A.D.? We know from Gildas, Bede, from examining the *Anglo-Saxon Chronicle*, and also from archaeology, that following Badon the

Britons experienced a period of some prosperity. We have now seen from the excavations of Viroconium that the city was the most sophisticated in Britain of this same period. It seems, therefore, that this could well have been the seat of the man who led the Britons to victory at Badon – and rebuilt either by him, or by his immediate successor with his inherited wealth and power. Our investigation has already concluded that Owain Ddantgwyn and then his son Cuneglasus ruled from the city during the period between 500 – 550. Which one of them rebuilt Viroconium is impossible to determine at this time. However, one way or the other, these excavations tend to confirm that Owain Ddantgwyn was indeed the British commander at Badon – the historical Arthur.

In the declining, strife-ridden years of the early sixth century, the splendid city of Viroconium must surely have seemed impressive, almost sublime, to the ordinary people of the countryside; an awe-inspiring place of wealth, mystery and power. Although the name Camelot appears to have been invented by Chretien de Troyes, it may have been from surviving legends of Viroconium that the medieval romancers formed their notions of King Arthur's magnificent city.

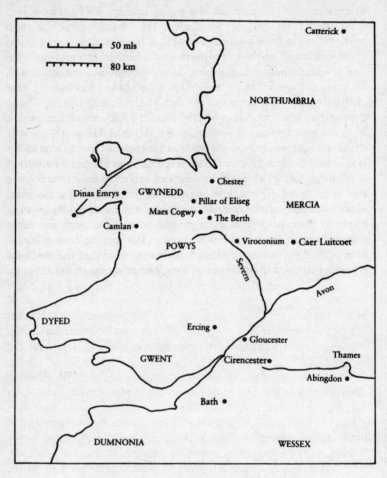

West Britain in the Mid-Seventh Century

8

The Isle of Avalon

The final stage in the search for the historical Arthur concerns the mystery of his burial site. In legend King Arthur was buried on the isle of Avalon, but if a place in the British Isles really did bear such a name during the Dark Ages, it has long been forgotten. Neither is there any contemporary evidence with which to locate the final resting place of Owain Ddantgwyn. Historical detective work is again needed – beginning with his most probable time of place of death.

From the *Welsh Annals* we learn that in the 93rd year there was the 'strife of Camlann in which Arthur and Medraut perished'. We are told nothing else, neither where nor why it occurred, nor even if Arthur and Medraut fought on opposite sides. Unfortunately, other than this entry in the *Annals*, no other Dark Age manuscript mentions Camlann. Before we attempt to locate the battle site, and consider the relationship between Arthur and Medraut, we must first establish a date for the battle.

The 93rd year of the *Annals* is somewhere around 539, which is almost certainly too late for the historical Arthur. Since Arthur was fighting when Hengist died in 488, he would have been well over seventy by 539. Although is it not impossible for Arthur to have died in battle in 539, it seems unlikely. Besides, we have already examined the inaccuracy of the *Annals* regarding the dating of Badon (see p 27).

If Arthur was Owain Ddantgwyn, a more reasonable date for his death would be around 520, when both his son Cuneglasus and his nephew Maglocunus came to power. As the *Annals* place the Battle of Badon around this time, in 518, it is possible that the writer had access to partly reliable information concerning Arthur's battles and knew the approximate year that one of them occurred. He may also have known that some two decades separated the events, but mistakenly located Badon at the time of Camlann.

Turning to Medraut, like the Battle of Camlann itself, he is not named in any other Dark Age manuscript beside the *Welsh Annals*: Gildas makes no mention of him; neither does Bede, and even Nennius fails to include him. However, Nennius does not refer to the Battle of Camlann at all, nor anything connected with Arthur's death. His list of Arthur's battles concerns only Arthur's victories, and since the Battle of Camlann appears to have been a disaster, it may not have been included because Nennius' source was a war poem praising Arthur's successful battles.

Geoffrey of Monmouth is the earliest writer to provide any details of Medraut and the Battle of Camlann. According to Geoffrey, Modred (Geoffrey's spelling of Medraut) was Arthur's nephew, who led a rebellion while Arthur was absent from the country. Arthur returns to confront Modred, but although he crushes the rebellion he is mortally wounded in the Battle of Camlann. Geoffrey uses the name Modred instead of Medraut, although he is clearly referring to the same man as the *Annals*. Welsh literature includes the character of Modred as Arthur's opponent at Camlann, but under the same spelling as the *Annals*, Medraut. The Medraut of the Welsh tales, however, is somewhat different to Geoffrey's Modred. Although he and Arthur are rivals, they are generally depicted as feuding equals or two chieftains involved in a struggle for supremacy.

The historical Battle of Camlann may well have been the result of an internal struggle between the Britons themselves. Gildas tells us that from the Battle of Badon until the time of his writing (*circa* 545) external warfare (war with the Anglo-Saxons) had ceased, although the country had been racked by internal feuding. Archaeology, supported by the evidence of the *Anglo-Saxon Chronicle* and Bede, clearly shows that by the mid-sixth century the Britons had been so weakened by internal squabbles that the Saxons were once more able to advance.

Gildas tells us that Maglocunus came to power by defeating his uncle the king in battle. As this appears to have been Owain Ddantgwyn – the historical Arthur – it is quite possible that the story of Modred mortally wounding his uncle, Arthur, may have derived from this historical event. It is possible that the Medraut referenced in the *Welsh Annals* did fall with Arthur, but fought on his side. Perhaps, many years later, Geoffrey of Monmouth learned that Arthur was overthrown by a nephew, and wrongly assumed that the Medraut recorded in the *Welsh Annals* was this nephew. Indeed, the most likely site for the battle of Camlann suggests that it was fought between Owain Ddantgwyn and Maglocunus.

Geoffrey sites the battle in Cornwall. However, we have already seen how his Cornish link seems to have been included to please his patron's brother, the earl of Cornwall. In light of the historical evidence suggesting an internecine conflict between Powys and Gwynedd around 520, a far more likely site would be somewhere between these kingdoms. Unlike Badon, there is still a location in Britain retaining the name Camlann (although it is spelt Camlan), a bleak and remote valley in the region of Merioneth in Central-West Wales. It lies approximately on the border of the kingdoms of Powys and Gwynedd as they existed during the early sixth century. Accordingly, it is where the battle between Owain and Maglocunus, referenced by Gildas, is likely to have occurred.

According to the medieval romances, after Camlann Arthur is taken to the isle of Avalon for burial. Where was Owain Ddantgwyn laid to rest? The answer to this, it seems, may be found with his descendants.

From the sixth century Britain moved progressively into a period of recorded history. The *Welsh Annals* no longer rely on Irish annals; the records which later formed the *Anglo-Saxon Chronicle* were compiled; and the gradual conversion of the Anglo-Saxons to Christianity from the end of the sixth century led to the founding of monasteries and the subsequent spread of writing skills. It is therefore easier to trace the decline of Powys than it has been to trace its rise.

In the mid-sixth century Gildas implored the British kings to cease their petty squabbles, for fear they would lose everything to the real enemy, the Anglo-Saxons. Within a few years his prediction began to come true. According to the *Anglo-Saxon Chronicle*, in 552 the Saxons moved north and defeated the British near Salisbury, and in 556 fought them forty miles further north at Barbury near Swindon. However, as the Chronicle records no victory for the Saxons at Barbury, it appears that the campaign was halted for a time. A new threat, however, came from the east, about fifteen years later.

According to the *Anglo-Saxon Chronicle*, in 571 the Saxon king Cuthwulf (of the Eslingas of south-west Cambridgeshire) routed the Midland British in Bedfordshire. Immediately after, he marched on Abingdon, where, although victorious, he died. He was succeeded by Cuthwine who seems to have formed an alliance with Ceawlin of Wessex in the south. The alliance marched west and in 577 beat the British at the Battle of Dyrham, seven miles north of Bath. With the cities of Gloucester, Cirencester and Bath now under Saxon control, the enemy had succeeded where they had failed at Badon over eighty years earlier. Dumnonia was effectively cut off from the rest of Celtic Britain and the heartland of Powys was now under direct threat from the Saxon alliance.

	POWYS	MERCIA	NORTHUMBRIA
480			
490	Owain Ddantgwyn (c488–c520)		
500			
510			
520	Cuneglasus (c520–c550)		
530			
540			
550	Brochfael Ysgithrog (c550–c580)		
560			
570			
580	Cynan Garwyn (c580–c598)		
590			
600	Selyf (c598–c613)		Aethelfrid (604–617)
610	Cyndrwyn (c613–c630)		Edwin (617–633)
620			
630	Cynddylan (c630–c656)	Penda (633–655)	Oswald (635–644)
640			Oswy (644–670)
650		Peada (655–658)	
660		Wulfhere (658–675)	
670			

The Struggle for the Midlands: 480–670
British and Anglian leaders

The Powys king responsible for the loss of Gloucester is unknown, but it was probably Cuneglasus' son Brochfael Ysgithrog. Although no record of Brochfael's campaigns survives, his son Cynan Garwyn seems to have halted the Saxon advance in the south. The *Book of Taliesin* contains a poem called *Trawsganu Cynan Garwyn*, believed to have been composed at the time by the bard Taliesin himself, which praises the prowess of Cynan in battle against the English.

With stalemate in the south, the theatre of the war then shifted to the north, where two Anglian kingdoms of the North-East joined forces against the British for the decisive Battle of Catraeth (Catterick in Yorkshire) about the year 598. There, King Aethelfrid of Bernicia (in modern-day Northumberland) and King Aelle of Deira (in modern-day Yorkshire) defeated the British; the subject of the *Gododdin* poem in which the Votadini fought with warriors from Gwynedd. As the *Gododdin* names a warrior called Cynan, this may imply that Powys was also involved in the Battle of Catraeth, for Cynan Garwyn seems to have been king of Powys at the time.

As the *Gododdin* relates, the Battle of Catraeth marked a decisive defeat for the Britons and the beginning of the end for the British kingdom of Rheged, which had been established some thirty years earlier across the north of England. However, the Anglo-Saxons were involved in one more battle before securing the north for themselves. In 603, according to Bede, the Irish king Aedan (who ruled in South-West Scotland) marched against them, but he too was beaten. The following year Aethelfrid decided to move against Aelle himself and occupied the Deira capital at York, so creating the huge Anglian kingdom of Northumbria which now covered much of northern England.

After a decade of consolidation, about the year 613 (according to the *Welsh Annals*) Aethelfrid attacked North Wales and defeated a joint Gwynedd/Powys army at Chester, where Cynan's son Cyndrwyn Selyf was killed. Northumbria had now driven a wedge between the British forces of north and central Britain.

However, within a couple of years the Angles began to fight amongst themselves again, when Aelle's exiled son Edwin marched with the army of King Redwald of East Anglia against Aethelfrid and defeated him. The *Annals* record the death of Aethelfrid around the year 617, after which Edwin became king of Northumbria and Aethelfrid's sons were exiled to Ireland. Edwin appears to have continued with the expansionist policy of his predecessor and invaded Gwynedd during the 620s. However, the internal wranglings of the enemy seem to have given the British a breathing space. After being besieged in 629 on an island the *Annals* call Glannauc (probably off the coast of Anglesea) Cadwallon, the King of Gwynedd, managed to fight back.

In alliance with the Anglian Prince Penda, who had broken away from Edwin and founded the Kingdom of Mercia in southern Northumbria, in 633 Cadwallon defeated Edwin who died in battle. Unfortunately for any new hopes of a British revival, two years later Aethelfrid's son Oswald returned from exile in Ireland and defeated Cadwallon with (according to Bede) a much smaller army. Gwynedd then seems to have been overrun by the Northumbrians, as the *Irish Annals* record the burning of Bangor in 634, while in the north, Gododdin was conquered four years later.

With the power of Gwynedd broken, in 644 a Mercian/Powys alliance finally defeated Oswald at a place the *Welsh Annals* records as Maes Cogwy at Oswestry. However, within a few years, only Powys remained as the last bastion of British power, as the *Welsh Annals* record the 'hammering of Dyfed' in 645 and the 'slaughter of Gwent' in 649, perhaps by the Irish and West Saxons respectively.

The last chance for Powys in central England came when its allies, Penda of the Mercians and Aethelhere of the East Anglians, were defeated by Oswald's brother Oswy at a battle which Bede describes as being near the River Vinwed, probably in the area of Leeds, about the year 655. With the defeat of Penda and Aethelhere, Penda's son Peada and Aethelhere's brother Anna were installed under Oswy's control in Mercia and East Anglia. It was then that Powys made its lone stand against Oswy's reprisals.

The details of these last days of greater Powys are recorded in a collection of early Welsh poems called the *Canu Llywarch Hen* – *The Song of Llywarch the Old*. Now preserved in the *Red Book of Hergest* at Oxford's Bodleian Library, the cycle of poems have been dated to the mid-ninth century. (The dating was derived not only on linguistic grounds, but also on the cycle's similarity to the *Juvencus Englynion*, three verses of ninth-century saga poetry preserved at Cambridge University.) However, although *The Song of Llywarch the Old* appears to have been committed to writing around 850, the poems evidence familiarity with names, places and events of the mid-seventh century, and so probably formed part of a saga composed much nearer that time – *circa* 660.

The Song of Llywarch the Old concerns the ruling family of Powys, and their king, Cynddylan's failing struggle against the invading Anglo-

The Historical Arthur: Dan Shadrake of Britannia in authentic armour of the late-fifth century. (Derek Rowe Photos Ltd)

ABOVE. Archaeologist Roger White discusses the Travail's Acre investigation with the geophysics team.

LEFT. Dr Susan Overden using the Proton Magnetometer.

ABOVE. Clare Stephens probing Travail's Acre with the Resistivity Meter.

LEFT. Dr Clare Adams using the Ground Sensing Radar.

ABOVE. John Gater prepares to reveal the geophysics findings at Travail's Acre to Brian Blessed during filming for *Schofield's Quest*.

LEFT. Authors Graham Phillips (right) and Martin Keatman (left) examine the site of the grave discovered at Travail's Acre.

Artist's impression of fifth-century Viroconium, the Dark Age capital of Powys. The real 'Camelot'.

The 'Old Work' at Viroconium.

Reconstructed Roman stockade at the Lunt, near Coventry. The defences of fifth-century Viroconium would have been similar in design.

n illo tempore saxones inualescebant in
multitudine & crescebant in brittannia.
Mortuo aut hengisto octha filio eius transi
uit de sinistrali parte brittannie ad reg
nu cantorum. & de ipso orti sunt reges cantor.
unc arthur pugnabat contra illos.
in illis diebus cum regibus brittonum. s. ipse dux erat
bellorum. Primum bellum fuit in ostiu flumi
nis quod dicitur glein. secundum & tertium & quar
tu & quintu. super aliud flumen quod
dicitur dubglas. & in regione linnuis.
Sextum bellum sup flumen quod uoca
tur bassas. Septimu fuit bellu
in silua celidonis. id est cat coit celidon.
Octauum fuit bellu in castello guinni
on. In quo arthur portauit imagine
sce marie ppetue uirginis sup hume
ros suos. & pagani uersi sunt in fuga in
illo die. & cedes magna fuit sup illos
per uirtutem dni nri ihu xpi & per uirtute
sce marie uirginis genitricis ei. Nonu
bellu gestu in urbe legionis. Decimu
gessit bellu in litore fluminis quod
uocat tribruit. Undecimu factu
bellu in monte qui dicitur agned. Duo
decimu fuit bellu in monte badonis.
in quo corruer in uno die nongenti sexa
ginta uiri de uno impetu arthur.

The earliest mention of Arthur, in Nennius' *Historia Brittonum* now in the
British Library.

Berth Pool, where the real 'Excalibur' may have been cast as a sixth-century votive offering.

The Pillar of Eliseg in Valle Crucis, Llangollen, North Wales, on which a ninth-century inscription recorded the descent of the rulers of Powys from the British king Vortigern.

Saxons. (Cynddylan was Cyndrwyn Selyf's son.) The first of Cynddylan's battles referred to in the poems is the Battle of Maes Cogwy, where the *Welsh Annals* record that Penda defeated Oswald in 644. In *The Song of Llywarch the Old*, the poet relates:

> I saw the field of Maes Cogwy
> Armies, and the cry of men hard pressed
> Cynddylan brought them aid

This evidence of Cynddylan's close ties with Penda is also echoed in Bede's writings where he names the Queen of the Mercians as Cynwise, and Penda's daughter as Cyneberga; the *Cyn* affix in the names inferring that an inter-family marriage had taken place between the kingdoms of Cynddylan and Penda.

The *Song of Llywarch the Old* also refers to what may well have been the last of Cynddylan's victories, at Caer Luitcoet (Wall near Lichfield). This must have been fought after Penda's death around 655, as the Anglo-Saxons are described as having Christian priests with their army. According to Bede, Penda died a pagan although Peada converted to Christianity under the guidance of Oswy.

The reference to this battle is of extreme importance, as the poet of *The Song of Llywarch the Old* includes a line describing the kings of Powys as actually being descended from King Arthur himself. Cynddylan and his family are described as:

> 'Heirs of great Arthur'

The dating of 850 means that, other than the *Gododdin* and Nennius' *Historia Brittonum*, *The Song of Llywarch the Old* may contain the oldest reference to Arthur in existence. It is certainly the oldest to place Arthur in a geographical context – in the Midland kingdom of Powys – centuries before Geoffrey of Monmouth and the romancers placed him in the south or south-west. After the Battle of Caer Luitcoet, the British of Powys were in retreat. *The Song of Llywarch the Old* relates how Cynddylan is killed and his kingdom sacked. During an elegy on Cynddylan's death, the poem describes Cynddylan's sister Heledd looking down upon the kingdom's pillaged capital, which it calls the White Town. This is almost certainly Viroconium as the poet describes Heledd looking down from Dinlle Wrecon, the Wrekin hill that directly overlooks the city ruins. Indeed, the most recent archaeological excavations have shown that Viroconium was finally abandoned in the mid-seventh century – the very period to which the poem refers.

This final defeat of Cynddylan and the sacking of Powys occurred around 658, and was probably the event referred to in the *Welsh Annals* when they record that in that year, 'Oswy came and took plunder'. The British of Shropshire were certainly conquered by the Anglo-Saxons by 661, as the people of the Wroxeter district around Viroconium are entered as *Wrocensaetna* in the census of Mercian territories in the Mercian taxation document, the *Tribal Hidage*. Also, a ford over the Severn near Melverley, fifteen miles west of Viroconium, is recorded as 'Wulfhere's Ford', bearing the name of Wulfhere, the Mercian king who succeeded Peada in 658.

Cynddylan must have been buried within a few years of his old ally Aethelhere of East Anglia, who died fighting Oswy about 655. The burial site of the East Anglian kings has been discovered at Sutton Hoo near Ipswich. Indeed Aethelhere himself is probably the famous 'Sutton Hoo Man', whose burial mound was excavated in 1939. The Sutton Hoo dig revealed one of the richest archaeological finds in Europe: the remains of an entire Anglo-Saxon ship, along with jewellery, armaments and other family treasures, now restored and on display at the British Museum. No British equivalent has yet been discovered, but *The Song of Llywarch the Old* may hold the secret to such a location.

The Song of Llywarch the Old not only calls the Powys kings 'the heirs of great Arthur', it also names the burial site of Cynddylan and the ruling dynasty of Powys. It may, therefore, reveal the most elusive secret of all, the burial site of Owain Ddantgwyn – King Arthur himself.

In one of the monologue poems of *The Song of Llywarch the Old*, the *Canu Heledd – The Song of Heledd* – the death of Cynddylan is mourned by his sister Heledd. She relates how after a final battle, the body of Cynddylan is taken to be buried at *Eglwyseu Bassa*, the Churches of Bassa. From the poem, it is clear that the Churches of Bassa has long been a sacred burial site, it also refers to 'the gravemound of Gorwynnion' and other 'green graves' to be seen there. In fact, in a second elegy on Cynddylan's death within *The Song of Llywarch the Old*, one of Cynddylan's family, Llywarch (after whom the cycle is named), says that he will 'grieve for the death of Cynddylan' until he too 'rests beneath the mound'.

Although *The Song of Llywarch the Old* refers to events over a hundred years after the death of Owain Ddantgwyn, its naming the Churches of Bassa provides crucial evidence for the lost burial site of the ruling family of Powys. The Churches of Bassa is almost certainly in the vicinity of the village today called Baschurch, some nine miles to the north-west of Shrewsbury. In secluded countryside on the edge of the village is the Berth, an ancient fortified hillock surrounded by marsh-land and linked to the mainland by a gravel causeway. The hill is completely encompassed by Iron Age earth and stone ramparts, and joined to a low lying oval enclosure by a second causeway some 150 metres to the north-east. Until the area was drained to claim arable farmland, the Berth would have been surrounded entirely by water, and in the Dark Ages it would have consisted of two islands – the Berth hill itself and a lower-lying, oval-shaped island (now called the oval enclosure) joined together by the causeway. Now, all that remains of this huge lake is Berth Pool, below the Berth hill to the south. As the village of Baschurch does not appear to have existed in the Dark Ages, and the Berth is the only contemporary site in the immediate vicinity, it must have been the original Churches of Bassa.

If this is the burial site of the Powys kings, it is probably the burial site of Owain Ddantgwyn. An isolated site, silent and eerie, the last resting place of the man who was Arthur could hardly be more appropriate: a forgotten island – could this be the real Avalon?

Only limited archaeological excavation has been carried out at the Berth in modern times. However, a dig in 1962-63, by Peter Gelling of Birmingham University, uncovered fragments of pottery dating from the sixth century – conceivably from the period of Owain's lifetime. Furthermore, in 1906, a workman cutting turf at the edge of the stream draining from the Berth pool discovered a bronze cauldron, some forty-five centimetres high and thirty centimetres wide, which was presented to the British Museum, where it was dated as first century. However, modern examination has dated it much later, around the sixth or seventh centuries. Consequently, the Berth does appear to have been in use during the period in question.

Exactly what the Berth was used for, however, has remained an archaeological mystery. Its name does suggests that it was a religious, rather than military or domestic site. The word *berth* comes from an old Welsh word meaning 'sacred', and until earlier this century the oval enclosure was still referred to as the Sacred Enclosure. It is currently impossible to gauge the degree of sacred associations the Berth may have had during the Dark Ages, since the modern archaeological work has been limited to that of Peter Gelling. However, according to the *Transcript of the Shropshire Archaeological & Historical Society* (Vol

XLIX 1937-38) the plural, Churches of Bassa, suggests a 'Celtic group of little churches'. These church groups, such as those more commonly found in Ireland, imply that at some time the Berth supported a monastic or religious community, which lends credence to the Berth being the genuine burial site of the Powys kings.

A legend that the Berth was an ancient burial site was recounted by archaeologist Lilly Chitty in 1925, who had been told by a village school teacher of a prince who was buried beneath in the area after a great battle. Also, that other warriors were buried there.

Returning to *The Song of Llywarch the Old*, the poem suggests that Cynddylan and his ancestors were buried somewhere at the Berth. But where? The Berth covers many acres.

In 1992 co-author Martin Keatman and I published our theory that Owain Ddantgwyn was the historical King Arthur in *King Arthur: The True Story* (Arrow). It created considerable controversy, particularly concerning the Berth as the burial site of the kings of Powys. Previously, few scholars took *The Song of Llywarch the Old* seriously. It was considered no more than a work of nostalgic Welsh fiction, and accordingly could not contain an accurate historical depiction of the sacking of Powys in the mid-seventh century. Few, it seems, appreciated just how much of the poem concerning the life and death of Cynddylan tallied with other historical sources and with modern archaeology.

The first of Cynddylan's battles referred to in *The Song of Llywarch the Old* is the battle of Maes Cogwy, a battle recorded in the *Welsh Annals* in the year 644. The poem also includes the last of Cynddylan's victories at Caer Luitcoet, a battle recorded in the *Anglo-Saxon Chronicle*. Additionally, the defeat of Cynddylan and the sacking of Powys by Oswy described in the poem is recorded in the *Welsh Annals* in the year 658, and evidenced in the Mercian *Tribal Hidage*. Most importantly, however, the poem refers to something that was not discovered until very recently – namely that Viroconium was finally abandoned at this time. Last but not least, *The Song of Llywarch the Old* tells us that Cynddylan was Arthur's heir, and our research suggests that Cynddylan's ancestor Owain Ddantgwyn was the historical Arthur. Another reason that scholars refused to accept the authenticity of *The Song of Llywarch the Old* was that Cynddylan is described as being buried with his shield, the objection being that during the mid-seventh century the Britons of Powys were Christian, and as such would not have buried their kings in this pagan manner. However, many pagan traditions continued in early Christian times. In fact, many have survived to this day, such as the tradition of Easter Eggs, derived from a pagan custom of egg painting to mark the start of summer; and the Christmas Tree, originally a pagan custom in which a fir tree was planted indoors during the festival of mid-winter. Few today would consider it sacrilegious to continue with these harmless pre-Christian customs; even less thirteen centuries ago. Cynddylan could very well have been buried with his shield, even if he were a Christian. He certainly appears to have had no reservations in forming an alliance with the pagan King Penda.

The only way to discover the truth about the Berth was an archaeological excavation. Unfortunately, that was out of the question for the foreseeable future. Even if we could persuade an eminent archaeologist that the Berth was the burial site of the kings of Powys, there were no funds for such an excavation in Shropshire. It seemed we would never know what lay beneath the Berth – until one day in 1994, when I saw the television series *Time Team* on Channel 4.

The series, hosted by actor Tony Robinson, involved a team of historians, archaeologists and other relevant experts visiting various historical locations, in an attempt to shed light on local historical enigmas. The investigation usually resulted in an archaeological dig, the excavation site often being determined by a scientific team called Geophysical Surveys of Bradford.

Geophysics is a hi-tech and revolutionary science, which has created something of a sensation amongst archaeologists. Put simply, geophysics enables archaeologists to see what lies below the ground without digging. With sophisticated equipment the geophysicists construct a three dimensional image of what is in the soil. In one *Time Team* episode the geophysics group revealed the complete outline of the foundations of an Anglo-Saxon church on their computer screen – something that had been hidden below farmland for centuries. It was obvious that the same technology could reveal what lay beneath the ancient soil of the Berth. I soon discovered, however, that the hi-tech team was well beyond our financial means.

However in late 1995 the opportunity to utilise geophysics at the Berth presented itself. Martin and I were contacted by Francesca Price, a researcher from the popular ITV television series *Schofield's Quest*. As the programme aims to provide answers to some of life's mysteries, our search for Arthur's burial site seemed an ideal subject for them to cover. Together with Francesca, we met with Mike Stokes, the curator of Rowley's House Museum in Shrewsbury, and Roger White, the

Shropshire archaeologist responsible for considering archaeological work in the Baschurch area. They confirmed that the Berth was an historical enigma, and both were happy to see a geophysics team examine the area. Once the farmer who owned the land granted his permission, Michael Hurl Television, the programme's production company, arranged for the same geophysics group who had appeared on *Time Team* to scan the area with the most sophisticated electronic equipment available.

The big question was, where to scan. Although *The Song of Llywarch the Old* suggests that the Berth was the burial site of the Kings of Powys, we are not told precisely where they were buried. The mound of Gorwynion, where Llywarch hopes to one day lie, could be anywhere, as could the other 'green graves'. However, when describing Cynddylan's burial, the poet provides an important series of clues. After Cynddylan's death, his sister Heledd surveys his burial site as she mourns his passing:

> The Churches of Bassa are his resting place tonight . . .
> I shall mourn till I enter my oaken grave . . .
> I shall mourn till I enter my quiet oak . . .
> I shall mourn till I enter the steadfast earth . . .
> I shall mourn till I enter circling staves . . .
> I shall mourn till I enter the field's surface . . .
> I shall mourn till I enter Travail's Acre . . .

The Churches of Bassa, 'his resting place', we had already identified as the Berth. Heledd goes on to relate how she will mourn for her brother till she too enters her 'oaken grave', her 'quiet oak', in the 'steadfast earth', probably referring to burial in an hollowed oak-trunk coffin, a common practice in post-Roman times. Heledd hopes to one day be buried with her brother, and we are told where this is – within a circle of staves, surrounding a field called Travail's Acre. During the seventh century, when Cynddylan was buried, the Berth consisted of two islands in a lake, connected by a gravel causeway: Berth hill and the smaller oval enclosure. The enclosure is encompassed by defensive earthen ramparts, which, judging by what is known of other Dark Age sites, would originally have been topped by a stockade of wooden stakes – circling staves? Within the enclosure is a field, about an acre in size. Could this be Travail's Acre?

As there was nothing else within the vicinity of the Berth which so precisely matched the description, we were sure that the oval enclosure was the site of Cynddylan's burial in the poem. If Cynddylan's grave remained undisturbed in the soil of the oval enclosure, it would certainly be detectable to the equipment of the geophysics team.

The geophysics team – John Gater, Dr Susan Ovenden, Dr Clare Adam and Clare Stephens – were to use three types of equipment. First, a Proton Magnetometer, which measures any magnetic anomalies beneath the surface, and reveals the presence of objects such as metal artifacts. Second, a Resistivity Meter, a double-pronged device which sends a current through the ground and measures any change in electrical resistance. It can detect different types of materials beneath the surface, and was the same device that revealed the foundation stones of the Saxon church on the *Time Team* programme. Finally, the most advanced equipment of all, Ground Sensing Radar, a scanner which can produce a three-dimensional radar picture of what lies deep below the ground.

The procedure took an entire day, and was filmed by the TV crew and narrated by the actor Brian Blessed, who also interviewed Martin, myself and Roger White. As I watched the geophysics people working in the rain, I began to wonder if it was all a wild goose chase. None of them seemed particularly roused by the findings. However, at lunch, when I joined the others in the dining bus at the farm, there was an atmosphere of excitement. Apparently the geophysics team *had* found something of considerable interest. Frustratingly, they would say no more until they had completed the Ground Sensing Radar scan later that afternoon, and run the combined data through their computer. By late afternoon the rain stopped and the sun came out; as if in response, the geophysics team announced that they were ready to be interviewed. The farmer, his wife and their two sons had arrived, and joined us all as everyone gathered round, listening intently as Brian Blessed asked the geophysics team's leader, John Gater, to reveal their findings.

The geophysicist explained that they had found evidence that two wooden buildings had stood on the site, plus a larger stone structure, and all might date from the Dark Ages. But was it a burial site? Although the type of soil meant that any bones would long ago have decomposed, a circular ditch had been revealed, right in the middle of the enclosure, some two meters deep, which appeared to be a burial ditch consistent with those of the post-Roman era. More remarkably, at the centre of the ditch was a diamond-shaped piece of metal, probably the central boss of an ancient shield. A series of gasps came from the onlookers – it could indeed be the grave of an important sixth or seventh-century chieftain.

Was this the grave of Cynddylan? The poem had not only revealed this as the precise location of Cynddylan's burial, but it actually said that Cynddylan was buried with his shield. The poem seems to have been right once again. It was right about the battles, the historical figures, the abandonment of Viroconium, and now, it appeares, the burial of Cynddylan. There is, therefore, every reason to believe that it is right about the graves of Cynddylan's ancestors also being at the Berth. The implications to the search for Arthur are remarkable: Owain Ddantgwyn, the man we identified as the historical Arthur, was Cynddylan's direct ancestor. It is now more likely than ever that he too is buried at the Berth. From the geophysics survey, it appeared that there was only one grave in Trevail's Acre itself. Perhaps, as the last king to be buried at the Berth before it was abandoned to the Anglo-Saxons, Cynddylan was buried in a part of the Berth that had previously been reserved for important religious ceremonies. The other graves may, therefore, be found on the larger island, which is now Berth Hill.

All the historical and archaeological evidence previously examined clearly pointed to Owain Ddantgwyn as the most powerful British king at the time when Arthur is said to have been Britain's most powerful king. From Gildas, who wrote within living memory of the time, we discovered that Owain Ddantgwyn was known as the Bear, the British *Arth*, from which the name Arthur almost certainly derived. Finally, *The Song of Llywarch the Old*, the earliest known reference to place Arthur in a geographical context, told us that Arthur was a king of Powys. As the historical evidence clearly showed that Owain Ddantgwyn was the king of Powys at the time of Badon, the period when Arthur appears to have lived, then if the poem was right, the historical Arthur can be no one other than Owain Ddantgwyn. By helping confirm the authenticity of *The Song of Llywarch the Old*, the geophysics survey of the Berth has provided the closest thing yet to scientific evidence for the existence of the historical Arthur.

As there is now compelling evidence of an important Dark Age burial site at the Berth, a full-scale archaeological excavation may soon follow. An excavation which may finally discover the earthly remains of the most mysterious figure in British history – King Arthur himself.

Appendix
The Historical Arthurian Era

The illustrations on the following pages have been prepared by Dan Shadrake of Britannia, an Arthurian re-enactment society based in Essex. The illustrations are based on his research into the weaponry, clothing and modes of warfare of the authentic Arthurian period.

1. British officer c. 493 A.D. The Roman style still persists. Often, well maintained, inherited weapons supplied the warrior elite.

2. Everyday life in fifth-century Viroconium.

3. Unhorsed British cavalry officer, wearing lamellar body armour, attacked by Pict.

4. British warlord outside a fortified settlement.

5. Saxon attack on a fortified British settlement.

6. Octha faces defeat at Badon.

PART TWO
THE SEARCH FOR THE GRAIL

9

The Grail Romances

Having gained an historical perspective on the Dark Ages, and the time and place in which Arthur seems to have lived, we turn now to the Middle Ages and the birth of the medieval Arthurian Grail romances. We have discovered how Geoffrey of Monmouth and the romancers of the eleventh and twelfth centuries re-created Arthur's life from half-remembered historical events; were the contemporary Grail romances similarly compiled?

The original Grail romances consisted of eight stories written within a period of about thirty years between 1190 and 1220. Although the Grail quest featured in many subsequent Arthurian romances, culminating in the most famous version by Thomas Malory in the late fifteenth century, any investigation into the birth of the legend must begin with these earliest versions. The first, Chretien's *Le Conte del Graal*, written around 1190, was followed within ten years by two so-called Continuations of his unfinished story, by anonymous authors. Robert de Boron's *Joseph d'Arimathie* then appeared around 1200, as did an anonymous French romance known as the *Didcot Perceval*. The German *Parzival*, by the epic poet Wolfram von Eschenbach, was composed by 1205. A revised version of the *Didcot Perceval*, called *Perlesvaus*, and two Grail stories in the Vulgate Cycle were the last versions in the series to appear, around 1220.

Chretien's *Le Conte del Graal*

Le Conte del Graal, the last of Chretien's five Arthurian romances composed somewhere between 1170 and 1190, was left unfinished when he died. Introducing the work, Chretien says that he obtained the story from his patron Count Philip of Flanders, in the form of a book given to him before Philip left for the crusades.

In the story the hero, Perceval, is introduced as 'Perceval of Wales', a sprightly young warrior who had been brought up by his widowed mother in a forest in Snowdonia. He travels to Arthur's court and trains for knighthood but, because of his naivety, his master Gornemant teaches him to keep quiet and to avoid asking questions. After training, Perceval sets out to return home to visit his mother, but during the journey meets two fishermen who direct him to a mysterious castle. Once inside, he is invited to a banquet held in honour of the castle's lord, a lame old warrior called the Rich Fisher. During the feast Perceval witnesses a strange procession in which he sees the Grail:

> While they were talking of this and that, a squire entered from a chamber, grasping by the middle a white lance. . . . all present beheld the white lance and the white point, from which a drop of red blood ran down to the squire's hand. . . . [Perceval] watched this marvel, but he refrained from asking what it meant . . . he feared that if he asked, it would be considered rude.

Shortly afterwards:

> A damsel came in with these squires, holding between her hands a graal [Chretien's spelling]. She was beautiful, gracious, splendidly garbed, and as she entered with the graal in her hands, there was such a brilliant light that the candles lost their brightness, just as the stars do as the moon or the sun rises.

Later the Grail is described in greater detail:

> [It was made from] refined gold, and it was set with precious stones of many kinds, the richest and most costly that exist in the sea or in the earth.

Although in awe, Perceval remembers what his master taught him about not asking questions, so he refrains from quizzing his hosts concerning the Grail. Eventually, he leaves the castle and cannot again discover its whereabouts. At length, he meets a hermit who explains the significance of what Perceval saw at the castle of the Rich Fisher and tells him of his foolishness in not having asked about the Grail:

> Great was your folly when you did not learn whom one served with the graal. The Rich Fisher was my brother; and his sister and mine was your mother. And believe me that the Rich Fisher is the

son of the king who causes himself to be served with the graal. But do not think that he takes from it a pike, a lamprey, or a salmon. The holy man sustains and refreshes his life with a single mass wafer. So sacred a thing is the graal, and he himself is so spiritual, that he needs no more for his sustenance than the mass wafer that comes in the graal. Fifteen years he has been thus without issuing from the chamber where you saw the graal enter.

Shortly after this encounter the story ends abruptly. From Chretien we learn that Perceval is, without knowing it, the grandson of the Rich Fisher, and that he is to inherit the Grail. To do so he must ask the right questions. However, the unfinished work leaves us mystified: what exactly is the Grail? Chretien neglects to describe the artefact's appearance, merely saying it is made of gold and decorated with precious stones. Indeed, he left many unanswered questions, which two anonymous writers attempted to address within ten years of his death.

The First Continuation

The so-called First Continuation is an anonymous story written in Old French around 1190. It is so named because it is the author's attempt to continue the story where Chretien left off, and consequently has Gawain taking over the role of the hero. When Gawain encounters the Grail in the Rich Fisher's castle we are given additional information concerning the relic, which in some ways is even more confusing.

Then Gawain saw entering by a door the rich Grail, which served the knights and swiftly placed bread before each one. It also performed the butler's office, the service of wine, and filled large cups of fine gold and decked the tables with them. As soon as it had done this, without delay it placed at every table a service of food in large silver dishes. Sir Gawain watched all this, and marvelled how much the Grail served them. He wondered sorely that he beheld no other servant . . .

Still we cannot tell what the Grail is supposed to be, merely that it seems to hover around the room serving food. We can only assume that it is some form of floating plate. We are, however, told its history.

It is true that Joseph caused it to be made: that Joseph of

Arimathea who so loved the Lord all his life, as it seemed, that on the day when he received the death on the cross to save sinners, Joseph came with the Grail which he had caused to be made to Mount Calvary, where God was crucified . . . He placed it at once below his feet, which were wet with blood which flowed down each foot, and collected as much as he was able in this Grail of fine gold.

Strangely, in the same story there is a second object also described as a Grail. This time we are told precisely what it is. When Joseph eventually leaves Palestine, he is accompanied by a companion, Nicodemus, who takes with him the second Grail:

Nicodemus had carved and fashioned a head in the likeness of the Lord on the day that he had seen him on the cross. But of this I am sure, that the Lord God set his hand to the shaping of it, as they say; for no man ever saw one like it nor could it be made by human hands. Most of you who have been at Lucca know it and have seen this Grail . . .

Having left this carved head – the second Grail – at Lucca, Joseph and his companions leave on a long journey.

Joseph and his company prepared their fleet and entered without delay, and did not end their voyage till they reached the land which God had promised to Joseph. The name of the country was the White Land.

This land we learn is somewhere in Britain. When Joseph eventually dies he leaves instructions that the original Grail – the one used to collect Jesus' blood – is to remain in the possession of his direct descendants.

At the end of his life he prayed sweetly that he would consent that Joseph's lineage would be rendered illustrious by the Grail. And thus it befell; it is the pure truth. For after his death no man in the world of any age had possession of it unless he was of Joseph's lineage. In truth the Rich Fisher descended from him, and all his heirs and, they say, Guellans Guenelaus and his son Perceval.

The First Continuation portrays the Rich Fisher and Perceval as direct descendants of Joseph of Arimathea, while the Grail (or at least one of them) once contained the blood of Christ. Neither of these themes was included by Chretien, so the author may have consulted a separate source, perhaps even the same book that Chretien obtained from his patron. Alternatively, it might have been pure invention.

Robert de Boron's *Joseph d'Arimathie*

We now come to the story that made the Grail famous: the most popular of all the medieval Grail romances, Robert de Boron's *Joseph d'Arimathie*.

Boron is a village near Montbeliard on the Swiss border, where the author wrote under the patronage of a crusader knight, Gautier de Montbeliard. As Gautier departed for Italy in 1199, and died in a subsequent crusade without returning home, Robert's poem was probably written around the same time (he records in his dedication Gautier leaving home). Unlike the authors of the two Continuations, Robert claimed to have a completely separate source from Chretien for his Grail story. He claimed it came from the book in which important Christian clerics had 'written the histories and the great secrets which one calls the Grail'.

For the first time we are given specific details about the appearance and origin of the relic, which Robert called 'The Holy Grail'. According to the author, after the Crucifixion, Joseph, who had been a secret follower of Jesus, teams up with another convert, Nicodemus, a Roman officer present at Jesus' death. Together they approach Pilate to request Jesus' body for proper burial. Eventually they succeed, also obtaining the cup that had been used at the Last Supper – the Holy Grail.

Accompanied by Nicodemus, Joseph uses the vessel to collect a few drops of blood from Jesus' body before laying him in the tomb. When, on the third day after the Crucifixion, the Jews discover the body missing, they accuse Joseph of removing it, throw him into prison, and confiscate the sacred chalice. There the resurrected Jesus appears to Joseph in a blaze of light, returns to him the Grail, and tells him he has custodianship of the holy relic. Christ also instructs Joseph in the saying of mass, and informs him that the vessel is to be called the 'calice'. Strangely, however, Robert thereafter refers to it as the Grail.

Joseph is eventually rescued after the sacking of Jerusalem by the Romans in A.D. 70, and escapes to Britain with his brother-in-law Bron. Bron has a son, Alein, whose own son is Perceval. Each of these men in turn is called the Rich Fisher, the secret title for the one who possesses and protects the Grail. Robert not only provides a complete history of the Grail and fully describes what it is, he even tells us what the word means: it comes, he claims, from the old French word *agree*, meaning to delight or satiate, indicating that the cup provides spiritual refreshment.

Confusion, however, arises over the time-scale. If Perceval is the grandson of Bron, Joseph's contemporary in first-century Palestine, how is he alive in the Arthurian era of the fifth century, the period in which Robert places Perceval? The answer is left to the next romancer, the anonymous author of the *Didcot Perceval*, who makes Bron immortal. By the time of Perceval, Bron is centuries old due to the Grail's powers of rejuvenation.

The *Didcot Perceval*

The prose romance Perceval, or the *Didcot Perceval* as it is now known, was written some time around 1200. It has survived into modern times in two separate manuscripts, the older found in the Didcot Manuscript in the French National Library in Paris. (The word Didcot has nothing to do with the original author, but is the name of a former owner of the manuscript, Firmin Didcot.)

In the manuscript the *Didcot Perceval* is preceded by a prose version of *Joseph d'Arimathie*; it was therefore once thought to have been a prose copy of a lost poem by Robert de Boron. However, on further examination of its style, it now seems that the *Didcot Perceval* is derived from another literary source entirely. Indeed, in the introduction the author claims to have discovered a more authentic source than his predecessors, including even Chretien de Troyes, the originator of the Grail romances:

> But of this Chretien de Troyes does not speak, nor the others who have composed of it in order to make their rhymes pleasant, but we tell only so much as appears in the story and as Merlin had written by Blayse his master . . . And he saw and knew the adventures that happened to Perceval each day, and had them written by Blayse in order that they may be spoken of to worthy men who would wish to hear them. Now know what we find in the writings that Blayse relates to us, just as Merlin made him write down and record it.

So according to the anonymous writer, the story was originally written by someone called Blayse. The story opens with Merlin explaining to Arthur the origin of the Round Table:

> It was made to signify the table where Our Lord sat on the Thursday when he said that Judas would betray him. And also the table was made after that of Joseph which was fashioned for the Grail when Joseph separated the good from the evil. Now I wish you to know that there have been two kings in Britain who have been priests and emperors of Rome. And also I wish that you should know that in Britain there will be a third king who will be priest and emperor ... But before you can be so noble and so valiant it is necessary that the Round Table should be exalted again by you ...
>
> It happened formally that the Grail was given to Joseph when he was in prison where Our Lord himself bore it to him. And when he had come from the prison this Joseph entered into a wilderness and many of the people of Judea with him ...
>
> Now, in truth, Our Lord made the first table, and Joseph made the second, and I, in the time of Uther Pendragon, your father, had the third made, which still will be much exalted ... So know that the Grail was given into the hands of Joseph, and upon his death he left it to his brother-in-law who had the name of Bron. And this Bron had twelve sons, one of whom was named Alain li Gros. And the Fisher King commanded him to be the guardian of his brothers. This Alain has come to this land from Judea, just as Our Lord has commanded him ...

Merlin goes on to say that, having lived since the time of Christ, Bron the Fisher King is now ill and will remain sick, unable to die, until a noble knight of the Round Table travels to his castle and asks:

> What it is that the Grail has served and what it is it serves, then immediately will the Fisher King be cured. And then he will tell him the secret words of Our Lord and he will pass from life to death, and this knight will have the keeping of the blood of Jesus ...

Perceval, as Bron's grandson, is chosen to embark on the quest to cure the Fisher King. However, no one, including Perceval himself, knows where Bron's castle is. After many adventures Perceval eventually discovers the castle and is made welcome by his grandfather. As in the previous romances, a banquet follows.

> Just as they seated themselves and the first course was brought to them, they saw come from a chamber a damsel very richly dressed who had a towel about her neck and bore in her hands two little silver platters. And after her came a youth who bore a lance, and it bled three drops of blood from its head; and they entered into a chamber before Perceval. And after this there came a youth and he bore between his hands the vessel that Our Lord gave to Joseph in the prison, and he bore it very high between his hands. And when the king saw it he bowed before it saying his mea culpa and all the others of the household did the same. When Perceval saw this he marvelled much and he might willingly have asked concerning it if he had not feared to annoy his host.

Perceval fails to ask about the Grail and, exhausted after his journey, falls asleep, awaking to discover the castle empty. On leaving the castle, he meets a damsel who tells him:

> You have been in the house of the rich Fisher King your grandfather and have seen pass before you the vessel in which is the blood of Our Lord – that which is called the Grail – and you have seen it pass before you three times, but you never enquired about it . . .

As in Chretien's story, Perceval cannot rediscover the Grail castle until he has proved himself a worthy knight. In this tale, however, he eventually succeeds. Not only does Perceval inherit the Grail, he is also told 'the secret words which Joseph taught', presumably the same secret words of Jesus referred to by Merlin in the opening passage of the story.

Within a few years of the appearance of the *Didcot Perceval* in France, Germany saw the first of its versions of the Grail romance, Wolfram von Eschenbach's *Parzival*.

Wolfram's *Parzival*

The Arthurian story found its way into Germany some time around

1200 in the form of two poems, *Erec* and *Iwein*, by the poet Hartmann von Aue. A year or so later, around 1205, the influential German poet Wolfram von Eschenbach composed his epic Grail romance *Parzival*, later to be immortalised in Wagner's opera *Parsifal*. It is essentially a reworking of Chretien's *Le Conte del Graal*, although Wolfram provides many details absent from Chretien's unfinished work. However, in *Parzival* the Grail is not a platter, a chalice, or even a head, but a magical stone called the *Lapsit Excillis*, from the Latin *lapis exilis*, meaning literally a small stone. According to Wolfram, it was with this stone that God had banished the angels who failed to support him in his battle with Lucifer.

In *Parzival*, the stone is in the keeping of a noble family who are entrusted with its protection. In return, they live in splendour on the food and drink that it miraculously provides. Additionally, the stone has the power to heal and preserve the life of its guardians. Contained within the walls of an impregnable castle, the Grail is protected by an order of knights, chosen as children when their names appear on the stone itself.

The story opens with Anfortas, king of the Grail castle, being mortally wounded, although the Grail's protection means that he cannot die. His only hope of freedom from the pain of his living death is if he can find a man to replace him. A message then appears on the stone telling the king that his heir, the son of his sister Herzelyde, will soon come to the castle. But only if the heir poses the right question will he prove himself worthy of succession.

Anfortas' nephew, and heir apparent, is none other than Parzival (the German rendering of Perceval), although he has been raised unaware of his true lineage. When he arrives at the castle he witnesses the same procession as Perceval in Chretien's story, although the Grail is now the stone. After failing to ask the correct question, Parzival leaves and spends the remainder of the story acquiring wisdom by enlisting as one of Arthur's knights. Finally, he returns to the Grail castle and proves himself worthy of succession.

Beside the Grail being a stone, there are a number of other differences between Wolfram's story and those of his predecessors. For example, the Grail guardian is called Anfortas rather than Bron, and the warriors who protect the castle are not Arthurian characters but the Knights Templar. Where did the story originate? Fortunately Wolfram reveals his source. In his epilogue he refers to Chretien's *Le Conte del Graal*, informing his readers that in it Chretien had failed to do justice to a tale that already existed. He goes on to say that his own full and accurate portrayal of the original legend came from an Arabic manuscript discovered by his friend Kyot in Toledo, Spain.

If Wolfram is to be believed, then the original Grail legend appears to have been an Arabian story, probably adapted by the crusaders for a European readership. Many such poems were composed during the crusades by the visiting soldiers, who took Arabian tales and transformed them, with medieval heroes replacing the original Arab characters. However, in this assertion, Wolfram stands alone amongst the medieval Grail romancers.

Perlesvaus

Perlesvaus is another early Old French Grail romance, its title meaning 'the disinherited Perceval'. The anonymous author says that he translated the story from a Latin work in a 'holy house situated in the isle of Avalon, at the head of the Adventurous Marshes'; where this might be he does not explain. Regardless of his claim, the tale is very similar to the *Didcot Perceval* and probably comes from the same source.

The story opens with Gawain meeting a hermit who appears many years younger than he really is because he has 'long served in the Chapel of the Grail where the Grail is kept'. Guided by the hermit, Gawain discovers the Grail castle and is welcomed by the Fisher King and made guest of honour at a feast. To see the Grail, however, Gawain must prove himself worthy by retrieving a sword from the pagan king Gurgaran which had been used to decapitate John the Baptist. When he arrives at Gurgaran's castle Gurgaran tells Gawain that he will relinquish the sword only if the knight rescues his son from a giant. Ultimately, the giant is killed while distracted during a game of chess; his head is cut off and Gawain returns with it to Gurgaran. The sword is then returned to the Grail castle and placed with a number of other holy relics in the Grail chapel. Gawain then sees the Grail itself:

> Lo, two damsels issued from a chapel, and one held in her hands the most holy Grail, and the other the lance of which the point bled into it . . . So sweet and so holy an odour accompanied the relics that they forgot to eat. Sir Gawain gazed at the Grail and it seemed to him that there was a chalice within it, albeit there was none at the time.

The second time the Grail appears Gawain sees a different vision within it:

> Lo, the two damsels issued from the chapel and came again before Gawain, and he seemed to behold three angels where before he had beheld but two, and he seemed to behold in the midst of the Grail the form of a child.

It is brought in for a final time, and again Gawain experiences a vision:

> Lo, the damsels came again before the table, and it seemed to Sir Gawain that there were three ... He looked up and there appeared aloft a man nailed to a cross, and a spear was fixed in his side.

Having failed to ask the right questions about the Grail, Gawain fails in his quest and Perceval takes up the challenge, having to prove his worth by slaying the worshippers of a golden bull. Ultimately, with the help of the magic of his uncle Pelles, Perceval enters the castle and sees the Grail in the chapel, where it is kept along with the sword that Gawain recovered, a bell cast by Solomon, 'and other relics in great plenty'.

In the chapel Perceval hears a voice telling him that the relics must now be distributed amongst the monks of monasteries and churches in the surrounding area. It is also declared that:

> The Holy Grail shall appear here no longer, but within a short time you will know well where it will be.

Finally Perceval sails away to a mysterious island, leaving Joseph, the son of King Pelles, to rule at the castle in his stead. We are not told where the Grail castle is, only that it is somewhere in Wales, as two Welsh knights many years later discover its ruins.

The Vulgate Cycle

Coming from the Latin word *vulgare*, meaning to make public or translate in a popular fashion, the Vulgate Cycle contains two anonymous Grail romances, *Lancelot* and the *Queste del Saint Graal*, composed around 1220.

Lancelot recounts how five of Arthur's knights fail in their Grail quest, while the *Queste* has Perceval ultimately succeeding. Much within the stories is taken directly from the others so far discussed. However, two additional themes are of particular interest. Firstly, regarding the setting of the story, the Grail castle is described as being near *Le Velle Marche* – 'the Old Border'. Secondly, as in the First Continuation, there are seemingly two Grails involved. In the prefatory introduction to *Lancelot* we are told:

> On the eve of Good Friday . . . Arthur lay in his hut in one of the wildest regions of White Britain, plagued by doubts about the Trinity. Then Christ appeared to him and gave him a small book, no bigger than the palm of his hand, which would resolve all his doubts. He, Christ, had written it himself and only he who was purified by confession and fasting might read it. On the following morning he opened the book, the sections of which were scribed as follows: This is the book of thy descent. Here begins the book of the Holy Grail.

Here the Grail is clearly described as a book – a book written by Christ himself. However, later in the same story, it is described differently:

> It was made in the semblance of a chalice . . . Sir Gawain looked on the vessel, and esteemed it highly in his heart, yet knew not of what it was wrought; for it was not of wood nor of any manner of metal; nor was it in any wise of stone, nor of horn, nor of bone . . . Then he looked upon the maiden, and marvelled more at her beauty than at the wonder of the vessel.

With the Vulgate Cycle we come to the last of the important original Grail romances. One or two others did appear before the end of the third decade of the thirteenth century, such as those by the French poets Gerbert and Maessier; however, they add nothing to the story in the way of themes. Although scores of other Grail romances were to follow, culminating in Thomas Malory's famous version in his *Le Morte D'Arthur*, they were essentially rewrites of these original eight stories. None of the later authors claimed convincingly to have consulted some external, earlier surviving documentation as did the composers of the first romances. Yet even these earliest surviving tales may not have been the original medieval popularisations of the Grail story, as they were all written by continental authors, mainly in France, although their setting is always Britain and they involve British legendary heroes. It is probable therefore that the story was initially taken from some native British romance. In other words, there probably existed at least one, now lost, Grail romance upon which they were all based. So where did the story truly originate?

10

The Heresy of the White Land

We know that by the late twelfth century the Grail story was widely disseminated, as the romance authors name a variety of different sources discovered all across Europe, from the Swiss Alps to southern Spain. This means that the legend must have been in existence for some considerable time before the surviving romances were compiled. What was the original legend upon which the Grail romances were based?

Firstly, we need to ascertain exactly what the Grail really was. In Wolfram's *Parzival* it is a magical stone. As we have seen, this was almost certainly based on an Arabian legend, and so seemingly had no connection with Christian tradition. Other crusader tales of similar sacred stones appeared throughout Christendom during the crusades. However, even though the other contemporary romances concerned Christian relics, like Wolfram's story the Grail itself is often something other than the cup of Christ.

In *Le Conte del Graal* it is far from clear what Chretien's Grail actually is. Obviously it is some form of holy relic associated with the mass, as the Rich Fisher is sustained by a mass wafer served from it. This has prompted speculation that the Grail was originally some form of dish or platter, as a mass wafer is unlikely to have been served from a cup. Additionally, Chretien gives the impression that graals were relatively common objects in his day, for he simply refers to it as *un graal*, 'a graal', and not *le Graal*, 'the Graal', as Robert de Boron later does. In fact, Robert de Boron goes on to describe it in even more venerating terms as *Le Saint Grail*, 'The Holy Grail'.

Chretien's lack of detail implies that *graal* was a word familiar to his contemporary readership, although the meaning has since fallen from use. It has been suggested that the word could be derived from *gradale*. A number of medieval French inventories of household possessions refer to items under this name, which possibly comes from the Latin *gradus* meaning 'in stages', and probably applied to a dish or platter that was brought to the table at various stages during a meal.

Whatever the word originally meant, it was quite clear, even from a cursory examination of the romances, that the Grail was different things to different writers. Chretien's Grail could have been the plate used by Christ at the Last Supper; the First Continuation has two Grails, one seemingly a floating dish and the other a carved head of Jesus; Robert and the *Didcot* author have it as the cup of the Last Supper; the *Perlesvaus* Grail seems to be a nebulous artefact in which visions associated with Christ's life appear; and the Vulgate version has the Grail as both a chalice and a holy book.

Apart from Wolfram's stone, which clearly came from a completely separate tradition, all these Grails seem to be holy relics associated with Jesus. Whatever it originally meant, around the year 1200 the word Grail seems to have become a collective word for holy relics associated with Christ himself, as opposed to the ordinary relics of mere saints. Indeed, in all the early romances the Grail is kept together with other holy relics; seemingly the most holy of relics, as they are each directly associated with the Bible, such as the sword that beheaded John the Baptist, the lance that pierced Christ's side, and the bell made by Solomon. *Perlesvaus* actually describes a chapel specifically built to house these relics, which the author collectively calls 'the Grail Hallows'. By the late thirteenth century, however, the word Grail applied almost exclusively to the cup of the Last Supper.

Something the original romances do have in common is that they all set their story in Britain, each associating the Grail with King Arthur and his knights. Is there therefore anything in early Welsh poetry, which existed before the romances, to couple Arthur with such a relic? Although neither the Holy Grail nor any other Jesus relic appears in the surviving Welsh Arthurian stories, we know that there are similar tales of Arthur searching for a magical cauldron. The two early Welsh tales, *Culhwch and Olwen* and the *Spoils of Annwn*, both include Arthur and his warriors searching for a cauldron which, like the Grail, has supernatural, life-preserving properties. As the quest for the cauldron is so similar to the later Grail quests, were the Grail romances influenced by these Celtic legends? Was the Grail originally a cauldron having no association with Christ or the Last Supper?

In the *Spoils of Annwn*, composed around 900, we read of Arthur's theft of the cauldron from the island of Annwn. It could have been from this poem that the legends of both the Grail and the isle of Avalon originated, perhaps as attempts to medievalise Celtic mythology. The similarities with the Grail and Avalon legends cannot be ignored, particularly when Annwn is depicted as a land which lies across the water – a mystical island containing the magical cauldron. In the romances Avalon is often depicted as the island where the Grail is hidden. Indeed, the link between Annwn and Avalon is further substantiated when we see that in *Spoils of Annwn* a citadel on the island is called the 'fort of glass', the same name used by Geoffrey of Monmouth to describe Avalon's castle. Moreover, as we have seen, there are many examples of magical cauldrons in Celtic literature, such as the cauldron of the legendary King Dagda in Irish folklore. Indeed, in the tale of *Culhwch and Olwen* it is to Ireland that Arthur goes in search of the cauldron. It therefore seems fairly certain that at least some aspects of the Grail story were taken from these Welsh Arthurian tales.

Historically, cauldrons were believed to contain magical properties and were treasured by Celtic chieftains, as described by Julius Caesar in the first century B.C. It can be argued that they were a pre-Christian equivalent of holy relics. Many Celtic traditions continued side by side with Christianity, so such a cauldron could have been associated with the historical Arthur of the fifth century. As discussed earlier, such a cauldron was actually found at the Berth, the site suggested by our research as the burial place of Owain Ddantgwyn – the warrior we believe to have been the historical Arthur.

Archaeologists have concluded that the cauldron was cast into the waters surrounding the Berth sometime in the sixth or seventh century as a votive offering to an ancient water spirit. It was therefore probably no ordinary cooking vessel, but a sacred cauldron such as that for which Arthur searches in the early Welsh tales. Its date means that it seems to have been cast into the water during the time of the kings of Powys investigated earlier. It may therefore have been in the possession of some important Powysian chieftain – conceivably even the historical Arthur himself.

These Celtic cauldron legends almost certainly influenced the development of the medieval Grail legend. As each successive romancer chose to embellish his story, relevant themes in early Welsh literature were probably adapted and medievalised for the purpose. However, Celtic mythology and Welsh cauldron legends only played a limited part in influencing the Grail tradition of the Middle Ages. The most important themes within all the early romances are purely Christian in concept.

In each romance the Grail or Grails are kept by the family of Perceval, the direct descendants of Joseph of Arimathea. The authors go to considerable lengths to explain this lineage and its significance – Joseph is appointed as Grail guardian by Christ himself. Here lies the Grail's importance – it is a visible, tangible symbol of an alternative apostolic succession.

According to Catholic doctrine, the Pope is the direct spiritual successor of the apostle St Peter who, according to the Bible, was appointed by Jesus as head of the Church. No one other than Peter's successor and his ordained priests can perform mass or hear confession. Called the apostolic succession, this idea is central to Catholic faith. Without the mass and confession there can be no salvation, hence the Catholic Church retains absolute spiritual authority.

In the Grail romances, however, we read that it is not Peter, but Joseph of Arimathea who is given the cup Christ used to perform the Last Supper – the very first mass. To the Church authorities of the Middle Ages, such a notion would be pure heresy. Surely if the cup had been given to anyone it would have been given to St Peter, and would still be in the hands of the popes. We are left in little doubt that this is the primary theme of the romances, as in the *Didcot* and Vulgate versions of the story Christ instructs Joseph in 'the secret words of Jesus'. Moreover, in *Perlesvaus* he is even taught the mysteries of the mass – something which according to the Church was strictly reserved for Catholic priests ordained through the apostolic succession from St Peter.

What the Grail romances are clearly implying is that there supposedly existed an alternative apostolic line of succession through Joseph of Arimathea and his family. Moreover, this line is claimed to have secret knowledge, unknown to the established Church. The Vulgate romances go so far as to make one of their Grails a book written by Jesus himself – something that no Catholic relic-hunter ever dared boast to have found. Most indicative of all is the hereditary name for the Grail guardian, the Rich Fisher or Fisher King. In the Bible Peter was a fisherman. Indeed, the papal legacy was, and still is, referred to as the 'shoes of the fisherman', meaning that, once appointed, the Pope, Christ's representative on Earth, has taken over the role originally given to Peter by Jesus himself. The Fisher King is seemingly, therefore, nothing less than an alternative pope.

This central theme of the romances seems to have been overlooked by the Church authorities at the time, otherwise the Inquisition of 1223, established by Pope Gregory IX to root out heresy, would have come crashing down on offenders. The romancers were lucky. All the same, for them to have risked papal wrath at a time when the Roman Catholic Church was at the height of its political power implies that there was more at stake than art for its own sake. Before we can begin to investigate what this might have been, we must first determine if there is any truth to the story of Joseph of Arimathea. Equally, is there historical evidence that the cup of Christ survived to become a Christian relic?

All four gospels tell how, after the Crucifixion, the rich disciple Joseph of Arimathea obtained Jesus' body from Pilate, wrapped it in a linen cloth and laid it in the tomb. St John's Gospel adds that another convert, Nicodemus, helped with the burial:

> And after this Joseph of Arimathea, being a disciple of Jesus, but secretly for fear of the Jews, besought Pilate that he might take away the body of Jesus: and Pilate gave him leave. He came therefore and took the body of Jesus. And there came also Nicodemus, which at the first came to Jesus by night, and brought a mixture of myrrh and aloes, about an hundred pound weight. Then took they the body of Jesus, and wound it in linen clothes with the spices, as the manner of the Jews is to bury.

This is virtually all the Bible tells us of Joseph and Nicodemus. There is nothing concerning their backgrounds, what became of them, nor any reference to Joseph in connection with the cup of the Last Supper. As we have seen, Nicodemus also appears in the Grail romances, and an early document, supposedly concerning his life as a Christian, proves that much of the Joseph story outlined in the Grail romances existed at least as early as the fourth century.

In the fourth-century *Evangelium Nicodemi*, now in the Vatican, we read that at the trial before Pilate, Nicodemus testified in Jesus' defence and became a converted follower. The manuscript is supposedly written by Nicodemus himself, and concerns the struggle of the early Christians in Jerusalem. Much of the opening section relates to Joseph of Arimathea, describing how, after he had deposited Jesus' body in the tomb, the Jews imprisoned him. However, on Easter Day Christ appeared to Joseph and set him free, after which he travelled to preach the word.

The *Evangelium Nicodemi* certainly shows that early Christians in the pre-Catholic empire considered Joseph of Arimathea to be one of the first leaders of Christ's Church. However, it does not show that any of them considered him to be *the* leader, neither does it mention the cup of the Last Supper. However, a second manuscript dating from the same period, the *Vindicta Salvatoris* (also in the Vatican), says that Joseph set out to found a Church in the far north, after the Roman plundering of Jerusalem in A.D. 70. In fact, this is exactly what we read in Robert de Boron's *Joseph d'Arimathie*. Although neither the *Evangelium Nicodemi* nor the *Vindicta Salvatoris* includes the cup of Christ, they do show that, in outline, the story of Joseph recounted in the medieval Grail romances was being told over eight centuries earlier.

Did Joseph of Arimathea really found a Church in Britain? It is recorded in the mid fifth century that an alternative Church still survived in Britain – just prior to the historical Arthurian era. Called Pelagianism, was this the Church of Joseph?

Pelagianism takes its name from the priest Pelagius, a Briton who preached a doctrine in opposition to the established Church. Where his ideas originated is unknown, but sometime around 380 he left Britain for Rome, where he came into conflict with the Pope. Although he disagreed with the establishment on a number of issues, it was his teachings throwing the apostolic succession into doubt that aroused the greatest anger. Although there is no direct evidence to link Pelagius with a Church founded by Joseph of Arimathea, he did question whether the true apostolic succession originated with St Peter. In 416, the Church responded by proclaiming his teachings a heresy. Not only the Church but the State itself stood to suffer if such dangerous ideas took hold, as they did for a while in Britain and Gaul. At this time Catholic Christianity was virtually all that was holding the empire together. Therefore, in 425 Emperor Honorius was persuaded by the Pope to issue an imperial command to the Pelagian bishops of Gaul. They must renounce their heresy before the Bishop of Arles within twenty days, or face the severest consequences.

Although the policy was successful elsewhere, the problem remained in Britain, over which Honorius had no direct control. St Germanus, the rich and powerful Bishop of Auxerre, was thus dispatched to Britain as a missionary to combat the Pelagian heresy. The contemporary writer Prosper of Aquitaine, who dedicated himself to attacking Pelagianism, wrote of the year 429:

> The Pelagian Agricola, son of the Pelagian bishop Severianus, corrupts the churches of Britain by insinuating his doctrine. But at the suggestion of the deacon Palladius, Pope Celestine sends

Germanus bishop of Auxerre as his representative, and after the confusion of the heretics guides the Britons to the Catholic faith.

As the Pelagians are known to have questioned the apostolic succession of St Peter, it is quite possible that Pelagius, Agricola, Severianus, and their followers were subscribing to a doctrine believed to have originated with Joseph of Arimathea. According to the *Vindicta Salvatoris* Joseph founded a Church in the far north of the empire; since Britain was the empire's northernmost province, it is possible that it was centred here.

Remarkably, Pelagianism may not only be linked with the Joseph of Arimathea story as it appears in the Grail romances, but also with the historical King Arthur.

In his *Historia Brittonum* Nennius relates how the British chieftain Vortigern came into conflict with Germanus shortly after he arrived in Britain to combat Pelagianism. According to Nennius, Germanus 'preached at Vortigern, to convert him to his Lord'. It seems, therefore, that Vortigern was himself a Pelagian. According to Germanus' biographer, Constantius of Lyon, the bishop's deputation to Britain was received in St Albans by a delegation of clergy from the city, who were soon reconverted to orthodox Catholicism. With the success of St Albans under his belt, Germanus moved on to preach across the country, converting not only the laity but also the troops, who chose to turn against the heresy of their leader. This again seemingly refers to the chief British warlord Vortigern.

According to Constantius, Germanus confronted Vortigern at the very heart of Pelagian heresy – his capital city. Constantius neglects to name the city, but since Bede, Gildas, Nennius and the *Anglo-Saxon Chronicle* all record that Vortigern ruled most of Britain shortly after the Romans left, it must have been the most important city of the time. As we have seen from both the historical and the archaeological evidence, Viroconium was the principal city of early-fifth-century Britain, and therefore was almost certainly the religious centre for Pelagianism. Again, we return full circle to Viroconium and the historical Arthur:

1. The Grail romances concern an alternative apostolic succession centred on Britain.

2. Pelagianism claimed an alternative apostolic succession and was centred on the British capital Viroconium.

3. Viroconium seems to have been the capital of the historical Arthur.

4. King Arthur and his knights are the central characters in all the Grail romances.

Perhaps Arthur was included in the Grail romances not simply to popularise the story, as previously thought, but because he was *genuinely* associated with historical events from which the Grail legend evolved.

Pelagianism offers only circumstantial evidence to couple the Grail romances with the city from where Arthur is most likely to have ruled. However, the romances themselves provide a direct link between the setting for the Grail quest and the Dark Age city of Viroconium. During the Dark Ages Powys was called the White Land and Viroconium was known as the White Town; in the Grail romances the Grail castle is said to be in or near the White Town in the White Land.

In the First Continuation we are told how Joseph founds his Church in Britain, in somewhere known as the White Land. The *Didcot Perceval* has Perceval and Gawain involved in a contest near the Grail castle, the location described as 'the White Castle in the White Town'. In *Perlesvaus* a similar contest takes place in the 'White Hall of the White Town', while the Vulgate Grail romances both refer to the Grail castle being the 'White Castle' in 'The Old Border'.

In addition to the Grail romances there survives a Welsh story, written in the mid twelfth century, which seems to be based on Chretien's *Le Conte del Graal*. Called *Peredur*, after its hero, it now survives in the *Red Book of Hergest* and appears to be a Welsh rendering of the Perceval tale. Peredur is invited to attend a banquet and witnesses a procession almost identical to that which Perceval sees in the Grail castle. In *Peredur*, however, the Grail is replaced by a head on a silver platter. In this particular story the banquet is held in the 'White Hall', in the 'White Town', in the 'White Land'. In Geoffrey of Monmouth's 1135 *Historia*, Arthur's kingdom is called the White Land. Furthermore, many of the early Welsh tales which include King Arthur, such as *The Dialogue of Arthur* (*circa* 1150), refer to Arthur's court as the 'White Hall'. These last three references were made some years before Chretien de Troyes introduced the name Camelot in the late twelfth century.

Although these references fail to provide a geographical location for the White Land and the White Town, they must have been respectively the kingdom of Powys and the Roman city of Viroconium. By the seventh century native Britons referred to Powys as the White Land and to Viroconium as the White Town. This is known from *The Song of Llywarch the Old*, which we have already demonstrated to be an accurate account of events in seventh-century Powys. The poem refers to the Saxon invasion of the kingdom in 658 as 'the plunder of the White Land' and the sacking of its capital as 'the burning of the White Town'. The name White Town probably originated from the time of the late Roman occupation, when the legion garrisoned at Viroconium was known as the White Legion. This legion is recorded in the *Notitia Dignitatum*, a Roman register of imperial officers compiled around 420. It seems that after the Romans departed, the rulers of Powys referred to their kingdom as the White Land and their capital as the White Town to emphasise their claimed succession from the former imperial governors.

The Song of Llywarch the Old also describes the royal palace in the town as 'the White Hall of Powys'. The White Hall, in the White Town, in the White Land – these are precisely the words often used in the Grail romances to describe the Grail castle and its locality.

From the archaeological evidence we know for certain that the White Hall of Powys historically existed. The latest excavations at Viroconium have shown that the city did have a splendid winged mansion at its heart, destroyed by the Saxons some time in the mid seventh century. There can be little doubt that *The Song of Llywarch the Old* is referring to this particular mansion as the White Hall, since the poet describes its character Heledd gazing down at the ruins from Wrekin Hill, which directly overlooks the site. Moreover, archaeologists have dated the period of the mansion's destruction to the mid seventh century, and the poem refers to the burning of the White Hall during the Saxon invasion of the kingdom in 658. (This date is known from both the tenth-century *Welsh Annals* and the ninth-century *Anglo-Saxon Chronicle*.)

The Grail story seems, therefore, to have been set in the kingdom of Powys. Both the historical evidence and the earliest legends locate King Arthur in Powys. Nearly all the Grail romances make specific reference to the White Land, White Town, White Castle or White Hall. In the Arthurian period, the White Town was the capital of Powys – Viroconium – where it is known from *The Song of Llywarch the Old* and from archaeology that there stood an historical White Hall. At the very least this suggests that the Grail romancers were basing their stories on much earlier tales which located Arthur in an historical setting. Remember, when the romances were written it was widely believed that Arthur came from Tintagel or Glastonbury. If the romancers were simply concocting their stories to please their readership, they would surely have set their scenes in the south of England – not in some mysterious White Town in a forgotten White Land.

Although there may be good reason to believe that the Joseph of Arimathea story was based to some degree on real events, and that a church or sect thought to have been founded by him may have had genuine associations with the historical Arthur, there is still no direct evidence to couple either of them with an historical Grail. Indeed, there is no reference to the cup of Christ anywhere outside the Bible predating the romances of the twelfth century. Maybe the Holy Grail was simply a medieval myth, after all, having no genuine associations with the historical Arthur or the original Joseph of Arimathea story. Perhaps the Celtic cauldron legends became the Holy Grail of Chretien and the other French romancers.

However, the Grail romances concern Christian relics: the lance that pierced the side of Christ, the sword used to behead John the Baptist, a book written by Jesus himself, a bell made by Solomon, and Christ's head carved by Nicodemus, and indeed, the cup. There is nothing pagan about any of these; the central themes of the Grail romances are entirely Christian. Even though the association of the Grail with Avalon appears to have been taken from the pagan cauldron and Annwn legends, the story of the Holy Grail itself must have originated with Christian tradition.

Regardless of any authentic associations with Biblical times, were these relics historical artefacts thought to be the genuine items at the time the romances were compiled? One of the Grails certainly was – the carved head of Jesus described in the First Continuation historically existed at the time the romance was written. It was housed at Lucca Cathedral in Tuscany and attracted pilgrims from all over Europe. Called the *Volto Santo*, it was believed to be the only true likeness of Jesus ever made, by either sculptor or painter. As this Grail was based on a relic that existed historically, perhaps the others were too.

Did a genuine relic, thought to be the cup of Christ, really exist during the Middle Ages? If so, where?

11

The Emperor King

Nearly all the romances place the Holy Grail in the White Land, in or near the White Town. As the First Continuation had been absolutely right about where the *Volto Santo* was to be found, perhaps an historical chalice, considered to be the Holy Grail, similarly survived in the vicinity of the White Town – the historical Viroconium. One verse in *The Song of Llywarch the Old* describes a remarkably similar event to a scene in the *Perlesvaus* Grail romance. According to the former:

> Cynddylan, vested in purple, divided the royal treasure. The abbots, vested in white, took each a holy relic. And all swore to protect them from heathen plunder.

In *Perlesvaus*, Perceval hears a voice telling him that the relics housed in the Grail chapel must be distributed amongst the monasteries and churches in the surrounding area. Could there be a connection?

The Song of Llywarch the Old gives no details concerning the nature of the relics or where they were taken. All we are told is that before the Saxons invaded, the Powysian king Cynddylan called a meeting of his clergy, handed over the relics, and ordered the abbots to preserve them. No contemporary records survive from pre-Saxon Powys, but a number of legends exist in Shropshire folklore which talk of the lost treasures of Powys, hidden when the Saxons invaded in the seventh century. This is the precise period to which *The Song of Llywarch the Old* refers.

We have seen how the Cynddylan named in the poem was an historical figure, a direct descendant of Owain Ddantgwyn, the warrior we believe to have been the historical Arthur. He was the last Briton to rule Powys before most of the kingdom was conquered by the Saxon king Oswy in 658, and died attempting to defend the kingdom while his people fled into what are now the Welsh Marches. The survivors established a new kingdom in central Wales, but the fertile English Midlands remained in Saxon hands.

As argued, *The Song of Llywarch the Old* appears to be an accurate account of the events surrounding the sacking of Powys. Both the leaders and the battles in the poem are recorded in contemporary Irish chronicles and in the tenth-century *Welsh Annals*, and are referenced in the ninth-century *Anglo-Saxon Chronicle*. Local landmarks and geographical features are accurately described, and the events in the poem are outlined in cold military terms, unfettered by myth or elaboration. There seems no reason to doubt, therefore, that the relics did exist, and were hidden as described.

Unfortunately, no subsequent record of these Powysian relics survives. However, they may be connected to the Marian Chalice, a cup around which legends had developed by the Middle Ages.

Although there is no historical evidence that the cup used at the Last Supper ever survived, the cup said to have been used by Mary Magdalene to collect drops of Christ's blood after the Crucifixion was believed to have been found in the early fourth century. According to legend, in 327, after the Roman Emperor Constantine the Great converted to Christianity, his mother, the Empress Helena, ordered an excavation of the presumed site of the Holy Sepulchre, Christ's tomb in Jerusalem. Along with a number of other purported relics, a cup was said to have been found which Helena believed to have been the actual one used by Mary Magdalene. Accordingly, it was called the Marian Chalice – the Chalice of Mary.

Although a number of reliable contemporary accounts do survive of the Empress Helena's excavations of the Holy Sepulchre, there is no historical record of the cup.

Medieval copies of the work of a fifth-century Greek historian Olympiodorus, however, said that it had been taken to Britain when Rome was sacked by the Visigoths in A.D. 410. Unfortunately, many medieval copyists tended to elaborate the works of classical writers, or alter them entirely, as we have seen with Geoffrey of Monmouth. Indeed later, more accurate, translations of Olympiodorus fail to mention the Empress Helena at all. However, it does appear that by the Middle Ages the legend of the Marian Chalice was accepted as genuine. Yet, even if such a cup *was* found by Helena, there is no way of knowing on what evidence the empress considered it to have belonged to Mary Magdalene. There are even conflicting stories concerning its appearance: in some it is a small stone drinking vessel, in others it is a larger silver cup, while the most popular tells how it had been incorporated by a Roman craftsman into a splendid gold and jewelled receptacle.

Whether fact or fable, the legends of the Marian Chalice seem to link with the Grail legend. The similarity between the Grail as the cup used by Christ, in which the wine became his blood, and the Marian Chalice, in which the blood of Christ was supposedly collected, seems too close a comparison to be mere coincidence. Moreover, according to the writings on the subject, both relics were eventually lost or hidden in Britain.

It is quite possible that important holy relics were brought to Britain when Rome was sacked in A.D. 410, as the province was considered relatively safe from the full-scale barbarian invasions threatening the rest of the Western Empire. Indeed, Britain was about the only safe place to where the Emperor Honorius could dispatch the relics. In 410 the Western Empire was technically in a state of civil war with the Eastern Empire based at Constantinople, and consequently no sanctuary could be expected anywhere in the East.

If the Marian Chalice and the other relics were brought to Britain as the medieval legend suggests, then their most likely destination would have been the city of Vironconium. In A.D. 410 northern and eastern Britain were already suffering incursions by the Picts and Germanic raiders. The three most important cities, London, Lincoln and York, were repeatedly threatened, which left Viroconium as the most important Roman city during the final years of Roman occupation. As we have seen, the archaeological evidence shows that the city was rebuilt around A.D. 400, while the previously more important cities were being abandoned. Viroconium was the last Roman capital of Britain, and so the most likely destination for the relics.

Two and a half centuries later, when the city of Viroconium itself was finally sacked, its ruler Cynddylan ordered the hiding of similarly important relics, and as we have seen *Perlesvaus* includes an identical account of the hiding of the Grail relics. It would therefore appear that either the author of *Perlesvaus* or his original source considered that Cynddylan's relics included the Grail. As the legends of the Marian Chalice also appear to link with Cynddylan's capital of Viroconium, it may be that the Grail and the Marian Chalice were considered to be one and the same.

If the Marian Chalice did inspire the theme of the Holy Grail as the cup of Christ, then the story of Joseph bringing the Grail to Britain would be inaccurate. Even if it existed, the Marian Chalice was only discovered in A.D. 327 by the Empress Helena in the Holy Sepulchre in Jerusalem. Neither was it associated with Joseph of Arimathea, but with Mary Magdalene. At some stage, however, there may have been a confusion of two separate traditions. The *Evangelium Nicodemi* says that Joseph escaped from prison to begin his ministry immediately after the Resurrection, whereas the *Vindicta Salvatoris* says that he remained incarcerated until the fall of Jerusalem some forty years later. Exactly the same discrepancy is echoed in the Grail romances, in which the First Continuation agrees with the *Vindicta Salvatoris*, while Robert de Boron's *Joseph d'Arimathie* tallies with the *Evangelium Nicodemi*. This shows that for at least eight centuries before the Grail romances were written there were conflicting accounts concerning Joseph's life. Perhaps there had been similar disagreements regarding the cup of the Last Supper.

It remains a mystery why anyone should have associated the Grail with Mary Magdalene. However, the Marian Chalice legend may have been influenced by surviving legends concerning the cup used by Joseph. St John's Gospel relates how Mary Magdalene had visited the Holy Sepulchre to find the tomb empty, and a late Grail romance written around 1225 by the French poet Gerbert de Montreuil (sometimes called the Fourth Continuation) says that Joseph had obtained the Grail from Mary on the day of the Resurrection. Although Gerbert's story adds little to the original eight Grail romances, it does address one important issue that the others neglect. Namely, how Joseph of Arimathea knew about the cup of the Last Supper in the first place. In the Biblical account he is not present at the Last Supper, neither is he previously named as a disciple of Jesus. For the Grail story to maintain its internal logic, it must be assumed that someone close to Jesus told Joseph of the cup's significance – presumably Mary Magdalene.

The Gerbert romance suggests that a legend could have survived that Joseph had obtained the cup from Mary. Perhaps it was thought that the cup remained in, or was later returned to the tomb by Joseph himself. Such a legend may have led to the belief that the cup had originally been used by Mary Magdalene to collect Christ's blood, while at the same time believing it to be the same vessel used at the Last Supper.

It is clear that the relics hidden by Cynddylan were considered by some during the Middle Ages to have included the Grail. However, whether this was thought to be the cup used by Mary or by Joseph is hard to say. The important point is that these relics were seemingly housed in the city of Viroconium. If they had been in Britain since the fall of Rome, they would have been in Viroconium at the same time that the city served as the capital for Owain Ddantgwyn. Accordingly, we must return to King Arthur's role in the Grail mystery.

One theme that the early Grail romances all have in common is their portrayal of a Grail family: only the Fisher King (or Rich Fisher) and his line can be the Grail's guardians. This, we are told, is the family of Perceval. So what exactly is King Arthur's role? Why was he so intrinsically linked with the Grail? The answer may be found in the *Didcot Perceval*, which describes Arthur as being the head of Christ's Church. According to the story, the Round Table represented the table of the Last Supper and, like Joseph of Arimathea before him, Arthur was to sit in the place of Jesus as rightful head of the Church. As the same story says that Jesus appointed Joseph as Grail guardian, it seems to imply that Arthur is also cast in this role.

However in the *Didcot Perceval*, Bron is the Grail guardian, Perceval is Bron's successor, and it is he who must eventually protect the Grail. The same paradoxical theme occurs in other medieval Grail romances. In *Perlesvaus* and the Vulgate *Lancelot* Arthur is as much the rightful Grail guardian as Bron or Perceval. In the Vulgate version, for instance, he is given a Grail – the book written by Christ himself. As the same romance has previously described Joseph of Arimathea as being given the cup of the Last Supper by Jesus to ordain him as head of the Church, Arthur is clearly being appointed as Joseph's successor. Not only is he given a Grail; more significantly he is being taught the inner mysteries of the Church.

But how can these romances cast Arthur in the role of Grail guardian, when Perceval and his family have the same honour? The answer to this riddle may be that the romances were derived from two separate traditions. One that the Perceval family were the Grail guardians, and the other that it was the family of Arthur. This might explain why different romances used different names for the guardian, the Rich Fisher and the Fisher King. Perhaps Perceval and Arthur had originally been portrayed as living in different eras of history, one succeeding the other many years later. Ultimately, they were confused as having lived at the same time. The evidence for this we shall examine later. For the time being, however, we must concentrate on Arthur's role.

How might King Arthur's portrayal as Grail guardian relate to the events surrounding the life of the historical Arthur? A relic thought to be the Grail may have been kept at Viroconium from 410 to 658. Arthur seemingly ruled from Viroconium from around 488, so the chalice may have been under his protection. But why do the romances also portray him as head of the Church? The answer may lie with the fact that he is also described as an emperor, for instance by the *Didcot Perceval*.

By the late fifth century Britain was the only part of the empire free from barbarian invasion. During the historical Arthur's time, around the 480s, it appears to have been the last surviving outpost of the former Western Empire. Arthur, therefore, may well have been considered the true Roman emperor, just as the romance asserts. The *Didcot Perceval* is certainly correct in that two earlier British leaders had become Roman emperors: the British imperial governors Magnus Maximus and Constantine III who had both seized the imperial throne, in 383 and 407 respectively.

If the historical Arthur was considered to be emperor at the close of the fifth century, then there is a strong possibility that the Britons would have perceived him as head of the Church. As we have seen, even as late as the fifth century the Pope was not universally believed to be its head. When the Church was officiallly recognised by the Emperor Constantine the Great in the early fourth century, the emperor himself became its head. At the First General Council of the Church, held in Nicaea in Turkey in A.D. 325, Constantine threatened to exile any bishop who refused to agree to the newly formed Church constitution. Many Christians did not accept Constantine's self-imposed authority and were branded heretics. One by one, however, the dissenting factions either dissolved or converted to Constantine's Roman Catholicism. Successive emperors remained head of the Catholic Church, although after their failure to halt the barbarian invasions from the early fifth century, the Church hierarchy began looking to the Bishop of Rome – the Pope – as their true leader. By the final collapse of the empire in the 470s, opinion was still divided, but soon, with no more emperors, the Pope assumed absolute authority. In free Britain, however, the Church probably continued to regard the emperor as its official figurehead. We have already seen how the British Church was in severe conflict with the Roman Church in the late 420s, when Germanus was sent to re-Catholicise the country.

To discover if Arthur really was appointed emperor in Britain, we must examine the period immediately preceding him. Although anarchy threatened the island after the legions left in A.D. 410, in many parts of Britain, particularly the west, a Roman way of life continued until the late fifth century. Indeed, as late as 470 a British contingent fought alongside the last true Roman emperor, Romulus Augustulus, when he tried to recapture Gaul. After the failure of this campaign in 476,

Romulus was defeated by the German warlord Odovacer and Rome fell. With the collapse of the empire, Britain was the last stronghold of Roman civilisation in the West.

Gildas explains that the British leader in the 470s was the Roman commander Ambrosius Aurelianus, and it seems to have been around 488 that Arthur succeeded him as the leader of the Britons, taking up the fight against the invading Anglo-Saxons. We might, therefore, learn something of Arthur's role by knowing more about Ambrosius. He does not seem to have been simply another chieftain, but an important Roman officer.

Gildas tells us that Ambrosius' parents 'wore purple', the imperial colour. This means that they were members of the imperial royal family. Perhaps his father was the emperor himself. Might Ambrosius have been the son of Romulus Augustulus, having fled to Britain after the collapse of Rome? Records of the final days of imperial Rome are sketchy, so it is quite possible that a son of Romulus went unrecorded. However, the situation is more confusing, for there were many people claiming to be the true imperial family. In the last century of the Roman Empire, would-be emperors were constantly usurping one another with alarming regularity. Indeed, at one point no fewer than six separate individuals all claimed to be the emperor at the same time.

A clue to which emperor Ambrosius might have been related to can be found in the legend recorded by Nennius, where Vortigern attempts to construct a fortress in the Snowdonia mountains in North Wales. Following the series of disasters, Ambrosius then appears before Vortigern, telling him that the problems were caused by two serpents that dwelt beneath the fort's foundations. When the serpents were found, Vortigern accepted Ambrosius as his equal, offering to share his throne. Although clearly legend, it provides important clues as to Ambrosius' background. On seeing the two serpents Vortigern is moved to pay tribute to Ambrosius. The serpents must therefore be an allegorical reference concerning Ambrosius' lineage and right to rule.

The dual serpent motif is recorded in the *Notitia Dignitatum* (*circa* 420) – which contains a list of the insignia of late Roman legions and important army officers – as the personal emblem of the Roman emperor Magnus Maximus. It may therefore be to Maximus' family that the Nennius legend is linking Ambrosius.

Maximus was a British-based general who seized the imperial throne in the closing years of the fourth century. In 376 the Roman emperor Gratianus executed his main rival Theodosius on the charge of high

The ruins of Viroconium – the historical Camelot.

Travail's Acre – the burial site of the historical Arthur.

Whittington Castle – the Grail castle in the earliest Grail romance.

The site of the Grail chapel at Whittington.

The Grail procession from *La Folie Perceval*
(Bibliothèque Nationale).

Surviving fragment of Wolfram's original *Parzival*
(Bayerische Staatsbibliothek).

'For thou art my rock and my fortress.'
The Red Castle at Hawkstone Park.

'They go down by the valleys.' The White
Cliff gorge.

'Lead me to the rock that is higher than I.' White Cliff, as seen from the Red Castle.

ABOVE. 'Thou art my hiding place.' The Grotto at Hawkstone Park where the chalice was discovered.'

LEFT. 'I looked on my right hand and beheld.' The window of the four Evangelists in Hodnet church.

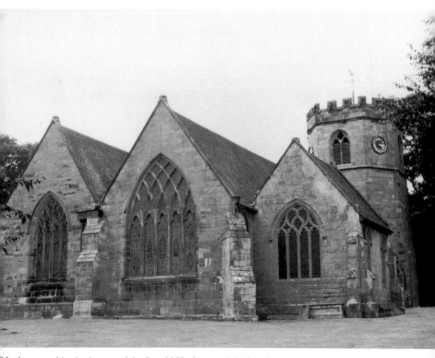

Ye that stand in the house of the Lord.' Hodnet parish church.

The trumps from the Marseilles Tarot pack – the key to the mystery of the Holy Grail.

LA ROUE DE FORTUNE

LA FORCE

LE PENDU

LA MORT

TEMPERANCE

LA MAISON DE DIEU

LE SOLEIL

LE IUGEMENT

LE MONDE

RIGHT. The historical Excalibur, re-created by Wilkinson Sword.

BELOW. The cup discovered at Hawkstone Park. Is this the Marian Chalice – the historical Grail?

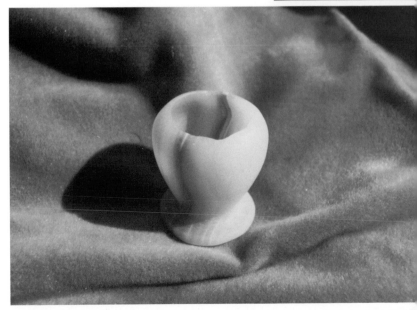

treason. Gratianus was considered by many high-ranking soldiers to be incompetent, and Theodosius had been seen as a possible replacement. The only other threat to Gratianus came from his general Magnus Maximus, but not daring to risk another execution the Emperor played safe. He ensured that Maximus remained in command of the imperial forces on the far-off island of Britain, posting him to the Segontium garrison at Caernarvon in north Wales.

It was only a few years before Gratianus made one mistake too many, and the army came close to revolt. In 383 Maximus was proclaimed emperor by the legions under his command. Taking his troops, he left Britain and sailed for the Continent. He won the support of the legions in Gaul, conquered Italy and marched on Rome. Gratianus was soon assassinated and Maximus took his place. The Eastern Empire, however, refused to recognise Maximus, instead proclaiming emperor the son of Theodosius, also named Theodosius. In the ensuing civil war Maximus was defeated and killed.

After the war the Western Empire was in tatters and Theodosius continued to rule from Constantinople. But there were many in Britain who still regarded the family of Maximus as the rightful heirs to the imperial throne. Theodosius, on the other hand, did not see them as a threat and, not wishing to risk another campaign, took no action.

As Maximus' family continued to live in north Wales, Ambrosius may well have been his descendant – according to Nennius, Ambrosius came from that very area. Descent from Maximus was certainly considered important in the post-Roman era. From a ninth-century inscription on the Pillar of Eliseg, near Llangollen in central Wales, we learn that Vortigern had married Maximus' daughter Severa, in an attempt to legitimise his own leadership.

The Nennius story may have been an allegory regarding Ambrosius' claim to a more direct line of descent than Vortigern, who was related to the imperial family by marriage alone. It is possible that Ambrosius was descended from another of Maximus' daughters. Indeed, Gildas' description of his 'parents', rather than just his 'father', was the usual way of implying matrilineal descent in early Christian times.

According to Nennius, Vortigern was ultimately forced to abdicate and Ambrosius became the sole British leader. Sometime around 488, Arthur then succeeded Ambrosius. Was he also a member of the Maximus family? If Arthur was Owain Ddantgwyn, as our research suggests, then he was not the son of Ambrosius. The *Welsh Annals* name him as the son of a Gwynedd warlord named Enniaun Girt. It is, however, possible that, like Vortigern before him, Owain married into the Maximus dynasty. Indeed, the originator of the Arthurian romances, Geoffrey of Monmouth, says that Arthur married a Roman princess.

In 1135 Geoffrey claimed to have discovered information about Arthur's life from 'an ancient book in the old British language', and wrote that Arthur's queen had been the daughter of a Roman emperor. Geoffrey calls her Ganhumara, from which the later romances derived the more lyrical-sounding name Guinevere. Interestingly, only a few miles from Owain Ddantgwyn's capital Viroconium survives a Guinevere legend telling how after Arthur's death the Queen retired to a priory close to what had been Camelot. In the most famous Arthurian romance, Thomas Malory's *Le Morte d'Arthur* (*circa* 1470), Guinevere retires to a secluded priory after Arthur's death. According to a sixteenth-century rendition of Malory's tale, it is White Ladies Prior, twelve miles to the east of Viroconium. Although the present ruins date from the Middle Ages, there may have been a prior on the site during the historical Arthurian period, as ecclesiastical buildings were often constructed on older sanctified sites.

As both Vortigern and Ambrosius seem to have married into the Maximus family, it is possible that Arthur did too. Indeed, there is historical evidence to suggest just this. As Ambrosius' successor, Arthur also appears to have employed the Maximus dual serpent as his standard. Not only has late-fifth-century royal Powysian jewellery bearing the device of two serpents been found in Shropshire but the same insignia is said to have been on Arthur's sword. The *Dream of Rhonabwy*, the twelfth-century Welsh work believed to be based on an earlier Dark Age war poem, contains the oldest known description of Arthur's sword, recording it as bearing 'a design of two serpents on its golden hilt'. If the historical Arthur's sword really did bear such a device, then it may have been a symbol of imperial authority.

Arthur may have inherited this sword from his predecessors. From Roman writers we learn that leadership disputes between rival British warriors were often resolved in single combat, the victor drawing a 'sword of office' from a stone altar – a practice that may have given rise to the Arthurian sword and stone legend. The importance accredited to Excalibur in the later legends may have arisen because the sword was originally a symbol of Roman imperial authority – the sword of Maximus, the inheritance of the true emperor. Remarkably, when co-author Martin Keatman and I created a replica of such a sword, it helped to provide confirmatory evidence to link the historical Arthur with the Maximus family.

In legend, Excalibur was a huge broadsword which bestowed kingship upon the rightful heir to the British throne. But what of the historical Arthur's sword? With the help of a leading authority on post-Roman military history, Dan Shadrake of the Dark Age battle re-enactment society Britannia, we reconstructed a fifth-century sword bearing a Powysian dual serpent design.

Archaeology has demonstrated that swords of the fifth century were not the huge, heavy broadswords erroneously associated with Excalibur, but the Roman *spatha*, of slimmer design with a stunted cross guard. This double-bladed Roman cavalry sword had an overall length of about sixty centimetres, including the hilt of about fifteen centimetres. Examples include two *spathas* found at Newstead on Hadrian's Wall (now in the Museum of Antiquities, Edinburgh), and a restored spatha in the Rijksmuseum in Nijmegen, Holland.

A ceremonial sword blade made for a high-ranking officer would have been of highly polished iron, inlaid with the kingdom's ornamental scrolling. The sword possessed by the historical Arthur – Owain Ddantgwyn – may therefore have been etched with the Powysian scrolling, known from a fifth-century inscribed stone in the British Museum. (Each kingdom had its own unique scrolling, just as Scottish clans have their own individual tartan.)

If Arthur came from Powys, the hilt would probably have been decorated with double serpents similar to those found on late Roman jewellery discovered in central Britain. Coming from the same time and place as the historical Arthur, this ornamentation is further evidence for the double serpents being an important royal insignia of the period. These rings, neck torcs and arm bands suggest that the hilt ornamentation would have been similar to the Maximus twin serpent design in the *Notitia Dignitatum*.

Ultimately, we approached the Queen's sword-makers, Wilkinson Sword, who agreed to reconstruct the weapon. When a photograph of the sword appeared in the *Daily Telegraph*, a reader wrote to reveal something that neither of us had previously known. In a late Roman document called the *Vistenium* (*circa* A.D. 400), now in the Turkish National Museum in Ankara, there is a drawing of a sceptre made for Magnus Maximus during his brief period as emperor. Around the shaft were entwined twin serpents, identical to those on the Excalibur replica. Consequently, if Arthur's sword really had been as the research indicated, then it was decorated with the royal insignia of Magnus Maximus. In other words, Arthur had inherited a sword of office which was a symbol of imperial succession.

The Song of Llywarch the Old not only confirms that the kings of Powys saw themselves as the true emperors in the early Dark Ages, it shows that Arthur himself was indeed thought to be one. The poem was committed to writing some time around the eighth century, but refers to events seemingly described first hand in 568. In the verse where King Cynddylan orders the relics to be hidden, he is described as 'Cynddylan, vested in purple'. Here he is being described as an emperor, in exactly the way that Gildas describes Ambrosius' parents. Since in the same poem Cynddylan and his family are also described as 'heirs of great Arthur', it clearly implies that Arthur himself had previously been considered an emperor.

History appears to link precisely with the medieval Grail romances: in the romances Arthur is portrayed as the head of the Church, a Roman emperor, and guardian of the Grail. The historical Arthur could well have been all three: the head of the Church in Britain, considered a Roman emperor, and the guardian of the Marian Chalice. The Grail romances refer to the Grail being in the possession of the Grail family, that of either Arthur or Perceval. Perhaps the true Grail family in the Dark Ages were the descendants of Owain Ddantgwyn.

What became of this dynasty? Although Owain's direct lineal heir Cynddylan died fighting the Saxons, Cynddylan's sister Heledd survived. It was her descendants who became the kings of lesser Powys, the kingdom that remained free from Saxon rule in central Wales. Was it from this royal family of Powys that the medieval romancers took their story? Were they considered the Grail guardians? To answer these questions we must now attempt to trace their successors to the time the romances were written in the late twelfth century.

12

The Heirs of Arthur

Cynddylan was the last of Owain Ddantgwyn's direct descendants to rule in greater Powys, by which time Britain had fragmented into a number of feuding kingdoms, and the Anglo-Saxons had invaded much of the country. The kingdom of Powys, in the west Midlands and central Wales, was virtually all that remained of what had been Arthur's Britain. In order to defend his kingdom against the Northumbrian Saxons, who were attacking from the north, Cynddylan formed an alliance with Penda of Mercia (the Anglo-Saxon kingdom which covered the east Midlands), and Aethelhere of East Anglia (centred in Norfolk and Suffolk). However, after the defeat of Penda and Aethelhere in 655, Powys stood alone. Around 658 Cynddylan died, Viroconium was abandoned and the British fled west into the Shropshire marshes and central Wales.

Unfortunately, Cynddylan's direct descendants are difficult to trace, and with his death we temporarily lose the trail of the Arthurian blood line. Returning to Owain Ddantgwyn, we turn to the Welsh genealogies, a series of Welsh family trees drawn up between the ninth and twelfth centuries. Some include the names of Owain Ddantgwyn and his son Cuneglasus. Owain's other sons – Meiryawn, Seiryoel and Einyawn – are named in a series of genealogies attached to the *Welsh Annals*. Unfortunately, other than their immediate offspring, nothing is recorded of their descendants.

With Owain's eldest son Cuneglasus, we discover three separate genealogies which record him as the ancestor of a ninth-century Welsh ruler, Hywel ap Caradoc. All three, including the earliest, in the *Welsh Annals*, give Hywel's descent from Cuneglasus' son Meic. By Hywel's time, around 830, the native Britons had been reduced to two pockets of resistance, in Wales and Cornwall. Ultimately, even Cornwall was conceded to the Anglo-Saxons, in 926, leaving only the area we now call Wales as the surviving homeland of the native Britons.

Wales itself fragmented into many small kingdoms, of which Hywel ruled Rhos, on the north coast of Wales in modern Clwyd. Although he left no heir, Hywel did leave what may be another intriguing legacy of the Arthurian era. The mountain hill fort from which he ruled, on Bryn Euryn near Llandrillo, was called Dinarth – the 'Fort of the Bear'. As it appears from Gildas that Cuneglasus adopted his father's battle name, the Bear, it would seem that this same name may have continued in the family for at least three centuries.

Interestingly, Nennius was not only a contemporary of Hywel, he also appears to have come from Bangor, only a few miles from Rhos. It may therefore have been from this direct descendant of the historical Arthur that Nennius obtained his information concerning Arthur's life.

We pick up the Arthurian trail in the Vale of Llangollen in central Wales. Here stands the Pillar of Eliseg, erected around 850 by the Powys king Cyngen. Its inscription celebrated Cyngen's line of descent from Maximus, telling how Vortigern married the emperor's daughter Severa, and through their son Britu their line ran unbroken down to Cyngen. One name on the Pillar suggests that Cynddylan's brother-in-law ruled lesser Powys after 658. From *The Song of Llywarch the Old* we learn that after her flight from the White Town, Cynddylan's sister Heledd married a prince named Concenn, a name recorded on the Pillar of Eliseg as the King of Powys around the same period. It would therefore seem that with Cynddylan's death, the rulership of Powys passed via his sister Heledd, the great-great-granddaughter of Owain Ddantgwyn, and ultimately through her to Cyngen by the mid ninth century.

The *Welsh Annals* record Cyngen's death on a visit to Rome in the mid 850s, during a rash attempt to claim the title of Holy Roman Emperor. After the fall of the Western Empire, Rome remained the centre of Catholic Christianity, and in 800 the Frankish king Charlemagne decided to utilise his influence. The Pope crowned him as Emperor, in return for accepting Catholicism as the State religion. Charlemagne's empire, which covered parts of Italy, France and Germany, became known as the Holy Roman Empire, and his successors inherited the title of Holy Roman Emperor. It seems that around 855 Cyngen travelled to Rome to dispute this claim.

He failed, and was executed by the Holy Roman Emperor, Louis II. The ninth-century Italian writer Ambrose Marca describes how Cyngen took an imperial sceptre to the Pope to prove his claim. Decorated with twin serpents, it was apparently the sceptre of Maximus described in the fifth-century *Vistenium*. What happened to the sceptre itself is a mystery but the story demonstrates once again that the family of Owain Ddantgwyn still considered themselves to be descendants of Maximus, and true Roman emperors.

As Cyngen died with no son to succeed him, the hereditary line appears to end. However, returning to 658 and Cynddylan, who also had no surviving son, we discover that the blood line continued through his cousin Cynwise, and an Anglo-Saxon dynasty. The British Library's *Cotton Vespasian* (the Saxon document compiled around 900) shows that Cynwise married Penda, Cynddylan's Mercian ally. After Penda's death in 658, their son Wulfhere formed a pact with the Northumbrian king, Oswy, and continued to rule Mercia as an Anglo-Saxon kingdom.

Wulfhere's hereditary line can be traced for 250 years, until it ends with the last Mercian king, Ethelred, in the early tenth century. Ethelred died without an heir, and so his wife Ethelfleda became queen, winning fame throughout Britain for defeating the invading Danes. In 914 Ethelfleda fortified the city of Warwick against the Danes. Although construction of the present Warwick Castle did not begin until the eleventh or twelfth century, this was the first fortified building on the site. The mound on which this earliest fort is thought to have stood is known as Ethelfleda's Mound, and lies within the grounds of the present Warwick Castle.

Ethelfleda's child from a second marriage became the Mercian leader. Subject to the Wessex King Athelstan, he and his descendants were demoted from Kings of Mercia to Earls of Warwick. However, although descended from Ethelfleda, the Earls of Warwick were not related to Ethelred, the last of the Owain Ddantgwyn line.

Although we confront another termination in the blood line, we do find what may be a surviving legacy of the Arthurian era. The crest of the medieval earls of Warwick is a bear holding a large ragged staff. Its origins are obscure, but the bear is generally thought to have been the emblem of the Saxon kings of Mercia, of whom Ethelred was the last. As 'Bear' seems to have been Owain's battle name, and the origin of the name Arthur, the Mercian kings may have adopted this title once their dynasty merged with that of the Powysian kings.

The earliest surviving reference to the origin of the Warwick crest supports its link with the historical Arthur. According to John Rous, a fifteenth-century Warwick priest, the bear device was first adopted by Arthgallus, an ancient earl of Warwick and one of King Arthur's knights. Although clearly legend, Rous' account may contain an element of truth. In his book, the *Rous Rol* (now in the British Library), written around 1480, he explains that arth is Welsh for 'bear'; the reason for the crest. He fails, however, to point out that in Welsh *gallus* means 'mighty'. Inadvertently, Rous seems to have discovered that the Warwick crest originated from someone called the 'Mighty Bear', who was somehow connected with Arthur. As there is no historical record of Arthgallus, it is possible that the name originally referred to Arthur himself.

It would support the Arthur/Warwick bear theory if Rous had simply written that the crest originated with a character called Arthgallus, but his association of Arthgallus with King Arthur renders the argument all the more compelling. Moreover, Rous' source material further supports the case, for he refers to a 'Welsh chronicle from the land of Powys', the kingdom of the historical King Arthur. It would therefore seem that Rous learned of both Arthgallus' association with Warwick and the origin of the bear crest in this Welsh Powysian chronicle.

As we have seen, it seems that Owain's descendants continued to inherit the battle name the Bear. The Saxon line of the family may also have used the name, which by medieval times had become an heraldic crest. Indeed, many medieval crests originated in this way. For instance, the sixth-century Cornish warlord Constantine was known as the Lion, and by the twelfth century the dukes of Cornwall had adopted the lion as their heraldic device.

Rous also tells us that Warwick was the site of Arthur's court, implying that the castle was Camelot itself. Although Warwick could not have been the seat of the historical Arthur, it may well have been where the romances originally set the scene for Camelot. The Arthurian story we know today is chiefly the work of Sir Thomas Malory, a fifteenth-century English writer from Newbold Revel in Warwickshire. Around 1480 Malory collected together scores of medieval tales concerning the legendary King Arthur, and compiled one epic tale of his life, *Le Morte d'Arthur*. Although the early medieval writers seem uncertain where Camelot is situated, Malory associates it with the Hampshire city of Winchester. Significantly, Rous' work, placing Camelot at Warwick, was written around 1480 – the same year as Malory placed it at Winchester. Could Warwick Castle therefore have been the traditional site of Camelot before it was accepted as Winchester?

Malory's publisher William Caxton, in his preface to *Le Morte d'Arthur*, actually writes that in his opinion Winchester was not the site of Camelot. Had Malory initially based his Camelot on Warwick

Castle, subsequently changing it to Winchester? As Malory knew Rous (he mentions him in his writings), and lived just a few miles from Warwick Castle, it is almost certain that he would have known of Warwick's Camelot claim. So why did Malory fail to include Warwick Castle in his work?

Sir Thomas Malory had fought in the Wars of the Roses, serving as a knight in the Earl of Warwick's army. Warwick's influence on the Yorkist side, in support of Edward IV, earned him the nickname 'the King Maker'. However, in 1470 he changed sides, exiled Edward, and placed the Lancastrian Henry VI on the throne. Along with others who continued to support Edward, Malory was arrested and incarcerated in Newgate Prison, where he was to write *Le Morte d'Arthur*. Here may lie the answer to Malory's Camelot's setting. As the Earl of Warwick had betrayed King Edward, it is possible that as Edward's supporter Malory would have relocated Camelot, replacing Warwick's seat with Edward's own castle at Winchester.

Another line of Owain Ddantgwyn descendants leads us to one of the greatest mysteries in Welsh history – the enigma of Owain Glendower.

According to a medieval Powys genealogy (discovered in St Asaph Abbey by the Welsh antiquarian Edward Lhwyd in 1696), when Cyngen of Powys died without issue about 855, his sister Nest's son Rhodri Mawr became king of Powys. His descendants were therefore of the Owain Ddantgwyn blood line. In 1400 Rhodri's direct descendant Owain Glendower was ruling in what was left of Powys. By the fourteenth century, however, the Normans had succeeded where the Saxons had failed: they had conquered Wales, leaving Owain Glendower merely a lord in the Norman province of Powys. Subjected to the authority of the English king Henry IV, Owain Glendower soon rebelled and was proclaimed King of Wales by his followers.

By 1405 he had raised an army from every part of the country, making his headquarters at Harlech Castle. However, the following year Henry IV retook Harlech, and Owain Glendower retreated into the mountains. By 1413 the last of the rebels had surrendered, but what became of Owain Glendower himself has remained a mystery. His followers never betrayed him, he was never captured, and his death was never recorded.

During the uprising, Owain Glendower claimed descent from King Arthur, and led his troops beneath a banner bearing a golden dragon. Although his claim was never taken seriously by the English, Glendower seems to have been justified in this assertion. If Owain Ddantgwyn was the historical Arthur, then Owain Glendower was Arthur's direct descendant. Moreover, he employed an emblem reminiscent of the Arthurian era, nine centuries later. But Glendower shares more in common with the historical Arthur than simply his banner and name. According to the sixteenth-century Welsh poet Gruffudd Hiraethog, Glendower still sleeps, awaiting the day that he will return to free Wales from English rule – a similar legend to that which surrounded the mystery of Arthur's death.

What really happened to Owain Glendower will probably never be known, although we can make an informed guess. In 1414, while he was in hiding, his surviving heir, his daughter Alice, married Sir John Scudamore of Kentchurch Court in Herefordshire. A legend survives telling how Glendower died in a secret room at his daughter's home. It may well be based on truth: a few years ago workmen renovating Kentchurch Court discovered a secret chamber, bricked up centuries ago behind wooden panelling.

The Owain Ddantgwyn blood line did not die with Owain Glendower: his daughter Alice had a son, whose present-day descendant, John Scudamore, is the current owner of Kentchurch Court.

There is one last line of descent which returns us directly to the Grail romances. According to the Lhwyd genealogy mentioned above, in 855, when King Cyngen of Powys died without issue, his second sister Cynddia married Ynyr, a prince of Gwent. The same genealogy traces the line directly to a Welsh baron, Cadfarch, whose daughter married the Norman baron Trevor, the Earl of Hereford, in the late eleventh century. Their sole heir, their daughter Lynette, then married another Norman baron, Payne Peveril, who had fought alongside William the Conqueror at the Battle of Hastings in 1066. So who was the head of the Peveril family around the year 1200 when the romances were written?

Payne Peveril's granddaughter and sole heir, Mellet, married a certain Fulk Fitz Warine; their son, also called Fulk, war baron of Whittington Castle in Shropshire at the close of the twelfth century. It is with Fulk Fitz Warine that we return to the Grail story. A prose romance, anonymously written around 1260, included the discovery of the Grail by the man who it claimed was the true heir of King Arthur. In this story, *Fulke le Fitz Waryn*, it is not Perceval, Gawain, or any of the other familiar Knights of the Round Table who discovers the Grail, but Fulk Fitz Warine, whom the story portrays as Arthur's living heir.

Fulk Fitz Warine was the direct descendant of Owain Ddantgwyn, and Owain Ddantgwyn seems to have been the historical Arthur.

Remarkably, here was a Grail romance claiming not only that Fulk Fitz Warine was a direct descendant of Arthur, but that he was the true guardian of the Holy Grail.

Fulk Fitz Warine was a rebel baron during the reign of King John. Born in the 1170s, he became lord of Whittington in Shropshire on the death of his father in 1197. However, in 1200 a rival lord successfully claimed Whittington Castle and Fulk was outlawed on a trumped-up charge of treason. For the next three years he fought against King John in the Shropshire Marches and north-central Wales. Pardoned in 1203, he re-inherited Whittington Castle, although in 1215 he again rebelled in support of the baronial revolt which led to the signing of the Magna Carta. He ultimately made peace with John's successor Henry III in 1217 and eventually died somewhere around the year 1256. (The life of Fulk Fitz Warine was outlined by the antiquarian R. W. Eyton in his *Antiquities of Shropshire* in 1860.)

After his death, Fulk became the focus of many legends and folk tales, and by the mid 1200s a romance of his life had been composed by an anonymous author. John Leland references the romance in his *Collectanea*, during the reign of Henry VIII, referring to it as 'an old French history in rhyme of the acts of the Warines'. This seems to have been the romance *Fulke le Fitz Waryn*, which still survives in the British Library in a manuscript known as the *Historia Rerum Anglicarum*. From the Anglo-Norman style of its French, it appears to have been composed in the mid thirteenth century, probably before the death of Fulk's son at the Battle of Lewes in 1265, as he is said in the author's preface to still be alive.

Fulke le Fitz Waryn focuses mainly on Fulk's life in the three years between 1200 and 1203, when he was engaged in a guerrilla campaign against King John. The story opens with Fulk being portrayed as a descendant and rightful heir of King Arthur:

> He shall have such great force and virtue.
> But we know that Merlin
> Said it for Fulk Fitz Warine;
> For each of you may be sure
> That in the time of King Arthur,
> That was called White Land.

We are told that Fulk must repossess the White Land of the Welsh Borders which was once the land of Arthur, but that to accomplish this he must first recover the Grail. Fulk eventually discovers the Grail in a chapel adjoining his castle at Whittington, and on his deathbed asks for it to be placed in a priory he founded in nearby Alberbury.

We have seen how the Grail romances describe the Grail kingdom as the White Land, and how the kingdom of Powys was called the White Land in Dark Age Welsh poetry. It is therefore not surprising to discover that Fulk's castle at Whittington stands in what was once the heart of Dark Age Powys, about twenty miles to the north-west of Shrewsbury. This reference to the White Land suggests that the author of *Fulk le Fitz Waryn* must either have been familiar with the Grail romances, written just a few years before, or have had access to some separate, earlier material. Moreover, we are told the name of Arthur's capital:

> It was the White Town
> Which is now called Whittington

We have seen how in *The Song of Llywarch the Old* Viroconium is the White Town. However, the author of *Fulke le Fitz Waryn* is telling us that Whittington, where Fulk's castle stands, is the White Town. Whittington is now in Shropshire, and until the seventh century the whole of Shropshire formed part of the British kingdom of Powys. Although the Roman city of Viroconium was the original White Town, it seems that the same name was applied to the new Powys capital once Viroconium was abandoned in 658. From the *Tribal Hidage*, the Saxon taxation document compiled in the 660s, we find reference to the new capital of the reduced kingdom of Powys. It is described as being near Oswestry, at the head of the Great March. This is precisely the location of Whittington, in the Welsh border marshes, about three miles east of Oswestry. We know from the Domesday Book, compiled for William the Conqueror in the late eleventh century, that Whittington had been the name the Saxons had used for the town. Indeed, Whittington is derived directly from the English words 'White Town'.

The *Anglo-Saxon Chronicle* records that Whittington was taken from the Britons when the Mercian king Offa advanced westwards in the late eighth century. After capturing the town Offa built a huge earthwork, now known as Offa's Dyke, to keep the Britons inside Wales. Thereafter, the kings of Powys made their new capital at Dinas Bran, a hilltop fort near Llangollen, a few miles to the west of Whittington. Whittington was thus the last Powys capital on what became English soil. It seems therefore that as lord of Whittington, Fulk was envisaged as a king of ancient Powys. Indeed, as we have seen, he did descend directly from its Dark Age rulers, although by his time the descendants of Rhodri Mawr were ruling in Welsh Powys.

Fulke le Fitz Waryn does not portray Fulk merely as the heir of any Powysian king, however, but of King Arthur himself. Just like Arthur, the coming of Fulk has been prophesied by Merlin:

> From that country the wolf issued,
> As the wise Merlin says,
> And the twelve sharp teeth
> We have recognised by his shield.
> He carried a shield indented,
> As the sayers have devised;
> In the shield are twelve teeth
> Of gules [gold] and of argent [silver].

Fulk's shield bears a design of twelve teeth, six above, six below, resembling the open mouth of an angry wolf. This, says Merlin, is the hero's mark:

> A wolf will come from the White Land;
> Twelve teeth he shall have sharp,
> Six beneath and six above.

Fulke le Fitz Waryn is a combination of historical events surrounding the life of the hero, merged with romantic fiction. In the fabulous sections of the story Fulk goes in search of the Grail, where he becomes an Arthurian-style knight, fighting dragons, rescuing damsels and outwitting witches. On a mysterious island he meets a shepherd, the porter to a magic castle cut into the mountain rocks. In order to enter the castle, Fulk is made to prove his worth by playing a bizarre game of chess with gold and silver pieces. Each time he is about to win the game, the shepherd's seven brothers, dressed as jesters, successfully distract him. Fulk finally loses his patience and runs them through with his sword.

With the jesters dead, Fulk enters the castle to discover an old woman and seven maidens, guardians of a magical horn which has the power to summon help in times of danger. Taking the horn Fulk leaves the island, travels to a land in the frozen north, defeats two serpents, rescues a damsel in distress, and finally returns home.

The story is not just similar to an Arthurian tale; Fulk's quest is almost identical to the Arthurian tales of early Welsh literature. The early Welsh stories *The Dialogue of Arthur*, the *Dream of Rhonabwy*, *Culhwch and Olwen* and the *Spoils of Annwn* all contain direct comparisons with episodes from *Fulke le Fitz Waryn*. Fulk's castle is on the Welsh/Shropshire border, from where 'he will drive away the boar'. The *Dream of Rhonabwy* sites Arthur's court precisely on the Welsh/Shropshire border, and *Culhwch and Olwen* tells of Arthur hunting down a boar. Fulk's final 'stronghold' is 'in the water', as is Arthur's on the isle of Avalon. To succeed Fulk must better an opponent in a bizarre game of chess, as must Arthur in the *Dream of Rhonabwy*. To gain entrance to the enchanted castle Fulk must outwit the shepherd guardian before being allowed inside, the same task set for Arthur in *The Dialogue of Arthur*.

Fulk's voyage across the western sea to the mysterious island where he discovers the magic horn is very similar to the *Spoils of Annwn*. The theme of this tale is a raid by Arthur and his men into the magical land of Annwn to steal a magical cauldron. In *Fulke le Fitz Waryn* the horn has replaced the cauldron, but just like the cauldron, it is guarded by a wise woman and a community of maidens.

Fulk's final adventure before he makes his peace with the king is to decapitate a giant in Ireland, returning with his head to Whittington Castle. Again this appears to be alluding to the Arthurian legend as it appears in the Welsh Triads. In *The Three Wicked Uncoverings* Arthur is blamed for the ultimate defeat of the Britons, being guilty of removing the head of the god Bran that had been buried on London's Tower Hill as a talisman against foreign invasion. The Norman keep of the Tower of London was (and still is) called the White Tower. Consequently, the original story may have referred to the White Tower in the White Town, as Fulk's castle is called in *Fulke le Fitz Waryn*. Moreover, Fulk's castle is even called the Castle of Bran in the opening verses of *Fulke le Fitz Waryn*. By returning the head of the giant, presumably Bran, it appears that Fulk is being portrayed as setting right Arthur's mistake.

Even the story of Fulk overcoming the two serpents is reminiscent of Ambrosius' task in Nennius' account. It may be alluding to Fulk's right to inherit the insignia of the Arthurian royal family, the dual serpents. In conclusion, the author of *Fulke le Fitz Waryn* clearly had access to earlier Arthurian material. Moreover, in the romance we discover what may well be verses from a lost Arthurian poem.

The author continually quotes verses from a poem in order to prove that they foretell the coming of Fulk Fitz Warine. The main text of *Fulke le Fitz Waryn* is written in Anglo-Norman French prose, but these poetic verses are in medieval Welsh. Linguistic analysis indicates that the Welsh sections date from the early twelfth century and seem, therefore, to be from an early romance which the author of *Fulke le Fitz Waryn* chose to include in its original language. Evidently, the author was portraying Fulk as an Arthurian successor in order to appeal to the Welsh, themselves in rebellion against the English king at the time the story was composed (*circa* 1260). As Fulk had successfully fought alongside Welsh barons in the early thirteenth century, the author apparently intended to influence the Midland barons and the Welsh princes to again join forces to defeat King Henry III.

The Welsh poem in *Fulke le Fitz Waryn* is now believed to be part of a lost medieval Welsh romance called the *Peveril*, named after its hero Payne Peveril, Fulk's great-grandfather. It is with the Peveril sections of *Fulke le Fitz Waryn* that the mystery of the Grail romances may be solved. It could be all that remains of the oldest Grail romance of all – the story upon which all the rest are based. Incredibly, the *Peveril* may reveal an historical Perceval and an historical Grail castle.

13
Perceval

Although much within the Grail romances is clearly fictitious – or at least allegorical – like Arthur, there may have been an historical character upon whom the legendary Perceval was based. A passage in the *Didcot Perceval* contains a vital clue that ultimately leads us to just such a figure. According to its anonymous author, the original Grail story had been taken from 'a book in the British language, which was dictated to Brother Blayse'. Who was this mysterious Brother Blayse?

A number of modern literary scholars have proposed that the author may have been a monk with the same name, recorded at the abbey of St Asaph in north Wales in the late eleventh century. Indeed, St Asaph is the very see to which Geoffrey of Monmouth was appointed bishop shortly after completing his History of the Kings of Britain around 1135. Some historians have gone so far as to suggest that the book from which Geoffrey claims to have taken his own work – 'a book in the ancient British Language' – was written, or at least translated, by Blayse himself.

If the Blayse named in the *Didcot Perceval* is the eleventh-century Welsh monk, however, then the author of the romance had placed him out of time. According to him, Blayse was a contemporary of both Merlin and Perceval. But, if this Blayse was the St Asaph monk of the late eleventh century, he lived some six centuries after the historical Arthurian period.

As discussed, it is possible that the medieval Grail story originated with two separate traditions, one holding that Perceval's family were the true Grail guardians, the other that this honour belonged to the family of Arthur. If there was an historical Perceval, perhaps he and Arthur lived during different eras, later being confused as living at the same time. If Blayse, the St Asaph monk, really was the author of the original Grail romance, then perhaps the historical Perceval was his contemporary. There has certainly been no historical evidence that anyone fitting Perceval's profile ever lived during the late fifth century.

Was there an historical figure, contemporary with the St Asaph Blayse, upon whom the story of Perceval was based? In the *Didcot Perceval*, it may be recalled, we learn the following about the Grail family:

> So know that the Grail was given into the hands of Joseph, and upon his death he left it to his brother-in-law who had the name of Bron. And this Bron had twelve sons, one of whom was named Alain li Gros. And the Fisher King commanded him to be the guardian of his brothers. This Alain has come to this land from Judea, just as Our Lord has commanded him . . . And well you may know that Alain li Gros was the father of Perceval, and for the merit of Bron his grandfather who is called the Fisher King.

The author is certainly confusing two different eras here. Joseph of Arimathea had lived in the first century, and the Arthurian period during which Perceval is said to live was over four hundred years later. The author seems to have conflated time for the purpose of his story. The situation is further confused in that neither Arthur nor Joseph was a contemporary of Blayse, the St Asaph monk. So were Bron, Alain and Perceval based on historical figures contemporary with Blayse in the late eleventh century?

In *Fulke le Fitz Waryn* there is compelling evidence that the legend of Perceval originated with an historical figure who was Blayse's contemporary in the late eleventh century. The romance begins the story a hundred years before Fulk's time, concentrating on Fulk's great-grandfather Payne Peveril. William the Conqueror, having recently been crowned king of England, is travelling the country:

> The king apparelled himself very richly, and came with a great host into the county of Shrewsbury . . . When King William approached the hills and valleys of Wales, he saw a town, formally enclosed with high walls, which was all burnt and ruined . . . Then the king inquired of a Briton what was the name of the town and how it came to be so named. 'Sire,' said the Briton, 'I will tell you. The castle was formally called Castle Bran, but now it is called the Old March . . . King Bran, the son of Donwal, caused the city to be rebuilt . . . and the town which is about it is still called White Town, in English Whittington.'

Fulke le Fitz Waryn continues with William rewarding Payne Peveril for his past services by making him lord of Whittington. Payne Peveril, who we are told is the son of an Alan le Crux, then builds 'the White Castle' at the centre of the town.

In the story Payne Peveril bears remarkable similarities to Perceval in the Grail romances. Not only is his name similar to Perceval, but he was the son of an Alan le Crux. In the *Didcot Perceval* Perceval's father is called Alain li Gros. (*Crux* is Latin for cross, and *groes* is Welsh for cross.) Payne Peveril's castle is called 'the White Castle', the name applied to Perceval's Grail castle in *Perlesvaus*. According to the *Fulke* romance Payne Peveril's castle had once belonged to someone named Bran, and nearly all the Grail romances give the Fisher King a very similar name – Bron. Also, we are told that Bran's castle was called the 'Old March', exactly the name used for the Fisher King's castle in the Vulgate *Lancelot*. Finally, three of the romances place the Grail castle in or near 'the White Town', and Payne Peveril's castle was in the White Town of Whittington.

Was Payne Peveril the historical Perceval? His life certainly pre-dates Perceval's first appearance in the Arthurian romances. Perhaps these startling similarities were merely due to the author of *Fulke le Fitz Waryn*, written around 1260, having lifted his character from the *Didcot Perceval*, composed about sixty years earlier. However, this seems highly unlikely: Payne Peveril and his father were not fictional characters, they were real historical figures. Both their names and Payne Peveril's lordship of Whittington are recorded in the Domesday Book and in the twelfth-century *Feet of Fines*. Equally, not only was Peveril a contemporary of the St Asaph Blayse, but the records of St Asaph Abbey show that Blayse actually became the priest of Whittington in 1090. It is surely beyond coincidence that the most likely author of the original Grail story, adapted by the author of the *Didcot Perceval*, was Payne Peveril's personal chaplain.

The references to Payne Peveril in *Fulke le Fitz Waryn* seem to have been taken from the Welsh *Peveril* poem composed around 1100 – a poem that was probably written by Blayse himself. It was even in his native, contemporary tongue. The Peveril was written in early-twelfth-century Welsh; Blayse lived in the early twelfth century and came from St Asaph in north Wales. As Blayse is also accredited with the story that inspired the *Didcot Perceval*, the two were most likely the same. In other words, the Peveril poem was the original Grail romance.

Unfortunately, the author of the *Fulke* romance only included brief passages from the *Peveril* in his narrative, so we know frustratingly little about Payne Peveril's life. What we do know for certain is that his wife Lynette was the direct descendant of Owain Ddantgwyn, the historical Arthur – the man who has always been associated with the Grail.

In *Fulke le Fitz Waryn* the Grail is discovered by Payne Peveril's great-grandson Fulk, who lived around a century later. After travelling halfway around Europe, Fulk eventually returns home to discover the Grail in the vaults of his own chapel in Whittington:

> And there in the chapel of St Augustine that is fair did Fulk look upon the Grail, which Our Lord and Saviour did give into the hands of his servant Joseph.

This chapel was an actual building destroyed after the dissolution of the monasteries in the mid sixteenth century. The ruins of Whittington Castle still survive, and the chapel site is now a scenic garden just outside the castle walls. From the records of Shrewsbury Abbey we know that the chapel was built around 1090 with an endowment from Payne Peveril himself.

Nearly all the Grail romances house the Grail in a chapel attached to the Grail castle. Perhaps the chapel at Whittington was the true Grail chapel. Perhaps, as Arthur's direct living heir, Payne's wife Lynette had requested the chapel built to house the relic.

The holy chalice, however, is not the only Grail in *Fulke le Fitz Waryn*. As in other romances, there is more than one Grail involved – a second relic, a book, is also described as the Grail. In the *Peveril* section of the *Fulke* romance we are told that a man must learn to balance his wisdom and his power if he is to achieve enlightenment. The verse goes on to say: 'This the Grail tells us, the book of the holy vessel'. As the words 'holy vessel' seem here to be describing Christ rather than the cup, like the book referenced in the Vulgate romance this Grail seems to be a secret text containing words spoken by Jesus himself. If the Grail romances were originally allegories concerning an alternative apostolic succession from Joseph of Arimathea, then this 'book of the holy vessel' might have been an alternative gospel. If such a book really did exist the threat to the teachings of the established Church would have been enormous. Unfortunately, *Fulke le Fitz Waryn* makes no further mention of the book.

Fulke le Fitz Waryn only contains extracts from the lost *Peveril*. However, the original may have directly inspired a fourteenth-century

French romance. Known as *La Folie Perceval*, it may contain the most complete translation of the Peveril poem still to survive.

La Folie Perceval now survives in a manuscript preserved in the Bibliothèque Nationale, Paris. Catalogued as *MS Fonds francais 12577*, the manuscript itself dates from around 1330 and contains a number of Arthurian tales copied by the same anonymous scribe. As other stories in the manuscript are prose versions of earlier Arthurian poems, such as Wace's *Roman de Brut* and Chretien's *Lancelot*, it seems that the scribe was attempting to translate into prose all the early Arthurian romances. The sources for the other works still survive in earlier copies, although an original *Folie* has not yet been discovered. The reason for believing that it may have been based on the same romance as the *Peveril* sections in *Fulke le Fitz Waryn*, however, is that the opening lines of both are almost identical.

The *Peveril* section of *Fulke le Fitz Waryn* opens with Merlin's prediction concerning the coming of a great warrior:

> The wolf will leave the woods and mounts,
> The leopard will follow the wolf,
> And with his tail will threaten him.
> The wolf will leave the woods and mounts,
> Will remain in the water with the fishes,
> And will pass over the sea,
> Will encircle the whole island.
> At last he will conquer the leopard
> By his cunning and by his art;
> Then he will come into this land
> Will have his stronghold in the water.

The *Folie* begins with virtually the same prophecy:

> The leopard will follow the wolf, and will threaten him with his tail and drive him into the sea. But the wolf will return from the sea to conquer the leopard by stealth and by cunning. Then he will come to the White land and build his castle on an island in a lake.

In *Fulke le Fitz Waryn* the passage is seen as a prophecy concerning Fulk's quarrel with King John, and his ultimate possession of Whittington Castle. In the *Folie* the same prophesy is said to refer to Perceval's quarrel with a Red Knight, and his eventual building of a new Grail castle in the White Town.

The inclusion of the same prophecy suggests a shared source of both romances, namely the original *Peveril*. But whereas *Fulke le Fitz Waryn* contains only a few verses from the poem, the *Folie* seems to continue with the full story. Although the hero in the romance is Perceval and not Payne Peveril, the two share many similarities. For example, Peveril built the castle at Whittington, the historical White Town, and it was constructed on a lake island in the Great Marche, just as Perceval's is. The author of the *Folie* may simply have changed the name from Peveril to Perceval as, by the time he was writing, in the fourteenth century, the Arthurian knight had become inseparably linked with the Grail story. We have already seen how other authors altered the name, such as Parzival in Wolfram's version, and Peredur in the Welsh.

Further indication that the *Folie* is based on the *Peveril* concerns the description of one of the Grails as a book. Like the *Peveril* section in Fulke, the *Folie* describes it as 'the book of the holy vessel'. No other surviving romance uses this precise description.

It seems likely that the *Folie* is a fairly accurate rendering of the original poem, since none of the other stories contained in the manuscript have been elaborated by the copyist, merely translated into prose. Accordingly, it may be a close rendition to the first medieval Grail romance.

The literal translation of *La Folie Perceval* is 'The Mad Perceval'. However, a more accurate interpretation is 'Perceval the Fool'. In the story, the foolish and naive young man must learn to become wise in the ways of the world before he can take his rightful place as the guardian of the Grail. Following Merlin's prophecy, the *Folie* continues with Perceval's encounter with a mysterious Red Knight. The knight tells Perceval that he must defeat him in combat if he is to pass over a bridge he is guarding, a theme that occurs in many later Arthurian romances, although the protagonists are then portrayed as Arthur and Lancelot. Although he fights bravely, Perceval is beaten. The knight, however, agrees to spare Perceval's life for one year, in which time he must acquire the skills to defeat his opponent or die. Once again, this theme occurs in a later romance, *Sir Gawain and the Green Knight* (*circa* 1400), in which the Green Knight offers the same bargain to Gawain.

After the knight leaves, Perceval is met by Merlin, who tells him that the only way to better the Red Knight is by seeking the wisdom of the Grail. At this point we are not told what the Grail actually is, or precisely what wisdom it might reveal. Merlin returns to the forest and Perceval sets out to find the Grail castle. Before long he meets a wise woman beside the road who tells him the whereabouts of the castle, 'the castle of the Fisher King in the Old Marche'. Once again the castle is in the Old Marche, the name for the Welsh borderland around Whittington, just as it is described in *Fulke le Fitz Waryn* and the *Didcot Perceval*.

When Perceval eventually finds the castle he is invited to a banquet held in honour of the Fisher King and his wife the Queen. During the feast a procession enters from a side chapel bearing 'the Grail Hallows'. The *Folie* manuscript includes an illustration of the procession showing a maiden carrying a chalice, followed by a page with a lance, and four servants bearing a draped box with a sword on top. Later in the story we are told the significance of the Grail Hallows: the holy chalice contained Christ's blood, the lance pierced his side during the Crucifixion, the sword beheaded John the Baptist, and the draped box holds the plate of the Last Supper. The servants place the box before the King and Queen and open it to reveal the sacred platter:

> And upon the platter was the book of the holy vessel, but Perceval could not look upon it for it shone with so great a light.

The King, however, is unaffected by the light and is able to read from the book. Again we find a link with the *Peveril* section in *Fulke le Fitz Waryn*, for the King tells Perceval that he must balance both power and wisdom if he is to make a wise king. Perceval is amazed at the spectacle, and mystified as to why the Fisher King should give him such advice but, as in the other Grail romances, he fails to question his host. The banquet then ends and the Fisher King retires alone to the Grail chapel where he intends to spend the night at prayer.

Later, Perceval decides to follow the King into the chapel, in the hope of seeing the Grail Hallows once more. Inside, he finds the King gone, and is confronted instead by a hooded man whom he assumes to be a priest. The man tells him that he must leave the castle as he has failed to ask about what he has seen and heard. Perceval is temporarily blinded by a brilliant flash of light, and when he recovers his sight he finds himself standing in the forest accompanied by the wise woman.

The story follows the same theme as the other romances when the wise woman tells Perceval that the Fisher King is his grandfather. However, it most closely corresponds to the *Peveril* in that the name of the Fisher King is Bran. The woman explains that Bran is the guardian of the Grail Hallows, and that he cannot die until he has been replaced by a successor. Like the other Grail romances, Perceval is that successor, although he cannot become the new Fisher King until he has asked the right question. The book, we are told, contains the secret words spoken by Christ himself, and only the Fisher King can read from it. When Perceval asks the woman how she knows these things, she explains:

> 'I was once as he who sent you here. I am the eagle who flew higher than any who dwelt in Rome. It is I who drank the wine of Peter and Joseph both.'

With this mysterious riddle, the wise woman vanishes into the forest.

Throughout the main body of the story Perceval experiences a series of adventures while searching for the Grail castle. He encounters a number of strange characters, each of whom sets him tasks to perform or riddles to solve. He meets two lovers sitting beneath a tree who ask him to retrieve a golden apple from a giant, a charioteer who holds a bleeding spear that seems to be one of the Grail Hallows, a hermit who reveals to him a vision of the Crucifixion, and a cowled figure who kills the grass over which he walks.

Eventually Perceval finds the Grail castle, which has been reduced to ruins by a lightning bolt cast down by the devil. Unable to die, the Fisher King is now alone amongst the rubble. Although frail and weak, he invites Perceval to dine with him. This time it is no banquet but a simple meal of bread and wine. When the Fisher King breaks the bread to share it with his guest, the Grail procession again enters the hall. This time as the sacred book is opened Perceval asks the right question: 'Whom does the Grail serve?' Satisfied that the conditions have been met for Perceval to take over his role, the King hands him the book, answering: 'The Grail serves the Fisher King.' Although it still shines brightly, Perceval can now read the text.

Unlike in the other Grail romances, where the significance of this strange question remains a mystery, the *Folie* makes it quite plain. When the King offers Perceval the book, telling him 'this Grail serves the Fisher King' it clearly shows that Perceval has proved himself worthy to become the new Fisher King. Moreover, the book itself seems to be the Grail, as Perceval is told that it serves the Fisher King while he hands it over.

The old King then teaches Perceval about the book, and how it contains the secret words of Jesus written down by Didymus, a disciple of Christ. He is also told about the characters he has met during his quest. The man whom he took to be a priest was in fact the Pope, the lovers were Adam and Eve, the hermit was Joseph of Arimathea, the charioteer was the Roman soldier who pierced the side of Christ, and the cowled figure was the Grim Reaper, death itself.

When the Fisher King has finished explaining, an angel appears to take him to heaven. It is then that the Red Knight returns to tell Perceval that his year is up, and he must fight for his honour. Perceval accepts the challenge, but is again defeated. The Red Knight runs him through with his sword but, as the new Fisher King, Perceval cannot die and immediately recovers. The Red Knight then laughs and announces that honour is satisfied. He removes his helmet to reveal that he is really Merlin. He set the year-long quest for Perceval so that he could learn to become a worthy Fisher King. The story ends with Perceval building a new Grail castle, 'the White Castle of the White Town', and a 'white maiden' taking the sacred book 'into another place', presumably heaven.

There can be little doubt that the *Folie* is an allegory concerning an apostolic succession. Just before his life on earth is over, the Fisher King invites Perceval to a simple meal of bread and wine, just as Jesus did with the disciples at the Last Supper. The Fisher King has taken the place of Christ, and like Christ he ascends bodily into heaven. Perceval then replaces him as Peter does Jesus. The fact that during Perceval's first visit the Pope himself is the only person in the chapel in which the Fisher King should have been praying surely symbolises that the Fisher King is himself the Pope. In other words, he is of the true apostolic line. Again Joseph of Arimathea appears in the story to impart a vision of the Crucifixion, presumably signifying that the succession is from Joseph and not from Peter, as taught by the established Church.

As we have seen, the source of the *Folie* is almost certainly the same source as the *Peveril* in the *Fulke* romance. However, was this source really the oldest Grail romance – the original upon which Chretien and his contemporaries based their versions of the story? The surviving copy of the *Folie* only dates from the 1330s, and so was transcribed almost a century and a half after the early romances. The general consensus among literary historians is that the *Folie* is a late romance, a compilation from the original eight. As the fifteenth-century Thomas Malory compiled his *Le Morte d'Arthur* from all the famous Arthurian romances available at the time, so the author of the *Folie* did likewise with the Grail stories. It is argued that even if the writer of the extant manuscript did adhere strictly to the story he was transcribing into prose, the story itself was already a much later romance than those of Chretien and his contemporaries.

Conversely, the *Folie* does have a feeling of authenticity about it. Whereas the allegorical significance and symbolism of the other romances remain vague and unclear, in the *Folie* it is far more apparent. Not only is the meaning of the final meal and Perceval's question more obvious, but the significance of the Grail is easier to understand. In all the romances the Grail seems to impart some special wisdom, but precisely how it does this is always obscure. For example: in the First Continuation the Grail is an unnamed floating object that somehow satiates a thirst for knowledge; the *Perlesvaus* Grail is a nebulous artefact in which visions somehow appear; while Chretien de Troyes fails to explain how his Grail works. We get the impression that the authors did not fully understand the significance of their material. The *Folie* author, however, leaves his reader with no doubt as to how his Grail discloses wisdom – it is a book containing secret words spoken by Christ. Although the Vulgate version does include as one of its Grails a book written by Jesus himself, this plays almost no part in the story. Indeed, the Grail seen during the banquet is the cup of the Last Supper.

Alternatively, the *Folie* author may appear more conversant with his subject matter simply because it was written much later. By the fourteenth century, the time of the extant copy, the Grail romances had been in circulation long enough for any imaginative writer to inject convincing interpretations of the symbolism into the existing story. All the same, the similarities with the Peveril sections of *Fulke le Fitz Waryn* still remain, and that seems to have been a poem written almost a century before Chretien and his contemporaries composed their works.

A similar either-way argument can be made concerning the characters in the saga. The figures that Perceval encounters during his quest to find the Grail castle in the *Folie* appear scattered through the other Grail romances. For example: the hermit is included in some, and the wise woman in others; the lovers appear in the *Didcot Perceval*, the charioteer features in the First Continuation, and the Grim Reaper is found in the Vulgate Cycle. This could either imply that the traditional romancers only had fragmentary knowledge of an earlier story upon which the *Folie* was based, or that the *Folie* author attempted to construct a complete story from all the others. Which is correct? If the hermit, the wise woman, the lovers, the Reaper, and the charioteer truly belong in the same story, then it would greatly strengthen the case for the *Folie* being the earliest of the Grail romances.

Each time I studied the *Folie* I had the distinct impression that these strange characters did belong together; I was sure I had come across them somewhere before. It was some time before I finally realised where – in the Tarot pack.

The oldest known Tarot pack dates from the mid-fifteenth century. Although the origins of the Tarot are obscure, there are references to the cards in the writing of a Swiss monk almost a hundred years earlier, in 1377. By the late sixteenth century they were being widely used as gaming cards all over Europe. Although today there are many different Tarot designs, the original cards, such as the French Marseilles pack dating from around 1500, consisted of four suits of fourteen cards, and a set of twenty-two named cards called the trumps. The four suits were similar to modern playing cards – which probably derived from the Tarot – but instead of spades, hearts, diamonds and clubs, they included swords, cups, coins and staffs. Each suit is similar to modern playing cards in that they are numbered from ace to ten, but they have four court cards instead of three: a page, a knight, a queen and a king. At some point during their development into modern playing cards the page became a jack and the knight was dropped. The twenty-two trump cards were also abandoned. It is on these trump cards of the Tarot that the characters from the *Folie* appear. The trumps consisted of a series of strange medieval figures and symbols, all but one, the Fool, having a number:

Number and Name	Brief Description
– The Fool	A journeying jester with a dog
1. The Magician	A conjuror performing before a table
2. The Female Pope	A woman wearing a papal crown
3. The Emperor	An enthroned man holding a sceptre
4. The Empress	A woman holding a shield and sceptre
5. The Pope	A pope with two attendants
6. The Lovers	A man, two women and a cupid
7. The Charioteer	A youth driving a two-horse chariot
8. Justice	A female holding a sword and scales
9. The Hermit	An old man with a staff and lantern
10. Wheel of Fortune	Three strange beasts on a spit wheel
11. Strength	A woman holding closed a lion's jaws
12. The Hanged Man	A tied figure hanging upside down

13. Death	A skeleton with a scythe
14. Temperance	A winged woman with two goblets
15. The Devil	The Devil with two bound imps
16. The Falling Tower	A tower struck by lightning
17. The Star	A naked woman under a star-filled sky
18. The Moon	Two dogs howling at the full moon
19. The Sun	The sun shining down on two children
20. Judgement	An angel summoning the dead to rise
21. The World	A bull, lion, eagle, angel, and maiden

Five of these characters – the Hermit, the Lovers, the Charioteer, Death, and the Pope – feature in the *Folie*; even the magician is present in the form of Merlin. Moreover, they even appear in numerical order. Perceval is advised by Merlin the magician to search for the Grail, and he later meets a pope, the lovers, and the charioteer in immediate succession. In the Tarot the Magician is number 1, the Pope is 5, the Lovers 6, and the Charioteer 7. Both the hermit and the Reaper appear later in the story; in the Tarot the Hermit is number 9 and Death is 13.

Did any of the other cards feature in the romance? The first character Perceval encounters after Merlin sets him on his quest is a wise woman – the Female Pope perhaps? He next meets the King and the Queen of the Grail Castle – the Emperor and the Empress? Some of the other cards could also be present. The Falling Tower and the Devil might be related to the devil destroying the Grail castle with a lightning bolt. The Judgement card might pertain to the Fisher King's ascension into heaven, and Perceval's inheritance of the sacred book might correlate with the final card, the World. This card shows an angel, a lion, a bull and an eagle, all surrounding a naked woman. Since early Christian times these four creatures have been used to symbolise the four gospels, Matthew, Mark, Luke and John. In the *Folie* the Grail is the book of Jesus' teachings written by the disciple Didymus – a fifth gospel. The book is eventually taken away by a mysterious maiden, possibly the naked woman of the World card. Finally, the unnumbered Fool card, showing a jester journeying with a pack on his back, might relate to Perceval himself, the naive quest hero who ultimately attains enlightenment.

Even the suit cards might be linked with the story. There is a king, a queen, a knight and a page in the *Folie*. Moreover, the symbols for the four suits are remarkably similar to the four Grail Hallows: the sword, the chalice, the lance and the platter. The sword and the chalice are present in the suits of swords and cups, and a lance is similar to a staff. The suit usually described as coins, or sometimes pentacles, is represented by a circular disc, possibly a plate.

I was convinced that there was some relationship between the *Folie* and the Tarot – the question was what. Initially I needed to discover which came first. Was the Tarot a pictorial representation of the Grail romance, or was the Grail romance a literary rendition of the Tarot?

14
The Mystery of the Tarot

The popular belief that Tarot cards arrived with the gypsies is historically unfounded. Originating in north-west India, these nomadic people migrated westwards into Europe during the sixteenth century. (The name gypsy stemmed from the erroneous belief that they came from Egypt.) The Tarot, however, was already in circulation in Europe at least a hundred years earlier.

There still survive a number of Tarot packs which pre-date the arrival of the gypsies, the oldest being seventeen cards from an Italian deck preserved in the Bibliothèque Nationale in Paris, dating from about 1470. The Visconti pack from Spain dates from around 1480, and the Marseilles pack from France was made shortly after. The fact that they were so widely dispersed over half a century before the gypsies arrived clearly shows that the Tarot was here first. Although the gypsies eventually became famous for their fortune-telling, they seem merely to have adopted the Tarot for the purpose. Indeed, it seems highly unlikely that the Tarot originated anywhere outside Europe, as the characters the cards portray, such as the Pope, the Devil, and the evangelical symbols on the World card, are purely Christian in concept.

The earliest recorded purchase of cards is found in the ledgers of the dukedom of Brabant in 1379, and in 1392 the court treasurer to Charles VI of France records payment for the artist Gringonneur to paint a private pack. Other records of the Tarot are found in legislation that either banned or permitted the cards' use for gaming purposes. In Regensburg in Germany they were banned in 1378, whereas they were permitted by a decree in Nuremberg in 1380, and were listed amongst the allowed games of Florence in 1393. These historical references demonstrate how widespread the cards had become by the end of the fourteenth century. This means that they were probably first introduced some time in the mid 1300s. As the manuscript containing *La Folie Perceval* was written around 1330, the Tarot and the romance appear to date from approximately the same period.

As the *Folie* romance was virtually unknown in fourteenth-century Europe (the romances of Chretien and his contemporaries were the popular stories), it seems unlikely that the Tarot would have been a game based around it. The other possibility is that someone decided to base a romance on the Tarot. However, as we have seen, the *Folie* seems to have been taken from a Welsh poem written around 1100. If there is a connection between the Tarot and the *Folie* – which there certainly seems to be – then some concept must have existed which inspired both.

Although the Tarot was widely used from the fifteenth century as a gaming pack, and more recently evolved into the popular playing cards, there have been many theories that it originally served a very different purpose. Over the years a number of scholars have proposed that the Tarot may hold religious or mystical significance.

In 1781 the French historian Antoine de Gebelin wrote *Le Jeu De Tarots*, in which he suggested that the Tarot contained occult symbolism from ancient Egypt. He proposed that the cards had originally been based on an Egyptian magical text called *The Book of Thoth*. The trump cards, he believed, had once depicted Egyptian gods and guardians of the underworld. Although de Gebelin's theory attracted a considerable following at the time, it was eventually discredited when the Rosetta Stone was discovered in 1799. A basalt slab containing inscriptions from the second century B.C., the Rosetta Stone became the key to deciphering Egyptian hierogliphics. It was soon shown that Egyptian mythology and The Book of Thoth bore little or no relationship to the symbolism of the Tarot pack.

One of de Gebelin's associates, Alliette, a Parisian antiquarian, published his own work on the Tarot in 1783. He also believed that the Tarot originally held important occult significance. However, his theory differed from de Gebelin's in that he believed that the cards had originally been used for fortune-telling. Before long, Alliette, or Etteilla as he later called himself, became the most famous fortune-teller in France. Thereafter, Tarot cards became popular for fortune-telling all over Europe, and were adopted by the gypsies some time in the early nineteenth century. The debate concerning the Tarot as ancient occult pictograms, or as a system of divination had thus begun.

In the mid nineteenth century the occultist Alphonse Constant, better known as Eliphas Levi, published a number of works on magic and occultism. Having studied theology, Levi believed that the Tarot trumps were associated with a mystical Hebrew system known as the Cabbala. Also called 'The Tree of Life', the Cabbala first appeared with a Jewish sect in twelfth-century Spain. In essence, the system concerned a pictorial design divided into a number of circles connected by a series of lines, or paths. Each circle (or Sefiroth) represented a different level of consciousness, while the paths represented the relationships between them. Although it has often been proposed that the Cabbala dated back to Biblical times, and was originally a secret, inner doctrine taught by Moses, there is no surviving historical evidence to date it earlier than the 1100s.

In the Cabbala, each of the twenty-two paths corresponded with a letter from the Hebrew alphabet, and Levi believed that the twenty-two Tarot trumps originally served a similar role. The symbolism of each card, he proposed, represented the path and the mystical experience involved in achieving the various levels of consciousness. He also linked the four suits with the four elements, earth, air, fire and water, and considered the entire pack to be the key to understanding ancient magic. Another occultist, Oswald Wirth, designed a pack of cards based on these ideas, although Levi's greatest exponent was an occultist who went by the name of Papus. In his *Tarot of the Bohemians*, published in he 1890s, he integrated Wirth's cards with Levi's theories to add a new dimension of Cabbalistic meaning to the Tarot.

Another school of thought which originated in England in the late nineteenth century came from the occult society, the Order of the Golden Dawn. The Golden Dawn followed Levi's lead by adopting the Cabbalistic concept of the Tarot, although they took the whole notion much further. The man largely responsible for this development was Samuel Mathers, later known as McGregor Mathers, who also incorporated the zodiac signs and the planets into the scheme. By this time new mystical names were also given to the trumps and suits of the Tarot – the major and minor arcana, from the word 'arcane', meaning secret knowledge. The ideas of Mathers and the Golden Dawn inspired a redesigned Tarot pack which included elaborate symbolic pictures on all of the fifty-six suit cards as well as the twenty-two trumps. Designed by Golden Dawn member A. E. Waite, and painted by the artist Pamela Coleman Smith, the pack first appeared in print in 1916. Having significantly influenced many subsequent Tarot designs, it is now called the Rider/Waite pack, and is probably the most popular Tarot deck in the world today.

We can see, therefore, that any magical associations with the Tarot are late developments. If there really was some mystical meaning to the Tarot it is more likely to be Christian than occult. The view of most modern historians is that the Tarot probably originated with the Albigenses, an heretical Christian sect who flourished around Toulouse in southern France between the eleventh and thirteenth centuries. (The word Albigenses comes from their stronghold town of Albi.) The Albigenses believed in the duality of good and evil, and envisaged Jesus as having rebelled against the cruelty of an uncaring God who had left the world to the whims of the devil.

Many surviving Albigensian texts show the cup of the Eucharist in exactly the same unique style as the cups drawn on the original Tarot decks, which have a symbol of four leaves descending from the bowl. Unknown outside Albigensian symbolism, it represented the Trinity with the added respect of the devil – or demi-urge – the imagined ruler of the earth in Albigensian philosophy.

The sect was subjected to the most appalling persecutions. From 1209 they were hunted down by an army appointed by Pope Innocent III, to be followed by wholesale and indiscriminate massacres initiated by the French king Louis VIII in 1219. By the time the atrocities ended, two and a half decades later, thousands had been killed. It is suggested that the Tarot cards were originally a pictorial book of Albigensian teachings, secretly concealed as gaming cards to avoid discovery by their persecutors. More likely, they had been a mnemonic device, a kind of mental shorthand, just as many students today use visual memory tricks to help retain key facts for examinations. The thirteenth-century theologian Thomas Aquinas refers to such cards being used in southern France shortly after the Albigensian persecutions had ended. He calls them the *Ars Notoria*, but unfortunately neglects to describe them.

The most telling clue to link the Tarot cards with the Albigenses is the Tarot trump the Female Pope. In 1206 Dominic Guzman, the founder of the Catholic Dominican order, began to preach against the Albigenses. He accused them of ordaining women priests and of claiming spiritual descent from a female pope. He referred to her as 'Joanna Aquila' – Joan the Eagle.

In 1245, shortly after the Albigensian persecutions had finally ended, the chronicler Martinus Polonus, who spent time in the area of Toulouse, referred to Pope Joan. He said that she had been a British woman who had travelled with her father to preach the gospel to the Germans during the Dark Ages. She eventually spent time around the monks of the monastery at Fulda, where she became an accomplished scholar. Ultimately, frustrated by the prejudice shown against her as a woman, she decided to leave the area and pose as a man. After journeying to Rome dressed as a friar, she was ordained a priest, and later became a cardinal. According to Martinus:

[In Rome] she opened a school and acquired such a reputation for learning and feigned sanctity that, on the death of Leo IV, she was made Pope. For two years and five months, with the name of John VIII, she filled the papal chair with reputation, no one suspecting her sex. Soon she came with child, some say, from a servant there.

Then at the Rogation, whilst the procession passed before St Clements, she was seized with pains, and fell to the ground amidst the crowd. Whilst her attendants ministered to her she was delivered a son. Some say the mother and child died. Others say that the child was to found the sect of Cathars, or be the Antichrist of the last days.

The Cathars was another name by which the Albigenses were known, and the reference to the Antichrist shows quite clearly how they were perceived by Catholics. The Church authorities vehemently denied the story of Pope Joan. However, two centuries before Martinus, around 1060, the Cologne monk Marianus Scotus wrote in his chronicle:

Lotharii 14 [in the fourteenth year of the Holy Roman Emperor Lothair I], Joanna, a woman, succeeded Leo, and reigned two years, five months and two days.

The fourteenth year of Lothair's reign was 854. If John VIII was really Joan, as Martinus asserts, then this dating is historically inaccurate. Pope Leo IV reigned from 847 to 855, and was immediately succeeded by Pope Benedict III. There was, however, an historical Pope John VIII, who was suspected of being a woman. Around 1100 another chronicler, Sigebert of Gemblours, wrote of John VIII, saying: 'It is reported that this John was a female.' This pope, who reigned from 872 to 882, did die under mysterious circumstances, murdered by a group of Italian nobles, seemingly under orders from the Holy Roman Emperor Charles III. Indeed, something very unusual seems to have been discovered about John VIII, as the entire papal electoral procedure was immediately changed after his death. Perhaps the Church intended to make certain they were never duped again?

It is with the story of the female pope that we find the most compelling evidence to link the Tarot with *La Folie Perceval*. Perceval is with the

Pope in the Grail chapel before he is mysteriously transported back to the forest to find himself accompanied by the wise woman. After she reveals his lineage, the woman explains how she is so knowledgeable: 'I was once as he who sent you here.' As it was the pope figure who seems to have transported Perceval from the Grail castle to the wise woman's forest, she appears to be saying that she too was a pope. Her next line is even more significant: 'I am the eagle who flew higher than any who dwelt in Rome.' According to Dominic Guzman in 1206, the female pope was called 'Joanna Aquila', Joan the Eagle, and as pope she would have ranked higher than anyone in the Roman Catholic Church. This clearly shows that not only is the wise woman of the *Folie* the Female Pope of the Tarot pack, but she is also perceived as Pope Joan.

For the Tarot to be linked so closely with the *Folie* and the Albigenses, there must be a connection between the Grail romances and this strange religious sect. If the Tarot did contain the coded teachings of the Albigenses, then presumably the *Folie* was another version of the same system. The Albigenses first appeared around 1100, and the *Folie*, in the form of the Peveril, seems also to date from about that time. However, the Grail romances concerned a British blood line, whereas the Albigenses can be traced back to their eleventh-century forerunners, the Bogomils of the Balkans. As there seems no medieval connection between the two, they must both have inherited the Tarot symbolism from some earlier source.

The central mystery of the Grail romances seems to have been an alternative apostolic succession; the Albigenses claimed something similar. They believed that they had the right to perform mass because their priests were ordained by priests with a line returning to Pope Joan. Here we have a direct cross-reference with the Grail romance. In the *Folie* the wise woman tells Perceval: 'It is I who drank the wine of Peter and Joseph both.' As the Papess, she is of Catholic apostolic succession from Peter, although she is also of the line of Joseph of Arimathea. Here, the Female Pope – who we have already established must be Pope Joan – is clearly portrayed as a member of the Grail family. Indeed, whenever the wise woman appears in the other romances, she is always portrayed as Perceval's relative. It seems that both the Albigenses and the historical Grail family were claiming descent from the same person. So who was this mysterious Pope Joan?

Marianus Scotus tells us that she became pope in 854, but this was eighteen years before the historical John VIII became pope. The date, however, may have concerned her arrival in Rome. If so, we discover a remarkable coincidence. This is precisely the year that according to the *Welsh Annals* Cyngen, the direct descendant of Owain Ddantgwyn – and possibly an historical Grail guardian – travelled to Rome to dispute the claim of Holy Roman Emperor. If Pope Joan really was a member of the historical Grail family, as the *Folie* implies, then she must have been a close relative of Cyngen, perhaps his daughter. Martinus actually says that Joan was British and that she initially travelled to the Continent with her father. The Welsh genealogies show that when Cyngen died he was succeeded via his sister Nest, so he obviously left no child in Britain. Perhaps Joan, the true heir, had chosen to enter the Church, be ordained a priest and thus join the two apostolic lines. Although this is mere speculation, the fact remains that in the early Middle Ages both the Albigenses and the initiators of the Grail romances seem to have held very similar beliefs.

Unlike the Peveril family tradition, enough has survived concerning Albigensian belief to know precisely where it originated – with an early Christian esoteric cult called the Gnostics. The Gnostics flourished in Alexandria, in Egypt, as early as the second century. Like the Albigenses, they believed in the duality of good and evil – Christ and the demi-urge. However, they rejected the redemption of the Resurrection, believing instead that the demi-urge created the body to imprison the soul. This could only be set free through knowledge and enlightenment as taught by secret words of Jesus. After the Roman Empire adopted Christianity as the State Religion, the Gnostics were considered heretics and progressively forced underground to become secret societies, such as the Bogomils from whom the Albigenses were descended. Consequently, if the Tarot contained Albigensian teachings, then they must have been Gnostic teachings. The *Folie*, therefore, may also be an enciphered Gnostic text.

A firm connection between the Grail romances and Gnosticism exists in the Gnostic claim to possessing secret words of Jesus. By the time Catholicism was established in the early fourth century, the Church chose to include only four gospels in the Bible: Matthew, Mark, Luke and John. There are known to have existed other supposedly first-hand accounts of Jesus' teachings, such as the Gospel of the Nazarenes, used by the early Church in Jerusalem. Constantine the Great outlawed all such gospels, and ordered copies destroyed. The Gnostics, however, still survived in the more remote areas of the empire, and continued to follow a gospel which they believed contained the inner teachings of Christ. As we have seen, the secret words of Jesus are a central theme in the Grail romances. The *Folie* even has such a book as its Holy Grail – a book containing secret words of Jesus written down by his disciple Didymus.

In the Bible we discover who this Didymus was – the apostle Thomas. In St John, Chapter 20, Verse 4, for instance, we find the disciple referred to as: 'Thomas, one of the twelve, called Didymus'. Remarkably, a Gospel of Thomas not only historically existed, but still survives. Preserved in a series of fourth-century parchments discovered in Egypt in 1945, is a Gnostic gospel which opens:

> These are the words which the living Jesus spoke and Didymus
> Judas Thomas wrote.

Was this Gospel of Thomas the true Holy Grail?

15

The Secret Gospel

In 1945 two Arab farmers were digging for topsoil in a cave in the hills around Nag-Hamadi in Upper Egypt. A few feet below the surface, they uncovered a number of clay pots, containing what they first took to be bundles of worthless card. In fact, they had made as important an historical discovery as the finding of the Dead Sea Scrolls: a volume Gnostic library of texts, dating back to the fourth century A.D. It had long been known that the Gnostics of the pre-Catholic era had claimed to have possessed a book of Jesus' teachings omitted from the Bible, but what it contained had remained a complete mystery. Now, after centuries, the world would know: the library included the Gnostic's secret gospel, the Gospel of Thomas.

The Gospel of Thomas was written in Egyptian Coptic, but seems to have been translated from a Greek edition dating back to the mid second century. Its verses matched precisely with a seven-verse fragment found in 1895 and dated from around A.D. 150. Linguistic analysis of the original seven-verse fragment (known as the *Oxytrhynchus Fragment*) indicated that it had in turn been copied from a first-century document.

Dating from the fourth century, the Gnostic texts had obviously been buried to prevent their destruction by the newly appointed Catholic authorities. The fourth-century cleric Epiphanius lists a number of other such works which were on the Church blacklist, like the Gospel of the Hebrews, the Gospel of the Egyptians, and the Gospel of the Ebionites. Whoever hid the Gospel of Thomas had managed to save the holiest of all Gnostic texts from vanishing forever.

The Gospel of Thomas contains 114 sayings of Jesus, some of which are included in the Biblical Gospels. Most, however, were completely unknown. The Nag-Hamadi discovery caused an uproar in ecclesiastical circles, with many Biblical scholars condemning the Gospel of Thomas as a Gnostic fraud. They pointed out that the Gospel is wholly devoid of detail. It says nothing of the Immaculate Conception, the Crucifixion, or the Resurrection. Even the everyday events surrounding the life of Jesus are absent. In their opinion, this list of teachings had nothing whatsoever to do with the historical Christ. However, its very simplicity might imply the precise opposite.

Before considering this argument, we must first examine the work itself. The full Gospel is too long for the present study, so included below are the opening passages of the text. (The text is printed without chapter or verse numbering, as none were included in the original. Indeed, even the first Bibles had no chapters or verses – they were an addition of the Middle Ages when most books were written in such a fashion.)

These are the secret words which the Living Jesus spoke and Didymus Judas Thomas wrote. And he said: Whoever finds the explanation of these words will not taste death.

Jesus said: Let him who seeks, not cease seeking until he finds, and when he finds, he will be troubled, and when he has been troubled, he will marvel and he will reign over all.

Jesus said: If those who lead you say to you: See, the kingdom is in heaven, then the birds of the heaven will precede you. If they say to you: It is in the sea, then the fish will precede you. But the Kingdom is within you and it is without you. If you will know yourselves, then you will be known and you will know that you are the sons of the living Father. But if you do not know yourself, then you are in poverty and you are poverty.

Jesus said: The man old in days will not hesitate to ask a little child of seven days about the place of life, and he will live. For many who are first shall become last and shall become a single one.

Jesus said: Know what is in thy sight, and what is hidden from thee will be revealed to thee. For there is nothing hidden which will not be manifest.

His disciples asked him: Wouldst though that we fast and how should we pray and should we give alms, and what diet should we observe? Jesus said: Do not lie; and do not do what you hate, for all things are manifest before Heaven. For there is nothing hidden that shall not be revealed and there is nothing covered that shall remain without being uncovered.

Jesus said: Blessed is the lion which the man eats and the lion will become man; and cursed is the man whom the lion eats and the lion will become man. And He said: The Man is like a wise fisherman who cast his net into the sea, he drew it up and from the sea full of small fish; among them he found a large and good fish, that wise fisherman, he threw all the small fish down into the sea, he chose the large fish without regret. Whoever has ears to hear let him hear.

Jesus said: See, the sower went out, he filled his hand, he threw. Some seeds fell on the road; the birds came, they gathered them. Others fell on the rock and did not strike root in the earth and did not produce ears. And others fell on the thorns; they choked the seed and the worms ate them. And others fell on the good earth; and it brought forth good fruit; it bore sixty per measure and one hundred twenty per measure.

Jesus said: I have cast fire upon the world, and see, I guard it until the world is afire.

Jesus said: This heaven shall pass away and the one above it shall pass away, and the dead are not alive and the living shall not die. In the days when you devoured the dead, you made it alive; when you come into light, what will you do? On the day when you were one, you became two. But when you have become two, what will you do?

The disciples said to Jesus: We know that thou will go away from us. Who is it who shall be great over us? Jesus said to them: Whenever you have come, you will go to James the righteous for whose sake heaven and earth came into being.

Jesus said to them: If you fast, you will beget sin for yourselves, and if you pray, you will be condemned, and if you give alms, you will do evil to your spirits. And if you go into any land and wander in the regions, if they receive you, eat what they set before you, heal the sick among them. For what goes into your mouth will not defile you.

Jesus said: When you see him who was not born of woman, prostrate yourselves upon your face and adore him: He is your Father.

Jesus said: Men possibly think that I have come to throw peace upon the world and they do not know that I have come to throw division upon the earth, fire, sword and war. For there shall be five in a house: three shall be against two and two against three, the father against the son and the son against the father, and they will stand as solitaries.

Jesus said: I will give you what eye has not seen and what ear has not heard and what hand has not touched and what has not arisen in the heart of man.

The disciples said to Jesus: Tell us how our end will be. Jesus said: Have you then discovered the beginning so that you enquire about the end? For where the beginning is, there shall be the end. Blessed is he who shall stand at the beginning, and he shall know the end and he shall not taste death.

Jesus said: Blessed is he who was before he came into being. If you become disciples to me and hear my words, these stones will minister to you. For you have five trees in Paradise, which are unmoved in summer or in winter and their leaves do not fall. Whoever knows them will not taste death.

The disciples said to Jesus: Tell us what the Kingdom of Heaven is like. He said to them: It is like a mustard seed, smaller than all seeds. But when it falls on the tilled earth, it produces a large branch and becomes shelter for the birds of heaven.

Mary said to Jesus: Whom are thy disciples like? He said: They are like little children who have installed themselves in a field which is not theirs. When the owners of the field come, they will say: Release to us our field. They take off their clothes before them to release the field to them and to give back their field to them. Therefore I say: If the lord of the house knows that the thief is coming, he will stay awake before he comes and will not let him dig through into his house of his kingdom to carry away his goods. You then must watch for the world, gird up your loins with great strength lest the brigands find a way to come to you, because they will find the advantage which you expect. Let there be among you a man of understanding; when the fruit ripened, he came quickly with his sickle in his hand, he reaped it. Whoever has ears to hear let him hear.

Jesus saw children who were being suckled. He said to his disciples: These children who are being suckled are like those who enter the Kingdom. They said to him: Shall we then, being children, enter the Kingdom? Jesus said to them: When you make the two one, and when you make the inner as the outer and the outer as the inner and the above as the below, and when you make the male and the female into a single one, so that the male will not be male and the female not be female, when you make eyes in the place of an eye, and a hand in the place of a hand, and a foot in the place of a foot, and an image in the place of an image, then shall you enter the Kingdom.

Jesus said: I shall choose you, one out of thousand, and two out of ten thousand, and they shall stand as a single one.

His disciples said: Show us the place where Thou art, for it is necessary for us to seek it. He said to them: Whoever has ears let him hear. Within a man of light there is light and he lights the whole world. When he does not shine, there is a darkness.

Jesus said: Love thy brother as thy soul, guard him as the apple of thine eye.

Jesus said: The mote that is in thy brother's eye thou seest, but the beam that is in thine eye, thou seest not. When thou castest the beam out of thine eye, then thou wilt see clearly to cast the mote out of thy brother's eye.

Jesus said: If you fast not from the world, you will not find the Kingdom; if you keep not the Sabbath as Sabbath, you will not see the Father.

Jesus said: I took my stand in the midst of the world and in flesh I appeared to them; found them all drunk, I found none among them athirst. And my soul was afflicted for the sons of men, because they are blind in their heart and do not see that empty they have come into the world and that empty they seek to go out of the world again. But now they are drunk. When they have shaken off their wine, then will they repent.

Jesus said: If the flesh has come into existence because of the spirit, it is a marvel; but if the spirit has come into existence because of the flesh it is a marvel of marvels. But I marvel at the body, at how this great wealth has made its home in this poverty.

Jesus said: Where there are three gods, they are gods; where there are two or one, I am with him.

Jesus said: No prophet is acceptable in his village, no physician heals those who know him.

Jesus said: A city being built on a high mountain and fortified cannot fall nor can it ever be hidden.

Jesus said: What thou shalt hear in thine ear and in the other ear, that preach from your housetops; for no one lights a lamp and puts it under a bushel, nor does he put it in a hidden place, but he sets it on the lampstead, so that all who come in and go out may see its light.

Jesus said: If a blind man leads a blind man, both of them fall into a pit.

Jesus said: It is not possible for one to enter the house of the strong man and take him or it by force unless he bind his hands; then will he ransack his house.

Jesus said: Take no thought from morning until evening and from evening until morning for what you shall put on.

His disciples said: When wilt thou be revealed to us and when will we see thee? Jesus said: When you take off your clothing without being ashamed, and take off your clothes and put them under your feet as the little children and tread on them, then shall you behold the Son of the Living One and you shall not fear.

Jesus said: Many times have you desired to hear those words which I say to you, and you have no other from whom to hear them. There will be days when you will seek me and you will not find me.

Jesus said: The Pharisees and the Scribes have received keys of knowledge, they have hidden them. They did not let those enter who wished. But you, become wise as serpents and innocent as doves.

Jesus said: A vine has been planted without the Father and it is not established, it will be pulled up by its roots and be destroyed.

Jesus said: Whoever has in his hand, to him shall be given; and whoever does not have, from him shall be taken even the little which he has.

Jesus said: Whoever blasphemes against the Father, it shall be forgiven him, and whoever blasphemes against the Son, it shall be forgiven him; but whoever blasphemes against the Holy Ghost, it shall not be forgiven him, either on earth or in heaven.

Jesus said: They do not harvest the grapes from thorns, nor do they gather figs from thistles; for they give no fruit. A good man brings forth good out of his treasure, an evil man brings forth evil things out of his evil treasure, which is in his heart, and speaks evil things.

Although there are a number of familiar parables in the Gospel of Thomas, such as the story of the sower, and although Jesus' sayings from the Biblical Gospels also occur, such as the beam in the eye, the lamp under the bushel, and the prophet not being recognised in his own land, much is completely new.

The Gospel is simply a list of Jesus' sayings, devoid of detail, which initially makes it seem less authentic than the more embellished Biblical Gospels. However, since the nineteenth century many eminent scholars have questioned the authenticity of the Evangelists' accounts. Matthew, Mark, Luke and John may have elaborated a similar list of Jesus' sayings based on second- or third-hand reports.

For centuries the four Gospels were unquestioned as contemporary, first-hand accounts. In 1835, however, David Friedrich Strauss published his *Life of Jesus Critically Examined*, which opened up the entire question of Biblical authenticity. Slowly but surely a number of mainstream Biblical scholars began to doubt that the Gospel writers really were eye-witnesses to the events they were describing.

No original manuscript survives from which accurately to date the Gospels. The oldest New Testament to survive is the fourth-century *Codex Sinaiticus* from St Catherine's Monastery at Mount Sinai. A few earlier fragments of the Gospels do survive, but even the oldest of these – the *Rylands Fragment*, containing six verses from St John's Gospel – only dates from around A.D. 125, almost a century after Christ is thought to have lived. As the oldest complete Bible dates from around the same time as the Nag-Hamadi text, and the *Rylands Fragment* dates from around the same period as the *Oxytrhynchus Fragment* (the passage from the Gospel of Thomas), from a purely historical perspective the Gospel of Thomas has as much claim to authenticity as the Biblical Gospels.

We are left with the content of the Gospels themselves to make their own case. From this standpoint, they do not bear close examination. Matthew, Mark, Luke and John all contain glaring discrepancies. A typical example is the account of Christ's healing of the centurion's servant at Capernaum. In Matthew's Gospel (8:5) it is the centurion himself who approaches Jesus for help:

> And when Jesus was entering Capernaum, there came unto him a centurion, beseeching him.

According to Luke, however, (7:3), the centurion sends a group of Jewish elders to meet with Jesus:

> And when he heard of Jesus, he sent unto him the elders of the Jews beseeching him.

There are many other discrepancies between the Gospels which suggest that the Evangelists had not known Jesus personally. Matthew, for instance, says that it is Joseph to whom Jesus' coming birth is first revealed, whereas in Luke's account the Annunciation is made to Mary. Matthew and Luke also disagree on the name of Joseph's father: Matthew calls him Jacob and Luke calls him Heli. Most remarkably of all, however, all four Gospels completely disagree about the most important event in Christian theology – the Resurrection. They each give very different versions of the discovery of the empty tomb. According to Chapter 16 of Mark's Gospel:

> And when the Sabbath was past, Mary Magdalene, and Mary the mother of James and Salome, had brought sweet spices so that they might come and anoint him ... And entering into the sepulchre they saw a young man sitting on the right side, clothed in a long white garment.

In Luke, Chapter 24, a woman called Joanna and 'other women' are also present with the two Marys when they enter the sepulchre. This time there is not one man in the tomb but two:

> And it came to pass, as they were much perplexed thereabout, behold, two men stood by them in shining garments.

In both these accounts, the women arrive to discover the stone already removed from the entrance to the tomb. In Chapter 28 of Matthew's Gospel, however, the two Marys actually witness the event:

> And behold, there was a great earthquake: for the angel of the Lord descended from heaven, and came and rolled back the stone from the door and sat upon it.

Finally, St John has a different version of events entirely. In Chapter 20, Mary Magdalene arrives alone to find the stone already removed and the tomb empty. She runs to tell Peter and another unnamed disciple, and they return with her. After they leave, Mary looks into the sepulchre:

> And seeth two angels, one at the head, and one at the feet, where the body of Jesus had lain.

At the very best, only one of these Gospels can be right.

It is now generally agreed by Biblical scholars that the Gospels were not written until some years after Jesus' time, in the late first or early second century. Even the earliest estimates place the oldest Gospel, John's, to around A.D. 50, some two decades after the events occurred. What probably happened is that sayings of Jesus were handed down verbally for a generation or two, until they were committed to writing by the Evangelists. This does not make them deceitful – they never claimed to have been present – they merely wrote what they had learned from others. The Gospel of Thomas, therefore, may have been an original list of Jesus' sayings, unfettered by the inclusion of half-remembered events.

The debate concerning the Gospel of Thomas will no doubt continue. However, the fact still remains that the Gnostics believed that the Gospel contained Jesus' secret words – a tradition that seems to have influenced the Grail romances. Here, the Gospel of Thomas almost certainly became the Holy Grail in *La Folie Perceval* – seemingly the original romance. In the story Perceval inherits the Holy Grail – the Gospel of Didymus – and the Gospel of Thomas is the Gospel of Didymus. Regardless of what the Grail later became, or even if the words in Thomas' Gospel were ever really spoken by Jesus himself, in reading the above passages we may have seen for ourselves the original Holy Grail.

16

Robin and Marian

Although the Gospel of Thomas may have been considered the Holy Grail when the first of the romances were written, by the late Middle Ages the true Grail was the cup of Christ. According to *Fulke le Fitz Waryn*, Fulk eventually asked his wife Maude to have the Grail cup relocated in what we are told was its final resting place, a wood about ten miles to the east of Whittington at Alberbury. He then paid for a priory to be built to contain it:

> Fulk founded a priory in the honour of our lady St Mary of the order of Grandmont near Alberbury, in a wood, on the river Severn; and it is called New Abbey. And not long after he died, and he and Dame Maude de Cause, his wife, were interred in this priory.

Just why he chose this site is not explained. However, it is a real historical location. The Priory of St Mary near Alberbury is recorded in the ecclesiastical archives of Canterbury Cathedral. It was eventually taken over by Cistercian monks, but was abandoned after the dissolution of the monasteries. Now called the White Abbey, its ruined walls were incorporated into a farmhouse erected in the mid nineteenth century which still stands beside the B4393, about eight miles west of Shrewsbury.

Did a splendid holy relic, once thought to be the Grail, still remain hidden in the foundations of the old farmhouse? Or had some later member of the Peveril family had it removed. Perhaps an outsider had discovered the artefact, having read *Fulke le Fitz Waryn*. However, *Fulke le Fitz Waryn* was not published until the mid nineteenth century. The surviving copy, now in the British Library, was discovered in the private collection of the Vernon family of Hodnet Hall in north Shropshire in the early 1800s. Interestingly, it was this same family who owned the site of the White Abbey until the farm was built.

It turned out that the Vernon family were directly descended from Fulk and the Peverils. During the reign of Henry VIII, the Fitz Warines sold Whittington Castle and moved to Bath, where their last son, Henry, the fifth Earl of Bath, died without issue. His sister Mary returned to Shropshire and married the squire of Hodnet Hall, Richard Vernon. It was via their son Robert that my investigation into the Grail mystery took on an astonishing new dimension.

Robert Vernon, it seems, became obsessed with the history of his mother's side of the family. He left many papers and diaries describing his research tracing back his lineage through the Fitz Warines to the Peverils. It seems to have been Robert Vernon who discovered the original copy of *Fulke le Fitz Waryn*. In the 1590s Vernon's sister Elizabeth married Shakespeare's patron, the Earl of Southampton, and Vernon himself became involved with the theatre. He even tried his hand as a poet and playwright, and for a time worked at the Shoreditch Theatre where Shakespeare himself was working. There is no evidence that he ever collaborated with Shakespeare, but he did patronise Shakespeare's fellow playwright Anthony Munday.

Robert Vernon was inspired to write his own romantic portrayal of Fulk Fitz Warine's life. Called *The Quest of Fulk Fitz Warine*, it is still preserved in the William Salt Collection in Stafford. Vernon must have based his story on *Fulke le Fitz Waryn*, as parts of the romance are included almost word for word. Like *Fulke le Fitz Waryn*, Vernon's quest concerns Fulk's adventures. However, he portrays Fulk in a remarkable way. He not only casts him as an Arthurian heir – but also as Robin Hood.

For some reason Vernon wrote the story in French, but in English translation his introduction reads:

> This Fulk was in truth the notorious outlaw Robin Hood. He was cast from his lands by the villainous King John, and was forced to join with rebellious cut-throats in the forest of Babbinswood. He took the name of Robin Hood as he would keep the truth of his identity a secret, lest the King did pursue him unto death . . . He was descended from Arthur, the great king of the Britons, but is reduced now to the life of an outlaw. Only should his quest succeed will he regain his inheritance, for he must find his Marian.

Robin Hood a descendant of King Arthur! This was a new one to me. I was familiar with a number of early Robin Hood stories, dating from the fifteenth century, but nowhere had I found him linked with Arthur. Vernon was not alone, however, in linking Robin Hood with Fulk Fitz Warine. The eighteenth-century Shropshire antiquarian Simon Pearson had also described Fulk as the 'Shropshire Robin Hood'. Additionally, in the late nineteenth century another Shropshire historian, William Cathrall, in his *History of Oswestry*, believed that the Robin Hood children's tale 'Babes in the Wood' originated with the name 'Babbins-wood', the forest around Whittington where Fulk Fitz Warine had been an outlaw.

As I continued to search through the available literature linking Robin Hood with Fulk Fitz Warine, I discovered something incredible. In the William Salt Collection there exists a Robin Hood poem thought to have been composed by an anonymous Shropshire ballad writer around 1550. Entitled *Robin and Marian*, all that now survives are a few verses scribbled on the back of a letter. Although Fulk is not mentioned by name, the theme is similar to Vernon's in that Robin goes in search of 'his beloved Marian'. Astonishingly, in this story Marian is not a person but 'a chalice, the most costly ever made'.

I had concluded that the historical Grail may have been based on the legend of the Marian Chalice; *Fulke le Fitz Waryn* had linked Fulk with the Grail; Vernon had linked Fulk with Robin Hood; and now another sixteenth-century writer had linked Robin Hood with a chalice named Marian. This must be more than coincidence.

Unfortunately, as only a few verses of the *Robin and Marian* poem survive, so there is no way of knowing what this chalice was meant to be. Nevertheless, where had the author got the idea to make Marian into a chalice? It was then that I realised that nowhere in *The Quest of Fulk Fitz Warine* does Vernon introduce Marian personally into his narrative. Vernon left the story unfinished; at least the surviving copy is incomplete. In what does survive we are simply told that Fulk 'must find his Marian', and the story continues with his adventures during this quest. Could Vernon's Marian also be a chalice?

Surprisingly, although the earliest surviving Robin Hood stories date from around 1400, Marian fails to feature in any of them for about two hundred years. The first writer to include her as Robin's lover was the playwright Anthony Munday – the very writer patronised by Robert Vernon.

I was definitely on to something: in the 1550s a Shropshire writer portrays Marian as a chalice; around 1600 Robert Vernon, another Shropshire writer, includes her in his story without saying what she is;

and almost at the same time Vernon's associate Munday first introduces Maid Marian into the Robin Hood story. Had Munday copied the name from Vernon, wrongly assuming Marian to be a woman? It certainly seems that something influenced Munday to introduce the name Marian as an afterthought, as his heroine's true name is given as Matilda. Only when she flees to the greenwood to join Robin as an outlaw does she adopt the name Marian in order to protect her true identity.

By the early weeks of 1994 my line of investigation had moved into totally unchartered waters. If Marian in the Robin Hood story was originally the Marian Chalice and not a woman, then the solution to the Grail mystery might be found not with the legend of King Arthur, but with the legend of Robin Hood. Was Fulk Fitz Warine really the historical Robin Hood as Vernon believed? Firstly, I needed to discover how the traditional Robin Hood legend originated.

In England in 1193, with Richard the Lionheart fighting in Palestine, the King's trusted friend Robin Hood, the Earl of Huntington, was cast from his lands by the treacherous Prince John. Outlawed and pursued into Sherwood Forest by the ruthless Sheriff of Nottingham, Robin raised a valiant band of followers, stole from the Norman rich to give to the poor, and became the hero of the Saxon peasants.

This, the story of Robin Hood as we know it today, originated with the Elizabethan playwright Anthony Munday in 1598. Contemporary with the works of Shakespeare, Munday's two plays, *The Downfall of Robert, Earl of Huntingdon* and *The Death of Robert the Earl of Huntingdon*, were as popular as any of Shakespeare's works, which ensured that this incarnation of the Robin Hood story survived. However, although Munday portrayed Robin as the Earl of Huntingdon, he did not invent the Robin Hood story. The oldest known reference to Robin Hood is contained in a work composed two and a half centuries earlier, in 1377, by the London cleric-poet William Langland. In his poems *Piers the Ploughman* Langland notes in passing, 'I know the rhymes of Robin Hood'. Unfortunately, Langland tells us no more about the outlaw, and the rhymes to which he refers have not survived.

The oldest extant Robin Hood story survives in the form of a ballad now preserved in the Advocates Library in Edinburgh. Called *A Gest of Robyn Hode* (or the *Gest* for short), it first appeared in print around

1510, but from linguistic analysis scholars have concluded that it might originally have been composed around the year 1400.

The *Gest* opens in the outlaw's camp, where Robin refuses to dine until he is accompanied by a guest of honour, a rich traveller whom they can rob to pay for the banquet. On Robin's orders Little John, Much and Will Scarlet waylay a downcast knight, who is brought to the camp. The knight says that he has little money, having been forced to sell his possessions to repay the abbot of St Mary's Abbey in York. He has mortgaged his estates to the abbot to secure the release of his son, unjustly imprisoned for murder. Sympathetic to the knight's cause, Robin lends him £400 and sends him on his way.

Eventually, the Sheriff of Nottingham decides to capture the outlaws by staging an archery contest to attract the finest archers of the north, the prize for the winner being a magnificent arrow of gold and silver. The band enter the contest in disguise, but when Robin is victorious the sheriff orders their arrest. Although Little John is wounded by an arrow in the leg, the outlaws escape and flee to the castle of the knight, who repays them by offering them protection.

When the sheriff arrives, the knight refuses to release Robin unless ordered to do so by the King himself. Petitioned by the sheriff, the King agrees to come to Nottingham to personally ensure the capture of Robin Hood and the renegade knight. However, while the sheriff is away, Robin and the outlaws escape and return to the forest. Ultimately, the knight is arrested, although he is later rescued by Robin, who kills the sheriff.

The King arrives in Nottingham and, discovering the sheriff dead, attempts to seize the knight's lands. Disguised as an abbot, with his men as monks, the King enters the forest to hunt down Robin himself. When the outlaws intercept the party, Robin unwittingly demonstrates his allegiance to the King, and the King reveals his true identity. Impressed by the show of loyalty, the King offers amnesty to Robin and his men, who return with him to Nottingham, while the knight returns to his castle.

Finally, Robin enters the King's service at court, where he remains for fifteen months until, homesick, he returns to the forest. For twenty-two years he lives as an outlaw in the greenwood; ultimately, he is beguiled by the treacherous prioress of Kirklees who betrays him to his enemy Sir Roger of Doncaster.

What can be deduced regarding the original Robin Hood legend from this early ballad? Composed over a century – perhaps two – before

Anthony Munday's plays gave us the modern version of the story, the ballad reveals a very different Robin Hood from the character we know today. He is portrayed not as a disinherited earl, but as a peasant who has taken up arms against the authorities.

The Kirklees prioress is the only woman to appear in the early ballads. As for Maid Marian, she had absolutely nothing to do with this original Robin Hood story. She is not recorded in any of the surviving stories of Robin Hood before Munday's plays in the late sixteenth century. Even then, as mentioned earlier, her true name is Matilda. The full title of the first of Munday's Robin Hood plays was: *The Downfall of Robert, Earl of Huntington, afterwards called Robin Hood of merry Sherwood: with his love to chaste Matilda, the Lord Fitzwater's daughter, afterwards his fair Maid Marian.* In the play Matilda assumes the disguise of a peasant woman named Marian once she has fled to the forest to join her lover.

The oldest reference anywhere to Marian in association with Robin Hood is in the poem fragment, *Robin and Marian*. As we have seen, it dates from around 1550, fifty years before Munday's play appeared. In this poem Marian is not a woman but a chalice. The next oldest references to Marian in association with Robin Hood are found in Robert Vernon's *Quest of Fulk Fitz Warine* and Munday's play, both of which were written around 1600. As we have seen, Munday may have got the name Marian from his patron, Vernon himself. In the latter's story we are not told anything about Marian, merely that Robin must find her in order to regain his inheritance. The Robin Hood in Vernon's story is not the Sherwood outlaw, however, but Fulk Fitz Warine. In *Fulke le Fitz Waryn* Fulk must find the Grail in order to regain *his* inheritance. Marian and the Grail seem, therefore, to be one and the same.

As the anonymous *Robin and Marian* of 1550 was also set in Fulk's home county of Shropshire, it seems that Marian originally had absolutely nothing to do with the Sherwood Robin Hood legend, but was associated solely with the story of Fulk Fitz Warine, where the name applies to a chalice. As Fulke is already associated with the Grail in *Fulke le Fitz Waryn*, his Marian, the original Marian, appears to have been the name for the Grail. There *must*, therefore, be a connection between this Peveril family's Grail and the legendary Marian Chalice.

Vernon's close friend Munday, however, used the name Marian for the assumed identity of Robin's lover Matilda; the name stuck, and to this day Maid Marian is still the heroine of the Robin Hood story. But what of Fulk Fitz Warine? Why did Vernon say he was Robin Hood?

Anthony Munday could well have based his disinherited earl, the sworn enemy of King John, on Fulk Fitz Warine. In Munday's play Matilda, lecherously pursued by King John, follows Robin to Sherwood and becomes an outlaw. Historically, King John had designs on Maude de Caus, Fulk's wife. She too joined Fulk in the forest as an outlaw. Also, like Robin, Fulk is eventually reinstated and helps force the King to sign the Magna Carta. Munday, however, sets his story in Nottinghamshire, and includes the familiar characters from the original ballads. Consequently, it is a hybrid story, mixing the legendary outlaws Robin of Sherwood and Fulk of Shropshire. Munday probably got the idea of basing his hero on Fulk Fitz Warine from Robert Vernon. But why should Vernon think that Fulk was Robin Hood in the first place? Is there any historical evidence that he was associated with the Robin Hood legend before Vernon's work? The early ballads are set in Sherwood in Nottinghamshire, and the original hero was a yeoman rather than an aristocrat. Was there, however, a parallel legend portraying Robin as a disinherited earl? If so, was it connected with Fulk Fitz Warine?

The oldest surviving reference to a Robin Hood having lived in the twelfth century was made by the Scottish writer John Major in 1521. Major was convinced that Robin Hood was an historical figure, stating in his *History of Greater Britain* that Robin was outlawed between 1193 and 1194 while Richard I was held captive in Germany after his crusade to the Holy Land. Major continued Robin's life through the reign of King John (1199–1216) and into the reign of Henry III (1216–1272), dating his death to 18 November 1247, aged eighty-seven.

Around 1560, some forty years after Major's reference, the printer Richard Grafton also announced that he had found evidence that Robin Hood was an historical outlaw during the reign of Richard I and King John. However, although Grafton claimed to have discovered an 'old and authentic pamphlet' dating Robin's life to around 1200, as well as records in the Exchequer rolls concerning the confiscation of the outlaw's lands, he failed to produce either as proof, or more importantly say where Robin originated. By the end of the sixteenth century, Major's and Grafton's dating had become generally accepted. Anthony Munday then set his plays during that period, thus establishing the historical setting for all the subsequent Robin Hood tales. In 1795 the

antiquarian Joseph Ritson gave the nineteenth-century romantic novelists their final authority for dating, also giving the year 1160 for Robin's
birth.

As the early ballads clearly concern a Robin Hood who had no
aristocratic connections, who did these later writers consider to have
been the original hero? The answer may lie with William Langland's
Piers the Ploughman. In it he wrote: 'I know the rhymes of Robin Hood
and Randolf Earl of Chester.' The Randolf referred to was the third Earl
of Chester (1172–1232), who lived during the reigns of Richard I and
King John. Since Robin and Randolf are coupled in the same passage, it
appears they were thought to have lived at the same time and fought side
by side. Who was the Robin Hood referenced in Langland's poem?

It may well have been Fulk Fitz Warine: he was the only historical
outlaw leader alongside whom Randolf fought. When Fulk was
dispossessed by King John in favour of John's friend Moris Fitz Roger,
he raised an army from among the local people of Shropshire and
reoccupied Whittington Castle. King John then sent Randolf, the Earl of
Chester, with an army to seize Whittington. However, Randolf changed
sides, joined with Fulk and fought along side him in his guerrilla
campaign against King John. The full story is included in *Fulke le Fitz
Waryn*; however, the story also includes far more to link Fulk with the
legendary Robin Hood.

Born in the 1170s, Fulk became lord of Whittington on the death of
his father in 1197. However, Moris Fitz Roger successfully claimed
Whittington Castle and Fulk was outlawed by King John on a trumped-
up charge of treason in 1200. For the next three years he fought against
the King in the forests of Shropshire and in the marshes of north-central
Wales. Pardoned in 1203, Fulk inherited Whittington, although in 1215
he again rebelled in support of the baronial revolt which led to the
signing of the Magna Carta. He quickly became a popular folk hero,
having successfully rebelled against the unpopular King John on two
occasions.

The romance *Fulke le Fitz Waryn*, composed around 1260, focuses
mainly on Fulk's life in the three years between 1200 and 1203, when he
was engaged in his first campaign against the King. After an initial
section outlining Fulk's right to Whittington Castle, the hero himself
enters the story. He is playing a game of chess with the future King John
when a quarrel erupts. Fulk assaults John and the prince swears
revenge. John is powerless to act immediately, as King Richard is a
friend of the Fitz Warine family. When Richard dies, however, and John

becomes king, he exacts vengeance by giving Whittington to Fulk's enemy Sir Moris Fitz Roger.

Disinherited and outlawed, Fulk and his followers flee from Whittington to nearby Babbinswood Forest. In the forest, Fulk gathers about him others who have grievances against the King and Sir Moris, and together they attack Whittington Castle. The siege fails and the outlaws flee, Fulk being wounded in the leg by an arrow. When his wound has healed, he continues to make trouble for Moris and the King by robbing wealthy merchants in the forests of Shropshire. He soon becomes a popular hero throughout the district, promising to steal only from the King's friends.

Fulk's brother John eventually tricks Sir Moris and lures him into the forest, where he is attacked and killed by the outlaws. The King's anger turns to fury when Fulk rescues and marries Maude de Caus, the richest and fairest lady in England, with whom the King is infatuated. With his new bride Fulk returns to the forest. Deciding to defeat Fulk himself, the King marches north from Winchester, but the outlaws are granted asylum at Castle Balham near Shrewsbury by a friendly knight called Sir Lewis. In the ensuing battle the King is forced to retreat and Fulk returns to his castle at Whittington.

Fulk's good fortune does not last, however, for the King appoints the ruthless knight Henry de Audley of Red Castle (at Hawkstone Park, near Hodnet) as sheriff. With ten thousand knights, Sir Henry besieges Whittington, and Fulk and his men barely escape alive. After a series of adventures the outlaws flee to the Continent, where they enter the service of the French king.

When they return to England, Fulk travels to Windsor where King John is holding court. Disguised as a peasant, he offers to lead the King to a good hunting spot in the forest. When the King accepts the invitation and enters the forest, he is captured by the outlaws and made to promise that he will no longer pursue them. Although he agrees, the moment he is free the oath is broken.

King John's final attempt to capture Fulk involves enlisting the help of Randolf, the Earl of Chester. Randolf is considered the greatest warrior in the land, but even this plan backfires on the King. Randolf joins forces with Fulk and they share many adventures together. Ultimately, Fulk captures the King in the New Forest, making him swear to reinstate him. On this occasion King John keeps his word, and Fulk and his family return to Whittington. It is at this point in the story that Fulk goes in search of the Grail.

It is clear that Munday acquired many of his themes for the later Robin Hood tale from the story of Fulk Fitz Warine; for example, the disinherited lord and his faithful lover, pursued by the lecherous Prince John until she herself becomes an outlaw. However, the tale of *Fulke le Fitz Waryn* has even more in common with the very earliest of the Robin Hood stories, the *Gest*.

Significantly, the stories of *Fulke le Fitz Waryn* and the *Gest* are in parts almost identical. Both Fulk and Robin's right-hand men are called John; Little John is Robin's lieutenant, while Fulk's is his brother John. In both stories John is instructed to waylay a party of wealthy travellers and bring them back to the camp to dine. In the *Gest* it is a party of monks from St Mary's Abbey:

> The monks had fifty two men,
> And seven laden horse full strong,
> There rides no bishop in this land,
> So royally, I understand.

In the tale of *Fulke le Fitz Waryn*, the victims are a group of merchants carrying the King's wealth:

> Then came from abroad ten burger merchants, who had bought with the money of the king of England the richest cloths, furs, spices and gloves . . . and they were carrying them under the forest towards the king.

In the *Gest* Robin instructs John to intercept the party:

> And wait for some unknown guest,
> And walk up into Sayles,
> And so to Watling Street,
> And wait for some unknown guest,
> By chance you may then meet.

In *Fulke le Fitz Waryn* the scene is thematically similar:

> When Fulk perceived the merchants, he called his brother John, and told him to go and talk with these people and inquire of what land they were.

In both tales, the respective Johns intercept the party and take them back to their leader's camp. The prisoners dine with the outlaws, thereafter being made to pay with their belongings. Both Fulk and Robin set their prisoners free, instructing them to thank their masters for the proceeds of the robbery. In the *Gest*:

> And bid him send me such a monk,
> Greet well your abbot, said Robin,
> And your prior, I you pray,
> And bid him send me such a monk,
> To dinner every day.

In *Fulke le Fitz Waryn*:

> He bade them adieu, and prayed them to salute the king from Fulk
> Fitz Warine, who thanked him much for his good robes.

In the initial section of the Fulk story the villain is Sir Moris, whose encounter with the outlaws bears a marked resemblance to that of the sheriff with Robin's men. In the *Gest* John goes to Nottingham in disguise to outwit the sheriff by becoming one of his men; in *Fulke le Fitz Waryn* John goes to the White Town in disguise, to trick Sir Moris in exactly the same way. Even the manner of the Johns' meetings with the respective villains are almost identical. In the *Gest* the sheriff questions John about his origins:

> In what country were you born,
> And where is your dwelling place.
> In Holderness, sir, I was born.

In *Fulke le Fitz Waryn*, Sir Moris questions John in precisely the same way:

> Moris asked him where he was born. 'Sir,' said he, 'in the march
> of Scotland.'

Subsequently, both Johns gain the confidence of their enemies, luring them into the forest and into a trap. In the *Gest* the sheriff is humiliated, but allowed to go free, but in *Fulke le Fitz Waryn* Moris is killed.

Earlier in the Fulk story, the outlaws are fleeing from Moris' men, in a similar manner to the flight of Robin's outlaws after the archery contest in the *Gest*. When Robin's outlaws are fleeing from the sheriff, Little John is wounded:

> Little John was hurt full sore,
> With an arrow in his knee.

In *Fulke le Fitz Waryn* it is Fulk himself who is wounded in the leg while fleeing from Sir Moris:

> At length came Morgan Fitz Aaron, and shot from the castle, and struck Fulk through the leg with an arrow.

In *Fulke le Fitz Waryn*, Sir Moris eventually goes to the King for help:

> Sir Moris made his complaint to the king . . . the king became so incensed that . . . he appointed a hundred knights with their company to go through all England, to seek and take Fulk.

In the *Gest*, the Sheriff of Nottingham also appeals to the King:

> I will be at Nottingham, said the king . . .
> Forth he rode to London town,
> All for to tell the king . . .
> I will be at Nottingham, said the king . . .
> And take I will Robin Hood.

Like the Sheriff, Moris is eventually killed by the hero. With Moris dead, King John comes personally to challenge Fulk, as does King Edward when the sheriff dies in the *Gest*. In the *Gest*, the outlaws find temporary sanctuary with the friendly knight, Sir Richard at the Lee, as do Fulk's men at the castle of Sir Lewis in Shrewsbury. Furthermore, when King John arrives in Shropshire, he finds it impossible to raise support because of the fear and respect the local people have for Fulk, just as King Edward discovers he can find no one willing to help him seize the castle of the knight who is protected by Robin Hood.

In *Fulke le Fitz Waryn*, with Moris dead, King John assumes the role of arch enemy. Once again, his encounters with the outlaws echo those of the sheriff in the *Gest*. In the *Gest* a disguised Little John meets the sheriff in the forest, telling him he knows where good hunting is to be found:

> It was one of the fairest sights
> I have been in this forest,
> A fair sight can I see,
> It was one of the fairest sights
> That I have ever seen.
> Yonder I see a right fair hart,
> . . . follow and come with me.

The same ploy is used by Fulk when he too encounters his enemy in disguise:

'Sir villain,' said the king, 'have you seen no stag or doe pass here?' 'Yes, my lord, a while ago.' 'What beast did you see?' 'Sir, my lord, a horned one; and it had long horns.' 'Where is it?' 'Sir, my lord, I know very well how to lead you to where I saw it.'

Both arch enemies are them led into a trap, captured and humiliated. Eventually, both the sheriff and King John promise to harm the outlaws no longer, in both instances immediately breaking the oath the moment they are free.

Towards the end of both stories, Robin and Fulk are reunited with their respective kings. Fulk's lands are returned and Robin enters the King's service. Ultimately, Robin wishes to return to the forest and visit a chapel he founded in Barnsdale. He appeals to the King to grant him leave:

> I made a chapel in Barnsdale,
> That seemly is to see,
> It is of Mary Magdalene,
> And thereto would I be.

Similarly, Fulk founds a priory dedicated to St Mary:

[Fulk] founded a priory in the honour of our lady St Mary of the order of Grandmont near Alberbury, in a wood, on the River Severn; and it is called the New Abbey.

Other early Robin Hood ballads are also echoed in *Fulke le Fitz Waryn*. Fulk leaves his men and goes to Canterbury Cathedral to pray alone, a remarkably similar theme to Robin's lone visit to St Mary's Church in Nottingham in *Robin Hood and the Monk*, another ballad written in the early fifteenth century.

The similarities occur too frequently, and too nearly identically, to be coincidental. Clearly one story has been taken from the other, but which came first? In its present form, the *Gest* was not committed to writing until the fifteenth century, whereas *Fulke le Fitz Waryn* was written around 1260. The surviving copy of *Fulke le Fitz Waryn* is thus certainly older. The writer of the *Gest* must, therefore, have drawn upon events from the life of Fulk Fitz Warine to elaborate his own story of Robin Hood, whether or not there was an historical outlaw who ever bore that name. By the sixteenth century Fulk's connection with the Robin Hood story seems to have been all but forgotten; Robert Vernon, however, evidently knew all about it.

As Vernon had been so accurate concerning Fulk and his link with the Robin Hood legend, perhaps he could shed more light on the Grail mystery. Remember, Vernon was Fulk's direct descendant, and therefore, if my theory was right, the successor to the Grail guardians. The more I discovered about Robert Vernon, the more I became convinced that he too believed that the Grail cup referenced in *Fulke le Fitz Waryn* was a genuine historical relic. Moreover, it seems that Vernon had attempted to find it for himself.

17

The Shepherd's Songs

The Shropshire County Records, in Shrewsbury Central Library, reveal that in 1596 Robert Vernon purchased the site of the White Abbey, where Fulk had hidden the Grail in *Fulke le Fitz Waryn*. The romance had probably been in the private collection of Vernon's mother's family since it was written around 1260. Vernon seems to have been the first member of the family for centuries to have taken any real interest in the story of Fulk and, since Fulk himself was apparently buried in the abbey, his purchase of the property may simply have been due to a desire to own the tomb of his ancestor. However, Vernon's interest did not end there. The abbey was just a ruin by the late sixteenth century, and he began to renovate the entire area. Parts of the crumbling structure were re-erected but, more importantly, large sections of the interior were excavated to landscape the ruins as a scenic garden. I began to wonder if there was more to it. After all, Vernon knew the Fulk Grail legend. Had he hoped to find the Grail in the abbey ruins?

Unfortunately, Vernon left no specific record of the renovation itself. However, he did write about the Grail, connecting it with the White Abbey. Around 1615, shortly before his death, he composed a poem based on the medieval Arthurian romance *Sir Gawain and the Green Knight*. In Vernon's poem, *Sir Gawain and the Red Knight*, he sets the story in the countryside around his home in north Shropshire, and even sites the Grail chapel at the White Abbey. In the story the monks of the White Abbey are the guardians of the Grail, but the Red Knight steals it and takes it to his fortress, the Red Castle. Once again, the Red Castle is an historical building; its red-brick ruins can still be seen at Hawkstone Park, about three miles south-west of Hodnet. Arthur's knight Gawain then offers to help the monks, eventually defeating the Red Knight and retrieving the Grail. However, instead of returning the Grail to the monks, Gawain decides to hide it in some unspecified location. (The original hand-written copy of Vernon's poem no longer survives, but it was published by the Shropshire antiquarian Thomas Wright in 1855.)

Mysteriously, Vernon claimed to have made a remarkable discovery which inspired him to write *Sir Gawain and the Red Knight*. In his introduction to the poem he wrote:

> As the Lord would deem it, I have made at the White Abbey of St Augustine, the finding which has led me to make such verse, for those who have eyes to see, and so worthy seen as I have seen.

Although the precise meaning of the passage is obscure, it seems that Vernon was claiming to have found the Grail. The poem was about the Grail, the White Abbey is where the Grail is kept in the poem, and Vernon says he has found something in the White Abbey which led him to write the poem. What else could 'the finding' be?

Anyone else reading this passage and concluding that Vernon was claiming to have found the Grail is unlikely to have taken him seriously. Even if they believed the Grail to have been a genuine historical relic, they are unlikely to have associated it with the White Abbey. But my research had, independently of Vernon's work, led me to the theory that the Grail was an historical artefact, and that it could well have passed into the hand of Fulk Fitz Warine, who in the romance did hide it in the White Abbey. So had Vernon really found the Grail?

The Vernon baronial line ended in the last century, and the present owners of the Vernon manor at Hodnet Hall, the Heber-Percys, inherited nothing of the Vernons' literary estate. The last person known to have possessed the Vernon family papers was the Shropshire antiquarian Thomas Wright in the mid nineteenth century. Nothing is known of what happened to them after he died in the 1860s. However, Wright did make sure that *Fulke le Fitz Waryn* and both Vernon's *Quest of Fulk Fitz Warine* and his *Sir Gawain and the Red Knight* were published in 1855 by the Warton Club in London.

When I examined the Warton Club edition of *Sir Gawain and the Red Knight* I became intrigued by something that I had first taken to be some kind of printer's reference. The poem ends with Gawain recovering the Grail for the monks, but instead of returning it to the White Abbey, he decides to hide it in a safer location. Strangely, the poem does not say where it was hidden, merely that Gawain stood on the battlements of the Red Castle contemplating its hiding place. The final lines of the poem read:

> The shepherd's songs to guide the way,
> The horn was blown, the treasure lay.

Following these final words there are two lines of letters:

> cxxxii xxxi lxi cii civ cxxxv cxlii cxxiii cxviii cxix cxvi
> xvii iii ii xix viii ii xix iv i xxii cxiv xiii

They appear to be Roman numerals:

> 132 31 61 102 104 135 118 142 123 118 119 116
> 17 3 2 19 8 2 19 4 1 22 114 13

Nowhere in the text or the preface does Vernon make reference to these mysterious numerals. There is no way of knowing if they were at the end of Vernon's original copy. But whoever inserted them, what did they mean? I asked a number of antique book dealers if they could explain, but they were as mystified as I. As the numerals did not seem connected with the printing of the book, I had to assume that they had formed part of the original poem. But why had Vernon included them? I was suddenly reminded of the words from Vernon's introduction to the poem:

> . . . For those who have eyes to see, and so worthy seen as I have seen.

An intriguing idea suddenly struck me: what if Vernon had hidden the Grail before his death and, seeing himself as some latter-day Merlin, left a coded message to reveal its location? In his poem, the Grail had originally been in the White Abbey, but Gawain had hidden it somewhere else. Perhaps Vernon, having found the Grail at the White Abbey, had himself concealed it in some other location. Did the poem secretly contain clues to where this might be? After all, Vernon finished the poem without saying where Gawain had hidden the Grail – all he left were the two lines of numerals. Were these coded instructions? Although I was excited by the possibility, I still expected that the numerals would eventually turn out to be some kind of printer's reference. As an experiment, however, I decided to regard the numbers as a code and began to try to decipher it.

The problem was deciding what the individual numbers might relate to. As the penultimate line of the poem referred to 'the shepherd's songs' guiding the way, 'the shepherd's songs' might be the key to the code. I spent many hours examining poems, rhymes, ballads and hymns which existed in the early seventeenth century when Vernon had written the poem. Eventually, I arrived at a plausible solution to the enigma. If Vernon intended his code to survive, he would surely have chosen references that would remain unaltered for decades, if not for centuries. Rhymes, poems, ballads and hymns are often changed or updated, even forgotten over time. However, one series of songs unlikely to be altered was that included in the Bible – the Psalms. Not only are the Psalms songs, they are shepherd's songs, attributed to Hebrew King David, a humble shepherd before he became the Israelite hero after slaying the giant Goliath.

There were two separate lines of numerals in Vernon's poem. Did the first line refer to the number of the Psalm and the second line to the verse? The first number in Vernon's first sequence is 132, and the first number in the second sequence is 17. Psalm 132, verse 17 reads:

There will I make the horn of David to bud: I have ordained a lamp for mine anointed

It seemed beyond coincidence that the verse should refer to the shepherd David and a horn – the poem actually ended with the line, 'the horn was blown'. Was Vernon assuring his reader that he or she was on the right track? The reference to the lamp in the verse may even have been used to indicate a guiding light, the following verses perhaps? Vernon would certainly have been able to use the same Bible translation that I was using, the King James edition printed in 1611, four years before he wrote his poem.

The second numbers in the sequences are 31 and 3. Psalm 31, verse 3 reads:

For thou art my rock and my fortress: therefore for my name's sake lead me, and guide me.

Again the reference seemed to correlate with a search – 'lead me, and guide me' – but where? The verse included a rock and a fortress, and in Vernon's poem Gawain stood on the battlements of the Red Castle. Significantly, the Red Castle, whose ruins still survive, some three miles from Hodnet at Hawkstone Park, is a fortress cut into the rocks. Is this what the conundrum was referring to?

In February 1994 I visited the Red Castle ruins to see if the remaining verses made geographical sense. If my reasoning was correct, then the third reference was Psalm 61, verse 2. The final line of the verse reads:

Lead me to the rock that is higher than I.

From the Red Castle there is only one higher location in the immediate vicinity, the White Cliff, which overlooks the castle about a quarter of a mile to the west. Above the White Cliff, facing the Red Castle, is a ruined chapel. The present ruin is a folly, but a much earlier chapel stood on the site, which is known from a drawing made by the Shropshire antiquarian John Street in 1620. This was within a decade of Vernon writing his poem, so again the location was historically sound.

From the chapel the next reference was consulted. Psalm 102, verse 19 begins:

For he hath looked down from the height of his sanctuary.

Until this point I had considered the associations coincidental. However, I was no longer so sure. 'The height of his sanctuary.' What better way to describe a chapel on the top of a cliff? I looked about me and found a narrow gorge cutting its way towards through the rocks. Did the next reference, Psalm 104, verse 8, refer to this gorge?

They go up by the mountains; they go down by the valleys unto the place which thou hast founded for them.

I followed the gorge to the valley at the bottom, continuing downward until I reached the nearby village of Weston, about a mile away. The next reference was Psalm 135, verse 2, which begins:

Ye that stand in the house of the Lord.

The house of the Lord surely referred to a church, so I made my way to the village parish church. It was medieval, so would certainly have been there in Vernon's day. Remarkably, the next four verses seemed to be telling me exactly what to do. Psalm 118, verse 19:

Open to me the gates of righteousness: I will go into them.

I entered the church. Psalm 142, verse 4:

I looked on my right hand and beheld.

I turned to my right. Psalm 123, verse 1:

Unto thee lift I up mine eyes.

I looked up into the church rafters. Psalm 118, verse 22:

The stone which the builders refused is become the headstone of the corner.

Had something really been hidden behind the highest stone in the north-west (back right) corner of the church? The penultimate verse seemed to confirm so. Psalm 119, verse 114:

Thou art my hiding place and my shield: I hope in thy word.

Everything seemed to fit. Unfortunately, if anything had been hidden in that particular church it was long gone. Although a church had stood on the site since the early Middle Ages, and could therefore have been included in Robert Vernon's conundrum, the present building dated only from the eighteenth century. Anything hidden there around 1615, the year Vernon wrote his poem, would probably have been removed and even destroyed.

I was now convinced that the numerals were a code, and that I had the solution. If just one or two of the verses had connected with the locality, then it might have been coincidence, but every single verse seemed to match precisely. Time and time again I kept opening the Bible at a random verse to see if I could make it fit with a location, but apart from once – even then with a stretch of the imagination – it didn't come close. This made the entire episode all the more frustrating. Some workmen in the 1700s probably found an ancient chalice, kept it from the vicar, and sold it to the local pawnbroker for the price of a drink.

Had an ancient holy relic believed to have been the Grail really been hidden in Weston parish church? The last reference in Vernon's list seemed very much to suggest so. Psalm 116, verse 13 reads:

I will take the cup of salvation, and call upon the name of the
Lord.

It was not until the summer of 1994 that I realised I might have been
looking in the wrong church. I was explaining the code to a friend, local
librarian Jean Astle. While reading through the list and following the
course I had taken on the map, Jean concluded that my trail did not fit
with the instructions. The fifth verse had read:

They go up by the mountains; they go down by the valleys unto
the place which thou hast founded for them.

Jean pointed out that I had only followed down a valley to reach Weston
church, whereas the verse had specifically told me to 'go up by the
mountains' before going 'down by the valleys'. I had assumed that the
mountains referred to the White Cliff on which the ruined chapel stood.
Indicating the map, Jean pointed out the mountains might refer to the
high hills directly facing the end of the rocky gorge. There I had turned
right, in order to continue following the valley downwards. If I had gone
over the hills I would have reached another valley about a mile away,
which did indeed lead to a second church, about three miles away in
Hodnet. I was sure we were on to something; Hodnet parish church
stands beside Hodnet Hall, the home of Robert Vernon. Moreover,
Vernon was actually buried in that church. It was certainly worth a visit.

Hodnet parish church was built in the Middle Ages, but the present
building is Tudor, dating from around 1550. Consequently it would
have been there in Vernon's day. It had been renovated in the 1850s but
these were only interior repairs. If anything had been hidden in the
church walls around 1615 then it could still be there.

Entering the church, I consulted the first reference I had followed in
the Weston church. Psalm 142, verse 4: 'I looked on my right hand and
beheld.' I found myself looking down the church aisle towards the
choir. The next reference, Psalm 123, verse 1, read: 'Unto thee lift I up
mine eyes.' I raised my eyes to see a stained-glass window depicting the
four Evangelists, Matthew, Mark, Luke and John. The next reference,
Psalm 118, verse 22, was: 'The stone which the builders refused is
become the headstone of the corner.' There was no headstone in the
corner; the window covered the relevant area of the church.

In order to have the church walls electronically scanned, I acquired
the help of Kerry Harper, a research graduate in archaeology at

Birmingham University. She managed to borrow a device that could differentiate between varying densities in stonework; if there were any cavities in which something could have been hidden it would find them. The entire church was swept but revealed nothing.

Then, when I had just about given up hope altogether, Kerry suggested that the stained-glass window might be important. She pointed out something that I had previously taken to be coincidence. The figure of St John, situated to the extreme right of the window, and so the nearest to the relevant corner of the church, held in his hands a golden chalice. The other three Evangelists merely held books. I had previously decided that the figure could not be related to the search as it only dated from the 1850s when the church was renovated, but Kerry suggested that it might have replaced an original bearing the same image. Sadly, no record survived of the original window; however, we discovered something equally fascinating. The window had been designed and donated to the church by the Shropshire antiquarian Thomas Wright, the same man who had translated and published *Fulke le Fitz Waryn*, Vernon's *Quest of Fulk Fitz Warine*, and *Sir Gawain and the Red Knight* – the poem which had contained the code that led us to the church.

Wright lived only a few miles from Hodnet in the village of Wollerton. Although he published a number of books on Shropshire history, almost no records survive of the man himself. However, it was fairly clear why he had had such an interest in the romance of Fulk Fitz Warine and the works of Robert Vernon: his wife, Frances, was the last of the Hodnet Vernons. The Wrights had had only one child, a son, Richard, who had died in infancy. Consequently, if my conclusions were correct, having descended from Fulk Fitz Warine, Wright's son would have been the last of the Grail family.

As the edition of Vernon's poem to include the numeral code was printed by Thomas Wright, perhaps the code had been his addition. In other words, it had been Wright who had hidden the chalice in the 1850s, once the family line had ended. If so, then the stained-glass window – commissioned by Wright himself – must be important. The four Evangelists: what could it mean?

The last of the Tarot trumps had shown the four evangelical symbols, the bull, the lion, the eagle and the angel, and the *Folie* romance had been based on the same symbolism as the Tarot. Was there a link? The stained-glass window even showed the four creatures above the heads of the saints. It was not until the spring of 1995 that I discovered that four statues depicting exactly the same evangelical symbols had once stood in a labyrinth of caves facing the Red Castle at Hawkstone Park. Again, they had been erected by Thomas Wright in the 1850s.

Beneath the arch of the ruined chapel, cut into the White Cliff, facing the Red Castle, are a series of tunnels and chambers. They were made in the 1780s by the owner of the estate, Richard Hill, who constructed a whole series of follies on his land. However, it is thought that Hill merely enlarged an already existing series of tunnels which were copper mines dating from Roman times. In 1934 Shropshire naturalist Mary Broquet described the tunnels in her book, *Shropshire Rambles*:

> The centrepiece of the labyrinth is a gallery eighty feet long, surrounded by pillars. Once the whole gallery was painted sea green, and the pillars were covered with shells. In the middle of the last century Thomas Wright, the antiquary, added to the grotto four statues, a winged angel, a bull, a lion, and an eagle, which stood beneath the arch. The lion and the eagle have now been moved to the Red Castle, but the bull and the angel have been lost. An interesting little tale concerns one of the statues. In 1920 Mr Wright's grandson, Walter Langham, found a tiny cup in the base of the eagle statue. It is thought to be a scent jar of some antiquity, but the reason for it being there is one of the mysteries that the present owner so loves to relate.

Wright had erected four statues depicting the evangelical symbols, and in one of them – the eagle – a *cup* had been discovered. In the stained-glass window the Evangelist St John holds a cup in his hand, and he is the Gospel writer represented by the eagle. Indeed, the eagle is actually shown above his head. Had the window been the last clue to reveal that the cup had been hidden in the eagle statue in the labyrinth? It made sense: anyone who had followed the Psalm trail in the 1920s would have seen the statues. All they had to do was make the connection. Perhaps Walter Langham had done just that. Unfortunately, none of the statues now survive to be examined. The last of them, the lion, was destroyed some years ago.

Mary Broquet calls Langham Wright's grandson. But Wright's only child, Richard, had died as a youngster. However, Wright's widow, Frances, remarried, and it was her daughter Edith who was Langham's mother. Since it was Frances from whom the Vernon line had descended, the blood line of the 'Grail family' had not ended after all.

Remarkably, if my theory was correct, the man who found the cup in the statue was the direct descendant of Robert Vernon, Fulk Fitz Warine, Payne Peveril, and Owain Ddantgwyn – he was the living Grail guardian. Had he discovered the cup which inspires the Grail romances?

The last of the line, Walter Langham's great-granddaughter, Victoria Palmer, is still alive today. The twenty-four-year-old graphic designer now lives in Rugby in Warwickshire, and she still possesses the cup found at Hawkstone Park. She had absolutely no idea of its importance, knowing only that it had been found by her ancestor, and that it was thought to be an old scent jar.

Remarkably, the artefact is only six centimetres high, with a round base and a stunted stem. Made from onyx, a semi-precious green stone, it resembles an egg cup, except that its rim is curled inwards. The reason for this, it has been suggested, is that it once had a lid. It certainly appears very old as it is worn away in places. Fascinated by our story, Victoria allowed Kerry to have the cup examined at Birmingham University. Unfortunately, there was no way of scientifically determining its age; only organic remains can be carbon-dated. Microscopy examination, however, revealed no evidence of machining, so at least it had been hand-made. Although that didn't prove that it was old, it suggested that it had probably been made before the Industrial Revolution.

Could this really be the Grail that inspired the grail romances of the Middle Ages – perhaps even the Marian Chalice? Although legends told how the chalice was made of gold and silver, no contemporary description survives. If it had been a cup used by Mary Magdalene in the early first century, it is more likely to have been a simpler artefact, such as a stone cup. In fact, a number of stone or pottery cups of similar size and design have been discovered at archaeological excavations around the Dead Sea, and are thought to have belonged to the first-century Jewish sect the Essenes. However, more significantly, when the cup was taken to the British Museum, it was suggested that it might have been a Roman scent jar. Unfortunately, no one was prepared to commit themselves; it could equally have been a nineteenth-century replica. On the positive side, Kerry made an interesting suggestion. If anything had been used to contain the blood of Christ – as the Marian Chalice was believed to have done – it was more likely to have been a jar of some sort than an open cup.

Whether or not this small onyx cup really is the Grail claimed to have been possessed by the medieval Peveril family will probably never be known. We may, however, have finally solved the age-old mystery of the Grail romances. They appear to have originated with a story written around 1100 – an allegory concerning an ostracised Christian sect, descendants of the Gnostics who claimed spiritual authority via an alternative apostolic line of succession. Because this original story concerned the lineage of King Arthur, and Arthur became a popular figure of romance in the twelfth century, other authors adopted the Grail story and adapted it to appeal to their own particular readership, seemingly having little understanding of its true significance. In conclusion, therefore, this may possibly have been the sequence of historical events which gave rise to the Grail legend we know today.

Until the early fourth century, various Christian sects existed throughout the Roman Empire. One of these, the Gnostics, claimed to have possessed a book containing secret words of Jesus – the Gospel of Thomas. In 327, however, the emperor Constantine the Great established Catholic Christianity as the State religion of the empire and, along with other nonconforming sects, the Gnostics were outlawed. Although within a few decades Gnosticism had successfully been suppressed elsewhere in the empire, it continued in the relative isolation of Britain. Here, Gnosticism seems to have inspired the fourth-century British priest Pelagius to established a breakaway Church. Unlike the Catholics who claimed spiritual descent from St Peter, the Pelagian Church evidently claimed spiritual succession from Joseph of Arimathea.

In A.D. 410, when Rome was sacked by the barbarian Visigoths, important Christian relics may have been brought to the safety of Britain, to the principal city of Viroconium. The relics may have included artefacts believed to be: the cup which once held Jesus' blood; the plate from the Last Supper; the lance which pierced Christ's side during the Crucifixion; and the sword used to behead John the Baptist.

When Britain broke from Roman rule in the second decade of the fifth century, the British leader Vortigern officially sanctioned Pelagianism, and the dissenting British Church refused to return the holy relics to Rome once the city had been reoccupied by the emperor Honorius. A succession of British kings continued to rule from Viroconium for some two and a half centuries, including the historical Arthur around the year 500. These rulers, who later became the Powysian kings, seemed to have remained head of the Pelagian Church, using their possession of the

Roman relics to legitimise their authority. The most important of these relics, the chalice (and possibly the others), seems to have remained in the possession of the Powysian kings until their descendants became Welsh barons under the control of the conquering Normans in the eleventh century. Lynette, the granddaughter of the last Powysian king, Cadfarch, married the Norman baron Payne Peveril who had fought with William the Conqueror at the Battle of Hastings in 1066.

Around 1100, Payne Peveril's chaplain, the St Asaph monk Blayse, wrote the *Peveril*, in which he describes his master as the holder of the Grail. Although only fragments of the *Peveril* now remain, the full story appears to have survived almost intact in a fourteenth-century translation, *La Folie Perceval*. The story concerns the spiritual descendants of Joseph of Arimathea – seemingly the Peveril family – and their role as Grail guardians, possessing the four Grail Hallows (the chalice, the sword, the plate and the lance) and the Holy Grail itself – the Gospel of Thomas. The portrayal of the Gospel of Thomas as the holiest relic, together with the inclusion of symbolism shared by the Gnostic Albigenses (in their Tarot pack), suggests that the Peveril was originally an allegory concerning the Peveril family inheriting the leadership of a secret Gnostic sect, presumably what remained of the Powysian Pelagian Church.

Within a few decades the *Peveril* story seems to have been copied and widely disseminated. Because the legendary King Arthur had become a popular figure of romance by the late twelfth century, and the *Peveril* included Arthur as the ancestor of the Peveril family, a number of European writers began to compose their own variations of the *Peveril* Grail story. It is unlikely that these authors understood the true significance of the original romance, as they each altered the story to suit their readership. The name Peveril was changed to Perceval and the story no longer concerned Arthur's medieval descendants, but his Dark Age contemporaries. Moreover, the Grail became different relics to different writers.

The four Grail Hallows continued to be included in most of the romances written a decade or so either side of 1200. However, the importance of the sacred Gospel was either played down or ignored altogether, presumably because reference to such a book would have been considered heresy by the powerful Catholic Church of the Middle Ages.

Around 1190 Chretien de Troyes included all four Hallows, but concentrated on the plate as the Grail itself. Although he does not specifically say so, his Grail is almost certainly being portrayed as the plate of the Last Supper, as the Grail guardian is served a mass wafer from it. Within ten years, the First Continuation followed Chretien's lead by making the plate a Grail, but did not portray it as the plate of the Last Supper. In this version it is made by Joseph of Arimathea specifically to collect blood from Christ's crucified body. The reason that the author chose to separate the artefact from Jesus himself was probably that he included another Grail in the story – one which he intended to have equal significance – the carved head of Jesus that could still be seen at Lucca Cathedral in Tuscany.

About 1200 Robert de Boron seems to have conflated all previous renditions of the Grail romance in his *Joseph d'Arimathie*. Possibly influenced by the legend that the Marian Chalice had been used to collect Christ's blood, he made the Grail a cup, and influenced by Chretien's association of the Grail with the Last Supper, he made it the original cup of Eucharist. Robert does not associate the Grail with Mary Magdalene, however, but follows the author of the First Continuation by having it being used by Joseph of Arimathea.

Unlike Chretien and the author of the First Continuation, Robert de Boron does allude to the secret Gospel by saying how the Grail guardian, the Fisher King, is taught the secret words of Jesus. About the same time, the author of the *Didcot Perceval* also concentrated on the cup as the Holy Grail and, like Robert, alluded to the Book of the Holy Vessel by having the Fisher King instruct his successor with Jesus' secret teachings. Around 1205 the author of *Perlesvaus* seems to have attempted to remain true to the original story by portraying the Grail as a secret Gospel, while cleverly disguising the fact. He does not say what the Grail is, merely that it mysteriously reveals episodes from Christ's life – possibly hinting at a Gospel which was not included in the Bible. By 1220 the Vulgate author was brave enough to directly describe the Grail as a book, in this case a book written by Christ himself. However, he also included the by now more familiar Grail, the chalice of the Last Supper.

To confuse matters, other legends seem to have influenced the development of the Grail story: Wolfram von Eschenbach incorporated a magic stone from an Arabian source as his Grail, whereas early Welsh tales of Arthur searching for a magical cauldron seem to have been interpolated into the Arthurian saga, resulting in modern speculation concerning the Grail having originally been such a cauldron.

Around 1260 an anonymous author, someone evidently linked with the Peveril family, appears to have attempted to put the record straight concerning the origin of the Grail story. In his *Fulke le Fitz Waryn* he describes Payne Peveril's great-grandson Fulk Fitz Warine discovering the Grail in his castle at Whittington. This Grail is a cup, although a more important Grail, the Book of the Holy Vessel, is also inherited by Fulk.

Although by the fourteenth century the Grail had become solely the cup of the Last Supper, we can clearly see that the word did not apply exclusively to that particular relic when the first Grail romances were composed. There were a number of Grails, and some of these have now either been found or identified, while others may be historical artefacts still awaiting discovery:

1. The Book of the Holy Vessel is seemingly the Gospel of Thomas. The only surviving copy is now in the Coptic Museum in Cairo.

2. The Marian Chalice, the cup said to have been discovered by the Empress Helena in 327, may have been the relic found and re-hidden by Fulk Fitz Warine in the mid thirteenth century. The same artefact was claimed to have been unearthed by Fulk's descendant Robert Vernon in the 1590s, and seemingly remained in the family until it was hidden at Hawkstone Park in the 1850s to be recovered by Walter Langham in 1920. The cup is now in the possession of Langham's great-grand-daughter Victoria Palmer, a direct descendant of the medieval Peverils, and of Owain Ddantgwyn – the historical King Arthur.

3. The *Volto Santo*, the carved head of Jesus said to have been made by Nicodemus, was an historical artefact kept at Lucca Cathedral in Tuscany.

4. The relic thought to be the plate of the Last Supper, the Grail in Chretien's version of the story, may have been amongst the relics inherited by the Peverils in the late eleventh century. Its subsequent whereabouts, however, remain a mystery. It was not mentioned in *Fulke le Fitz Waryn* in the thirteenth century, neither was it claimed to have been discovered by Fulk's descendant Robert Vernon. Perhaps it still remains to be discovered where Fulk is said to have found the chalice, in Whittington Castle – the historical Grail castle in the medieval romances. The same may also apply to the relics believed to

have been the lance of the Crucifixion and the sword which beheaded John the Baptist.

5. The *Lapis Excillis*, the magic stone of Wolfram von Eschenbach, was claimed to have been possessed by a number of medieval alchemists who believed that it could be used to transform base metals into gold. What happened to it, if it ever existed, is open to further investigation.

6. Although not included as a Grail in the medieval romances, certain aspects of the Grail story may have been influenced by early Welsh tales of Arthur's search for the cauldron of Di-Wrnach. If based on events associated with the historical Arthur, the cauldron in question may just possibly have been the one discovered at the Berth at Baschurch, the burial site of the Powysian kings. It is now in the British Museum.

Today the Grail is no longer simply an artefact – it has come to represent a search for truth or enlightenment. From this perspective, the present investigation has indeed proved successful. This search to discover the truth behind the Grail legend has thrown invaluable new light upon the historical King Arthur and the mystery of the medieval romances.

Chronology

43–7   Britain conquered by Emperor Claudius and becomes an island province of the Roman Empire.

380   Pelagius leaves Britain for Rome and comes into conflict with the Church.

383   Magnus Maximus proclaimed emperor by the British legions, invades Gaul and Italy but is defeated by Theodosius I.

401   Alaric, king of the Visigoths, invades Northern Italy.

408   Alaric lays siege to Rome and Emperor Honorius is forced to withdraw troops from Britain.

410   Alaric sacks Rome. Marian Chalice leaves Rome. Honorius unable to respond to the British plea for reinforcements. Last of the Roman legions leave Britain.

416   The Roman Church proclaims the teachings of Pelagius heresy.

420   Mass rebuilding of Viroconium.

429   Germanus, Bishop of Auxerre, visits Britain as an envoy of the Catholic Church.

447   Germanus' second visit to Britain.

451   Attila the Hun defeated at Chalons.

455–60   Anglo-Saxons take control of eastern Britain. Vortigern deposed.

460   Ambrosius leader of British forces. British defences reorganised.

470   British contingent fights for Emperor Anthemius in northern France.

476   Odovacer defeats Emperor Romulus Augustulus and proclaims himself King of Italy. Final collapse of the Western Roman Empire.

480   Military stalemate between the Britons and the Saxons in the south of England. The Angles suffer defeat in the north. Cunorix buried in Viroconium.

488	Hengist dies and is succeeded by Octha. Arthur succeeds Ambrosius.
488–93	The Arthurian campaigns.
493	The Battle of Badon. Anglo-Saxons retreat into south-east England.
519	Possible date for the death of Arthur. Maglocunus becomes King of Gwynedd. Cuneglasus becomes King of Powys.
530	Byzantine emperor, Justinian I, fails to recapture the Western Empire.
545	Gildas writes *On the Ruin and Conquest of Britain*.
549	Death of Maglocunus.
610	The poem *Gododdin* composed.
658	Owsy sacks Powys. Death of Cynddylan. The British lose Staffordshire and Shropshire and the Mercians occupy western Powys. Wulfhere King of Mercia.
731	Bede writes the *Ecclesiastical History of the English People*.
800	The Pope crowns Charlemagne of the Franks Holy Roman Emperor.
830	Nennius writes the *Historia Brittonum*.
850	*The Song of Llywarch the Old* is composed in its present form. Cyngen, King of Powys, erects the Pillar of Eliseg.
871–99	The *Anglo-Saxon Chronicle*, under the supervision of Alfred the Great, compiled from early monastic records.
900	*The Spoils of Annwn* is originally composed.
927	Athelstan effectively unites the Anglo-Saxon people and becomes first king of all England.
950	*Culhwch and Olwen* is originally composed.
955	The *Welsh Annals* are compiled.
1100	Possible date for the *Peveril*.
1135	*The History of the Kings of Britain* is completed by Geoffrey of Monmouth.
1160	*The Dream of Rhonabwy* composed.
1170	Birth of Fulk Fitz Warine.
1190	Chretien de Troyes writes *Le Conte del Graal*.
1189	Accession of Richard I.
1190	The monks of Glastonbury Abbey claim to have discovered the grave of King Arthur.
1193–4	Richard I held captive in Germany.
1195	First and Second Continuations of *Le Conte del Graal* are written.

1197   Fulk Fitz Warine becomes Lord of Whittington.

1199   Accession of King John.

1200   Fulk Fitz Warine outlawed on charges of treason. Robert de Boron composes *Joseph d'Arimathie*. He introduces the theme of the Holy Grail as the vessel used by Christ at the Last Supper.

1203   The *Didcot Perceval* is composed. Fulk Fitz Warine pardoned by King John.

1205   Wolfram von Eschenbach writes his epic Arthurian story *Parzival*, in which he depicts the Grail as a magical stone.

1215   Fulk Fitz Warine joins the baronial revolt. King John signs the Magna Carta at Runnymede.

1216   Death of King John. Accession of Henry III.

1217   Fulk Fitz Warine makes peace with Henry III.

1220   Vulgate Cycle *Lancelot* and the *Queste* composed, as is *Perlesvaus*.

1256   Death of Fulk Fitz Warine.

1260   Probable date for the composition of *Fulke le Fitz Waryn*.

1264   Death of Fulk's son at the Battle of Lewes.

1265   *The Book of Aneirin* is compiled, containing the oldest surviving copy of the *Gododdin*.

1275   *The Book of Taliesin* is compiled, containing *The Spoils of Annwn*.

1322   The Lancastrian revolt.

1323   Edward II's royal progress, leading to Nottingham in November.

1325   *The White Book of Rhydderch* is compiled, containing the earliest section from *Culhwch and Olwen*.

1330   The surviving copy of *La Folie Perceval* is written.

1377   William Langland's poem *Piers the Ploughman* mentions Robin Hood rhymes.

1400   Possible date for the composition of the *Gest*. *Sir Gawain and the Green Knight* composed by an anonymous writer from the north-east Midlands. *The Red Book of Hergest* is compiled, containing the *Dream of Rhonabwy*, the tale of *Culhwch and Olwen*, and the surviving copy of *The Song of Llywarch the Old*.

1420   Andrew de Wyntoun, in his *Original Chronicle of Scotland*, says that 'Little John and Robin Hood, as outlaws were renowed' in the early 1280s.

1470   Sir Thomas Malory completes *Le Morte d'Arthur*, the most famous of all Arthurian romances.

1510   *A Lyttel Geste of Robyn Hode* is published by the English printer Wynken de Worde.

1515   A second edition of the *Gest*, entitled *A Gest of Robyn Hode*, is published.

1521   Scottish writer John Major, in his *History of Greater Britain*, states that Robin was outlawed between 1193 and 1194, while Richard I, following his crusade to the Holy Land, was held captive in Germany.

1542   John Leland, Henry VIII's chief antiquarian, refers to Robin Hood as a nobleman in his *Collectanea*.

1550   Anonymous Shropshire poem *Robin and Marian* composed.

1562   Publication of Richard Grafton's *Chronicle*. Grafton claims to have discovered an 'old and authentic pamphlet' recording Robin's life as a lord, along with 'records in the Exchequer' referencing the confiscation of his lands.

1567   The surviving copy of *Diarebion Camberac*, containing the Welsh Triads, is compiled.

1598   Elizabethan playwright Anthony Munday writes *The Downfall of Robert the Earl of Huntingdon*.

1600   With Henry Chettle, Anthony Munday writes *The Death of Robert the Earl of Huntingdon*. Robert Vernon writes *The Quest of Fulk Fitz Warine*.

1615   Robert Vernon writes *Sir Gawain and the Red Knight*.

1852   The sub-commissioner of public records, Yorkshire antiquarian Joseph Hunter, publishes his *Mr Hunter's Critical and Historical Tracts. No IV. The Ballad Hero Robin Hood*, subtitled *Robin Hood: His Period, Real Character, Etc., Investigated and Perhaps Ascertained*.

1850   Hodnet church renovated.

1855   Thomas Wright publishes a translation of *Fulke le Fitz Waryn*. He also publishes Robert Vernon's *The Quest of Fulk Fitz Warine* and *Sir Gawain and the Red Knight*.

1920   A small cup, believed to be a Roman scent jar, discovered at Hawkstone Park.

Bibliography

Source Material, in the
Original and in Translation

The Anglo-Saxon Chronicle, trans. G. N. Garmonsway, Everyman's Library, London, 1967.

Bede, *The Ecclesiastical History of the English Nation*, trans. J. A. Giles, Everyman's Library, London, 1970.

L. T. Topsfield, *Chretien de Troyes: A Study of the Arthurian Romances*, Cambridge University Press, Cambridge, 1981 (for *Le Conte del Graal*).

The Continuations of the Old French 'Perceval', trans. William Roach, University of Pennsylvania Press, Philadelphia, 1983 (for the Continuations).

The Romance of Perceval in Prose, trans. Dell Skeels, University of Washington Press, Seattle, 1961 (for the *Didcot Perceval*).

Fulke le Fitz Waryn, trans. Thomas Wright, Warton Club, London, 1855.

Robert Vernon, *Sir Gawain and the Red Knight*, ed. Thomas Wright, Warton Club, London, 1855.

Geoffrey of Monmouth, *History of the Kings of Britain*, trans. Lewis Thorpe, Penguin, London, 1966.

The Gest of Robin Hood, ed. W. H. Clawson, Toronto University Press, Toronto, 1909.

Gildas, *On the Ruin and Conquest of Britain*, Latin & trans. Michael Winterbottom, *History from the Sources Vol. 7*, Phillimore, Chichester, 1978.

Nennius, *Historia Brittonum*, Latin and trans. John Morris, *History from the Sources Vol. 8*, Phillimore, Chichester, 1980.

Olympiodorus, *The Works of Olympiodorus*, trans. D. C. Scott, Chicago University Press, Chicago, 1952.

Perlesvaus, trans. William Nitze, Chicago University Press, Chicago, 1937.

Robert Vernon, *The Quest of Fulk Fitz Warine*, ed. Thomas Wright, Warton Club, London, 1855.

The Oxford Book of Welsh Verse in English, ed. Gwyn Jones, Oxford University Press, Oxford, 1977. Also: *The Age of Arthur*, John Morris, Phillimore, Chichester, 1977 (for *The Song of Llywarch the Old*).

Jane E. Burns, *Arthurian Fictions: Re-reading the Vulgate Cycle*, Ohio State University Press, Columbus, 1985.

Hugh D. Sacker, *An Introduction to Wolfram's 'Parzival'*, Cambridge University Press, Cambridge, 1963.

Welsh Annals, Latin and trans. John Morris, *History from the Sources Vol. 8*, Phillimore, Chichester, 1980.

The Mabinogion, trans. Gwyn Jones and Thomas Jones, Everyman's Library, London, 1975 (for *Culhwch and Olwen, The Dream of Rhonabwy* and *Peredur*).

Poems from the Book of Taliesin, ed. G. J. Evans, Tramvan, Llanbedrog, 1915 (for *The Spoils of Annwn*).

Joseph Clancy, *The Earliest Welsh Poetry*, Macmillan, London, 1970 (for *The Dialogue of Arthur*).

Thomas Parry, *A History of Welsh Literature*, trans. H. Idris Bell, Oxford University Press, Oxford, 1955 (for *The Triads*).

Selected Bibliography

Alcock, Leslie, *Arthur's Britain: History and Archaeology A.D. 376–634*, London, 1971.

Arbert, Edward (ed.), *A Transcript of the Registers of the Company of Stationers of London 1554–1640*, London, 1875.

Ashe Geoffrey, *The Quest for Arthur's Britain*, London, 1968.

Ashe Geoffrey, *Camelot and the Vision of Albion*, London, 1971.

Ashe Geoffrey, *A Guidebook to Arthurian Britain*, Wellingborough, 1983.

Ashe Geoffrey, *Avalonian Quest*, London, 1984.

Ashe Geoffrey, *The Discovery of King Arthur*, London, 1985.

Baildon, W. P. (ed.), *Court Rolls of the Mannor of Wakefield*, Yorkshire Archaeological Society Records Series, 1945.

Baildon, W. P. *Notes on the Religious and Secular Houses of Yorkshire*, Yorkshire Archaeological Society Records Series, 1931.

Barber, Richard, *King Arthur in Legend and History*, London, 1973.

Baugh, G. C. & Cox, D. C., *Monastic Shropshire*, Shrewsbury, 1982.

Bellamy, John, *Robin Hood: An Historical Enquiry*, London, 1985.

Benham, W. G., *Playing Cards: Their History and Secrets*, London, 1931.

Bindhoff, S. T., *Tudor England*, Harmondsworth, 1950.

Bogdanow, Fanni, *The Romance of the Grail*, Manchester, 1966.

Boulton, Helen (ed.), *The Sherwood Forest Book*, Thoroton Society Records Series, 1965.

Bradbrook, Muriel, *The Rise of the Common Player*, London, 1962.

Bronson, Bertrand, *The Traditional Tunes of the Child Ballad*, Princeton, 1966.

Brown, W. (ed.), *Yorkshire Deeds*, Yorkshire Archaeological Society Records Series, 1955.

Bryant, Frank, *A History of English Balladry*, Boston, 1913.

Camden, William, *Annales*, London, 1625.

Cavendish, Richard, *King Arthur and the Grail*, London, 1978.

Chadwick, Nora K., *Celtic Britain*, New York, 1963.

Chadwick, Nora K., *The Age of the Saints in the Early Celtic Church*, London, 1981.

Chadwick, Nora K., *The Celts*, Harmondsworth, 1970.

Chambers, E. K., *English Literature at the Close of the Middle Ages*, Oxford, 1945.

Chambers, E. K., *The Elizabethan Stage*, Oxford, 1923.

Chambers, E. K., *The English Folk Play*, Oxford, 1933.

Chambers, E. K., *Oxford Book of Sixteenth-Century Verse*, Oxford, 1961.

Child, Francis J. (ed.), *The English and Scottish Popular Ballads*, New York, 1956.

Clancy, Joseph, *Pendragon: Arthur and his Britain*, London, 1971.

Clawson, W. H., *The Gest of Robin Hood*, Toronto, 1909.

Comfort, W. W., *Arthurian Romances*, New York, 1914.

Copley, Gordon K., *The Conquest of Wessex in the Sixth Century*, London, 1954.

Crossley-Holland, Kevin, *British Folk Tales*, London, 1987.

Davidson, H. E., *Gods and Myths in Northern Europe*, Harmondsworth, 1964.

Delaney, Frank, *Legends of the Celts*, London, 1989.

Dillon, Myles & Chadwick, Nora K., *The Celtic Realms*, New York, 1967.

Dodson, R. B. & Tylor, J., *Rymes of Robin Hood*, London, 1976.

Dugdale, William, *Antiquities of Warwickshire*, London, 1656.

Dunning, Robert, *Arthur – King in the West*, London, 1988.

Empson, William, *Some Verses of Pastoral*, London, 1935.

Fife, Graham, *Arthur the King*, London, 1990.

Ford, Patrick, *The Mabinogi and Other Medieval Welsh Tales*, Los Angeles, 1977.

Frere, S., *Britannia*, London, 1967.

Fryde, N., *The Tyranny and Fall of Edward II*, Cambridge, 1979.

Fuller, Thomas, *The History of the Worthies of England*, London, 1662.

Gable, J. H., *Bibliography of Robin Hood*, Lincoln (Nebraska), 1939.

Garmonsway, G. N. (trans.), *The Anglo-Saxon Chronicle*, London, 1967.

Gerould, Gordon, *The Ballad of Tradition*, New York, 1932.

Giles, J. A., (ed.), *The Ecclesiastical History of the English Nation* (trans. from Bede), London, 1970.

Goetinck, Glenys, *Peredur: A Study of Welsh Tradition in the Grail Legends*, Cardiff, 1975.

Grafton, Richard, *Grafton's Chronicle*, London, 1809.

Green, Miranda, *The Gods of the Celts*, Gloucester, 1986.

Hales, J. W. & Furnivall, F. J., *Bishop Percy's Folio Manuscript*, London, 1868.

Harding, A., *The Law Courts of Medieval England*, London, 1973.

Hargrave, Catherine, *A History of Playing Cards*, New York, 1966.

Harris, P. V., *The Truth About Robin Hood*, Mansfield, 1973.

Hart, D. F., *The Legend of Pope Joan*, London, 1966.

Hodgkin, R. H., *A History of the Anglo-Saxons: Vol. 1*, London, 1952.

Hodgkin, R. H., *A History of the Anglo-Saxons: Vol. 2*, London, 1952.

Holt, J. C., *Robin Hood*, London, 1991.

Hunter, Joseph, *The Ballad Hero: Robin Hood*, London, 1852.

Jarman, A. O. H. & Hughes, Gwilym Rees, *A Guide to Welsh Literature*, Swansea, 1976.

Jewell, H. M. (ed.), *The Court Rolls of the Mannor of Wakefield*, Yorkshire Archaeological Society Records Series, 1982.

Keen, Maurice, *The Outlaws of Medieval Legend*, Toronto, 1961.

King, Francis, *Ritual Magic in England*, London, 1970.

Lacy, Norris (ed.), *The Arthurian Encyclopedia*, London, 1988.

Langland, William, *Piers Plowman* (ed. W. Skeat), London, 1886.

Leland, John, *The Itinerary of John Leland* (ed. Lucy Toulmin Smith), London, 1909.

Loomis, Roger Sherman, *Arthurian Literature in the Middle Ages*, Oxford, 1959.

Loomis, Roger Sherman, *The Grail: From Celtic Myth to Christian Symbol*, London, 1993.

Loomis, Roger Sherman, *Wales and the Arthurian Legend*, Cardiff, 1966.

McGrath, Patrick, *Papists and Puritans under Elizabeth I*, London, 1967.

Markale, Jean, *King Arthur: King of Kings*, London, 1977.

Morris, John (ed.), *The Age of Arthur: Vol. 1*, Chichester, 1977.

Morris, John (ed.), *The Age of Arthur: Vol. 2*, Chichester, 1977.

Morris, John (ed.), *The Age of Arthur: Vol. 3*, Chichester, 1977.

Owen, D. D. R., *The Evolution of the Grail Legend*, London, 1968.

Painter, S., *The Reign of King John*, Baltimore, 1952.

Page, W. (ed.), *Victoria County History, Nottinghamshire*, London, 1906.

Parry, Thomas, *A History of Welsh Literature*, (trans. H. Idris Bell), Oxford, 1955.

Percy, Thomas, *Reliques of Ancient English Poetry*, London, 1765.

Phillips, Graham & Keatman, Martin, *King Arthur: The True Story*, London, 1992.

Pollard, Alfred, *The Romance of King Arthur*, London, 1979.

Salway, Peter, *The Frontier People of Roman Britain*, Cambridge, 1965.

Sinclair, Andrew, *The Sword and the Grail*, London, 1993.

Stephens, Meic (ed.), *The Oxford Companion to the Literature of Wales*, Oxford, 1986.

Thomas, Charles, *Britain and Ireland in Early Christian Times*, London, 1971.

Thomas, W. J., (ed.), *Early English Prose Romance*, London, 1858.

Thomson, E. A., *A History of Attila and the Huns*, Oxford, 1948.

Treharne, R. F., *The Glastonbury Legends*, London, 1967.

Thorpe, Lewis (ed.), *History of the Kings of Britain* (trans. from Geoffrey of Monmouth), London, 1966.

Topsfield, L. T., *Chretien de Troyes: A Study of the Arthurian Romances*, Cambridge, 1981.

Walker, J. W., *The True History of Robin Hood*, Wakefield, 1973.

Westwood, Jennifer, *Albion: A Guide to Legendary Britain*, London, 1987.

Whitelock, Dorothy (ed.), *English Historical Documents: 500–1042*, London, 1955.

Wiles, David, *The Early Plays of Robin Hood*, Cambridge, 1981.

Wilson, R. M., *The Lost Literature of Medieval England*, London, 1952.

Williams, A. H., *An Introduction to the History of Wales*, Cardiff, 1962.

Winterbottom, Michael (ed.), *De Excidio Britanniae: History from the Sources Vol. 7* (trans. from Gildas), Chichester, 1978.

Wyntoun, Andrew, *The Original Chronicle of Andrew de Wyntoun* (ed. F. J. Amours), Edinburgh, 1907.

Index